Australian Plants for Small Gardens and Containers

Gwen Elliot

Hyland House Melbourne

First published in 1979 by
Hyland House Publishing Pty Limited
10 Hyland Street
South Yarra
Melbourne
Vic. 3141
Revised Edition 1982
© Gwen Elliot 1979

Elliot, Gwendoline Margaret
Australian plants for small gardens
and containers

Index
ISBN 0 908090 14 5

1. Wild flower gardening — Australia. 2. Container gardening. I. Title.

635.9676'0994

Designed by Peter Yates

Typeset by Meredith Trade Lino Pty Ltd
Printed by Toppan Printing Company (HK)

Contents

Introduction

Interest in Australian native plants has increased dramatically over recent years. We have become quite familiar with seeing native trees and shrubs in street plantings and home gardens. The main places where this interest has developed are the outer-suburban and rural areas, but it is not surprising that we are now seeing Australian plants becoming popular in inner-suburban areas, and right in the heart of our major cities.

We also now see an increasing number of cluster-housing areas, where each resident has a small garden, rather than the earlier trend of multi-storey flats with a garden area professionally maintained, or no garden at all.

The fact that a garden area is small restricts the number of plants suitable for planting, and makes the choice of plants much more important than in a larger area. As there can be only a limited number, each plant chosen will need to be for a specific position, and is individually of considerable significance in the total garden. Plants must therefore be carefully chosen, having regard to the needs of the plant species as well as the size and shape of the fully grown plants.

Not all Australian plants are giant forest trees. Some are delicate little species that could be grown in an egg-cup if desired. There are also, fortunately, many species between these extremes, and it is from these that a wide range of plants suitable for smaller gardens, or for growing in various types of containers, can be selected.

While container gardening is ideally suited to areas of restricted garden space, many owners of larger gardens are also realizing the advantages to be gained with container-grown plants.

Information is not readily available about the suitability of a wide range of Australian plants for growing in containers. This book is designed to help fill that gap.

For easy reading and reference, a series of charts has been included. These will give a quick reference to the plants suitable for particular containers or garden conditions. The detailed descriptions that follow in Section 3 give additional information to enable a choice of plants that add beauty or perform a desired function.

Whether you plan a totally Australian garden or a combination of native and introduced species, no garden is too small for Australian plants.

A lot of Australian plants have comparatively small leaves, and their fine foliage tends to give a garden a soft and relaxing character. Fragrance, of both foliage and flower, is another important and very often enjoyable consideration; the charts list specifically plants that are renowned for their perfumes.

The flowering season for our native plants is not confined to any limited period of the year, and all-year colour can be obtained with the minimum degree of planning. There are plants that will attract insects and butterflies to a garden, while others attract honey-eaters and other birds. For those who wish to add these extra dimensions of interest and enjoyment to their garden, charts have been included to give easy reference to suitable plants from which to choose.

There is much pleasure to be derived from gardening with our fascinating Australian flora, and the aim of this book is to help readers gain this enjoyment, by being able initially to make a wise choice of plants, and then by perhaps avoiding some of the frustrations that can eventuate along the way.

Acknowledgements

Firstly I would like to express sincere appreciation to my husband Rodger, who has been of immense help throughout this project. In addition to information provided, he has also contributed the line drawings and photographs used, and without his help this book would certainly not have been written.

I would like to thank David Jones, for information supplied, and Beryl and Trevor Blake, for their assistance in reading through the manuscript.

Many native plant growers have been extremely helpful in supplying information regarding plants grown, thus making possible a publication of this nature. I would like to thank Kath Deery, whose excellent ceramic containers and hanging baskets have been a source of inspiration, as well as the subject of several colour photographs; and A. Ross Lloyd for sharing his expertise on bonsai cultivation. I am also grateful to Beth and John Armstrong, Annette and Bob Bangay, Bill Bond, Elizabeth and Neville Bonney, Glad and Rae Elliot and Gwynnyth and Ron Taylor, for permitting the use of photographs taken within their gardens.

Finally, to Sue and Grant, who were tolerant and understanding when mum was busy writing, my warmest thanks.

Gwen Elliot

Gardening in Containers

The use of containers makes it possible for us to have and enjoy a garden in even the smallest of areas. There is much enjoyment to be gained from the inclusion of container-grown plants in paved areas, or from a carefully planted and tended window box.

It is certainly the unavailability of large garden areas that leads some people to container gardening, but others choose this method of cultivation for the versatility it gives. It is possible to grow in containers plants that would not normally survive in local conditions, simply by adjusting the soil mix to suit the needs of the plant, and if necessary by varying the position of the container from season to season.

Nurseries have found that when a new species is introduced to cultivation it is wise to grow stock plants in containers while experiments are carried out as to the best garden conditions for the species. It is one of the most reliable methods of cultivating difficult-to-grow plants, and therefore it is of equal value to the hobby gardener who likes to experiment with unusual plants.

Those whose occupation or way of life involves moving from house to house will find that container growing allows plants to be transported. This can be useful for a large number of plants, or just for specially prized or favourite species.

A plant selected to grow in a container immediately becomes very special, in the same way as a feature or specimen plant in a garden. The use of containers allows plants to be singled out for individual display. The most attractive feature of a plant in many cases is the flower, but foliage, shape or form of the plant, buds, berries or fruits, and fragrance, are also aspects worth considering, and in many cases constitute the main attractive feature.

Container gardening never ceases to be full of interest and enjoyment to the keen gardener. Pots may be moved around to obtain maximum enjoyment of each plant at its best, and by a careful choice of species a small number of containers can give year-round beauty.

Choosing a container

A feature of major importance to the beauty of a container-grown plant is of course the container. Individual taste will dictate preference here, as it also will do in the choice of plants. It is good that this is so, otherwise our gardens could be monotonous in their similarity. While some growers will choose a container with smooth uncluttered line, others will prefer a more ornate pot, either in shape, colour or texture.

Try to choose a container that will complement both the plant and the surroundings. If selecting a coloured container, keep in mind the colour of the plant's flowers and foliage. The size of the container in relation to the plant is also important. Try to create a mental picture when choosing your combination of container and plant — or even have a go at sketching the desired effect, using graph paper if available. Remember that most plants will not grow to their full

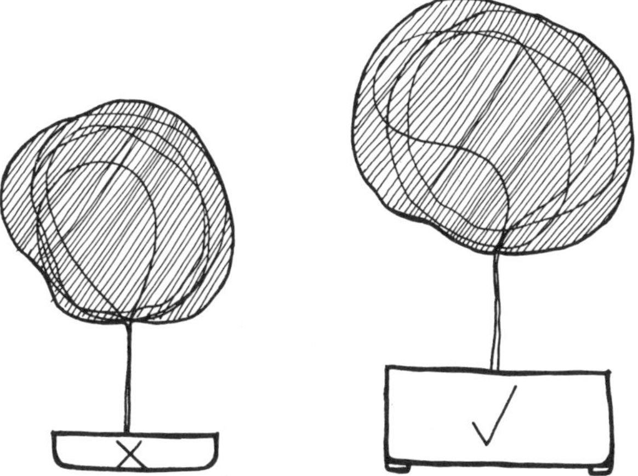

Containers must be of adequate size to enable satisfactory root growth of plants.

size in containers, and almost without exception, plants grown in containers will respond well to light pruning.

The position from which a plant will be viewed should also be considered in initial planning. You may plan to look down on the container, as would be the case if it were on the ground, or it could be that it will be placed at a higher elevation, such as on a low wall, a bench, a table or other pot stand. It may even be a hanging basket which will be viewed from below.

You may choose or be given the container first, and then look for a suitable plant, or you may seek a container for a particular plant. Whichever is the case, choosing carefully will result in infinitely greater satisfaction than when containers and plants are poorly matched.

Types of containers

Any container chosen should be functional. It should be able to retain moisture for sufficient time to allow absorption by the plant, but it must also be well drained. It should be durable and able to withstand regular watering without breaking down or decaying. It should be adequate in size to accommodate the plant or plants to be grown.

Ceramic

Ceramic containers are amongst the oldest used by man, and they are still very popular as plant containers today.

Unglazed terracotta pots have been used for many years as planters, and their earthy colours can be most attractive. These pots are very porous and dry out fairly rapidly. Some peat moss added to the soil mixture will help retain moisture. (Further information about this will be found under Soils and other potting mixes.) Glazed pots have a non-porous surface, and do not dry out as quickly as unglazed pots.

The use of unglazed terracotta pots can sometimes result in a build-up of salts, seen as a white powdery substance on the exterior of the container. This can be detrimental to the growth of the plant. (Further information about this will be found in the sections on Maintenance and Re-potting.)

Ceramic containers are obtainable in a large range of sizes and designs.

A wide range of ceramic pots is usually available from nurseries and stores. With the current interest in arts and crafts, many potters are producing excellent pots for plant growing. You may also be able to buy imperfect pots from some of the major potteries. In many cases drainage holes are drilled in the base, and these pots are then sold specifically for planting purposes.

For those who cannot find what they are looking for, or who like to design and make their own containers, very attractive clay pots may be made without the use of a potter's wheel. It is necessary for these pots to be fired in a kiln, and many potteries provide this service for amateur potters. It is also possible for unglazed earthenware pots to be glazed according to your own taste, providing you have access to a kiln. Ceramic glazes in a wide range of finishes and colours are available from handcraft and ceramic suppliers.

In making or choosing a ceramic container an important aspect to consider is the size of the opening. Some very attractive pots have an opening that is narrower than the overall width of the container, and this can present difficulties if it is necessary to re-pot the plant.

The main disadvantage with ceramic containers is that they can be broken.

Plastic

In contrast to the ceramic container, plastic is one of the most recent materials to be used in plant cultivation. Plastic is now, without a doubt, the most widely used material for plant pots in the nursery trade. It is non-porous, with an almost unlimited range of colours and textures. On the debit side, plastics can tend to become brittle and break after long exposure to the elements; however it will usually be found that black pots will give the greatest service in this regard.

Plastics would seem to be of greatest use in the smaller to medium size pots. They are relatively inexpensive and their light weight allows ease of handling.

If you have a feature container of wood or ceramics, or a large indoor or outdoor planter box, try growing a selection of plants in plastic pots of suitable size. You can then select a plant with attractive growth and place it in the tub or planter, alternating the various plants as

above: A young plant of *Correa reflexa*, in a container that will allow for good growth and development.

right: A showy container-grown plant such as this pink form of *Lechenaultia formosa* can be used to add colour to a garden area.

below: The suckering habit of *Dampiera diversifolia* makes it ideal for a pocketed container.

The Fishbone Water-fern, *Blechnum nudum*, in an unglazed terra-cotta pot.

A section of hollowed tree-fern has been used as the container for this plant of *Asplenium simplicifrons*.

A hand crafted ceramic hanging basket, with a young plant of *Grevillea alpina* 'Tooborac' in bloom.

The graceful fronds of *Asplenium bulbiferum* complement the soft lines of this ceramic basket.

Contrasting foliage of two water-loving plants is featured in this container, with *Restio tetraphyllus*, the Tassel-cord Rush, and the low growing Running Marsh-flower, *Villarsia reniformis*.

One of the cycads, *Lepidozamia peroffskyana*, growing successfully indoors.

Individually designed ceramic baskets containing plant groupings.
The trailing plant with yellow flowers is *Hibbertia dentata*.

above: This plant of *Grevillea glabella* is growing in a container. It is a dwarf species, highly suitable for garden or container cultivation.

left: Rhododendron lochae appreciates a warm, shaded and moist position, and can be readily grown in a container.

below: The Beech Orchid, *Dendrobium falcorostrum* is readily cultivated in containers. As well as being spectacular, the flowers are also highly fragrant.

you wish. The plants will appear as if permanently grown in the larger container if they are immersed in peat moss, gravelly sand, indoor plant mix or other available material. This also means that they do not dry out quite as quickly, and therefore require less watering.

Timber

Some of the most attractive planters are made from timber. Here we have a natural material that blends perfectly with plants, and the ways in which timber may be used are as wide as the ingenuity and inventiveness of the craftsman or home handyman.

Wooden tubs or barrels are excellent containers.

While timber may be used for small containers, its main use is in the area of planter boxes and large tubs. Wooden barrels are often obtainable, and make ideal tubs.

Timber provides good insulation, thus protecting the roots of a plant from excessive heat and drying out in summer.

Some timbers are more durable than others. Red gum, jarrah, cedar and treated pine are noted for their durability. Treated timbers should be used with caution. Although some plants will tolerate the presence of the preservative chemicals, others will not. Less durable timbers may be coated with a preservative to prevent rotting, or the interior of the container can be lined with black plastic sheeting. Holes must be made in the base, to permit drainage. Timber decay can also occur if a container is allowed to sit on the bare earth.

Wooden or ceramic containers, with provision for the insertion of plants in smaller and perhaps non-decorative pots. These can be used indoors or outdoors, and plants can be changed as desired.

The use of house bricks or a concrete slab under the container will prevent this, but you should make sure that good drainage and air movement beneath the container are still allowed.

The aspect of weight is important when planning large timber containers. In many cases it will be necessary to leave the container in a permanent position once it is filled with soil.

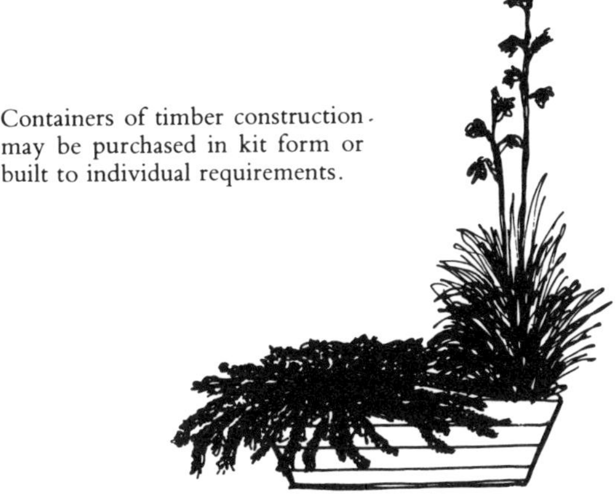

Containers of timber construction may be purchased in kit form or built to individual requirements.

Logs, stumps, fern fibre

These materials may be used as containers, since they blend well with the plants and surrounding garden, but using too many of them can reverse the effect and give a very superficial and unnatural appearance.

Metal

Plant containers made of metal are not widely used, but in certain circumstances metal objects can serve a useful purpose. Containers of copper, brass and cast-iron are not uncommon.

Metal is an efficient conductor of heat, and therefore a hot, sunny position would not be ideal for a metal plant container. Protection would also be desirable in areas of heavy frost or extreme cold.

Rust is a problem with iron containers because they are constantly exposed to moisture.

Other containers

Almost any item around the house or garden can be used as a plant container if it meets these needs:

Design. The size must be suitable for the plant it contains.
Durability. It must be of a lasting material.
Drainage. This must be adequate.

Terracotta and concrete pipes of various sizes give good drainage and are useful, particularly for trailing plants, which will hang down over the side.

Concrete is often used for large moulded tubs, and can be aesthetically pleasing. With the use of concrete, it is important that there is not an excessive amount of

lime still present, which would adversely affect the plant. To avoid this situation, and to help neutralize any excessive lime, new concrete containers can be washed with a diluted solution of spirits of salts. Thoroughly rinse several times after washing.

Large bricks with hollow interiors are useful, and reasonably priced.

The range of suitable containers goes on and on. It is necessary only to re-emphasize the desirability of choosing a container that will complement both the surrounding area and the plant or plants grown.

A miniature garden in a moulded container.

Soils and other potting mixes

An open, friable mix is recommended for container-grown plants. Mountain soil and clay loams, which look ideal when freshly cultivated and slightly moist, can turn to a soggy, claggy mass when wet, and then become almost rock-hard after drying out. This is not a well drained mixture, but it can be adjusted to form an excellent potting mix by adding coarse sand. The particles of sand separate the soil particles and permit good drainage.

Plants require a certain amount of moisture, and as the roots of a container-grown plant cannot penetrate deep into the soil to obtain this, it is desirable that an amount of peat moss, or other moisture-retaining substance, be added to the mixture. Peat moss is a material that can absorb moisture, then be squeezed out in a similar way to a sponge. The addition of peat moss still permits good drainage, but retains moisture to assist the survival of the plant.

A basic potting mixture would therefore be about 3 parts friable soil, 5 parts coarse river sand and 4 parts peat moss or organic material.

Several other potting ingredients are used by nurseries and gardeners, and while it is not planned to discuss these in detail here, they are worthy of consideration. They include vermiculite, perlite, exploded polystyrene, rice hulls, straw, pine chips (not from treated pine), aged or rotting sawdust, scoria, fern fibre and mushroom compost.

You may wish to obtain the ingredients and make your own potting mix, but prepared mixes are available from many nurseries and stores, and for small quantities it is often easiest and cheapest to obtain a prepared mix.

In most cases commercial potting mixes are pre-sterilized or pasteurized. This eliminates the possibility of introducing to your garden disease or soil fungus, which can be fatal to many plant species. The majority of undesirable weeds are eliminated by pasteurization, and any seeds that later germinate can be readily removed.

The plant species to be grown in a container should be considered when preparing the soil mix. Some ferns, for example, may require a mix with greater moisture retention than a plant or group of plants from a dry area. It may also be desirable to vary the potting mix under particular circumstances. Additional peat moss may prove to be desirable for plants in hanging baskets, or in unglazed terracotta pots in a warm situation. The basic mix could be altered to 2 parts soil, 3 parts sand and 3 parts peat moss, or a small bag of peat moss could be added proportionately to a commercially prepared mix.

Hydroponics

Hydroponics is a specialized method of plant cultivation that involves the growing of plants in containers without the use of soil. Materials such as sand, gravel, peat moss, vermiculite, perlite and sawdust are used to support the plant roots, and the plants are fed with a nutrient solution according to their needs. Hydroponic cultivation may be used outdoors or indoors, and can be used in association with fluorescent lighting.

While some Australian plants respond well to hydroponic cultivation, comparatively few species have been grown this way, and there is wide scope for experimental work in this area. Specialized publications on hydroponic cultivation are obtainable.

Fertilizers

Fertilizing is a very important aspect of growing plants in containers. Because of regular watering and efficient drainage, plant food is more readily leached from the potting mix than from garden soils.

Feeding at the time of planting can present some difficulty. If plants have been bought from nurseries, it is not always possible to know what fertilizer they have received, and how recently. Slow-release fertilizers are now used quite extensively in nurseries. These can continue to provide nutrients to a plant for many months, and further application of fertilizer when planting can result in over-feeding. If you have propagated your own plant, you will know exactly what fertilizer, if any, has been used, and can act accordingly.

Types of fertilizers

There are a large number of suitable fertilizers to choose from. They include the following.

Slow-release fertilizers These are usually marketed as small balls with a hard coating, or in pill or tablet form. It is best to buy those described as complete fertilizers, as some will only supply a limited number of essential nutrients.

Blood and bone A recommended fertilizer.

Hoof and horn Has less phosphorus than *blood and bone* and is highly recommended. In most cases these fertilizers will provide the required plant nutrients and will also release them to the plants fairly slowly. They are usually obtained and applied in powder form. An approximate initial application rate for these fertilizers incorporated into potting mixes is 1 to 3 kilograms per cubic metre, or 1 to 2 tablespoons per 5 medium-sized shovelfuls.

Liquid fertilizers Several different types of fertilizer are obtainable, either as a liquid, or in powder form to be mixed in the recommended quantities with water. Fertilizers of this type can be used at the time of potting plants, but their main value for container-grown plants is in the area of maintenance, and they are further discussed under that heading.

Excessive use of fertilizers can result in container-grown plants becoming root bound, and therefore heavy feeding of plants at the time of potting is not recommended. Additional nutriment can be readily applied at a later date, and further information in this regard will be found under the section on Maintenance.

Potting of plants

When you have gathered together your container, potting mix and selected plant or plants, the next stage is relatively simple.

If you are using small or medium size containers, clear a table or work bench for your use. Large tubs or planters may need to be placed in their permanent position before filling with soil and planting.

The container you wish to use may have been previously used for other plants. If this is the case, make sure it is washed or scrubbed. Soak the container in a disinfectant for several minutes, then thoroughly remove any residue before planting, by rinsing in water a number of times. This is particularly important if the previous plant happened to die, and it will minimize the possibility of any disease being passed on to the new plant.

Small plants can be successfully potted directly into large containers if desired. It is not necessary to progressively re-pot plants from small to medium pots over a period of time before finally placing them in containers of larger size, although some growers prefer this method. It is often a matter of personal preference, and with adequate care and maintenance plants can be successfully cultivated by either method.

Potting procedure

1 Water plant thoroughly. If it is very dry or difficult to remove from the nursery pot, immerse it in a bucket of water until the bubbles cease to rise. This will usually make removal easier.

2 Check that containers will allow good drainage. A piece of broken pot or coarse gravel placed over the drainage hole will prevent potting mix falling through if the hole is large, or prevent the holes becoming clogged up if there are a number of smaller holes.

3 Partly fill the container with potting mix. The level to which you fill will depend on the size of the plant being potted.

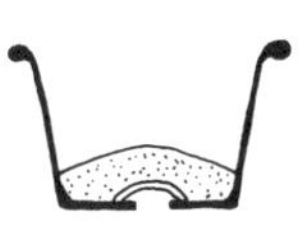

4 Remove the plant from its nursery pot. Plants may be tipped from containers with sloping sides (A) or from plastic bags (B). Straight-sided tins should be cut with tinsnips to avoid root damage to the plants (C).

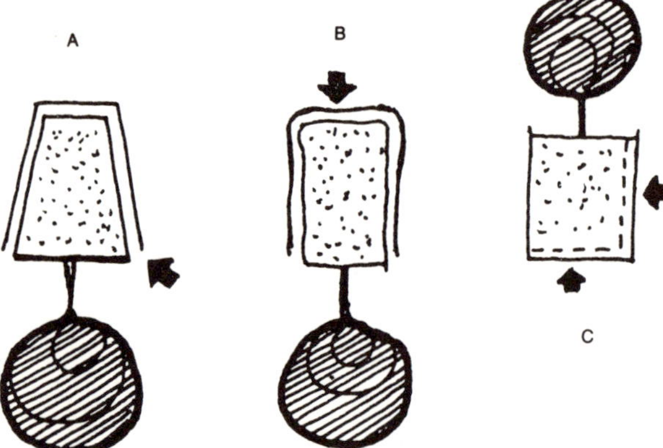

5 The roots may have formed a matted ball. If this is so, tease the edges of this ball, so that small feeder roots will be able to penetrate into the new potting mix. Straighten any coiled roots, and if too long for the new container, cut with secateurs. Don't panic if the soil breaks away more than you intended at this stage. Provided the plant is handled with care, and adequately watered and protected after potting, it is not likely to be adversely affected.

6 Place plant on potting mix, and add further mixture to fill container to desired level. Most plant species should be planted with a soil level just slightly higher than that of their original nursery pot. A degree of settling of the potting mix will later take place. Planting a plant too deep can cause collar-rot, while too high can result in the roots drying out excessively.

7 Firm down the potting mix in the container, paying particular attention to the outside edges.

8 If desired, a mulch can be placed on top of the potting mix to help retain moisture, to maintain a more even temperature around the root system, or for aesthetic reasons. A detailed listing of the various mulching materials available is given in Section 2, but coarse river sand, pebbles and gravel have been found to be excellent for container-grown plants.

9 Water well.

Care of plants after potting

After potting or re-potting, plants will appreciate protection for a period, particularly if there has been major disturbance of the roots.

Place containers in a sheltered position for several days, to avoid full exposure to sun, wind and frosts. The period of protection will depend on climatic conditions at the time; for example, if potting is done in midsummer, protection will be more necessary than during spring or autumn.

For large tubs or planters, protection can be given by a temporary screen, using a material such as hessian or shadecloth.

Incorrect watering is undoubtedly the major cause of fatalities with container-grown plants. Over-watering is a common cause of plant death, as also is drying out. How then can this situation be remedied? First let's look at some DON'Ts.

Watering of containers.
A — A soft broad flow is best.
B — A hard narrow flow can dislodge soil and expose roots.
C — If soil has dried out, shrinkage occurs, which allows water to drain out quickly without penetrating the soil.

DON'T water plants in the heat of the day. Water in the early morning, or wait until late evening.

DON'T leave pots standing permanently in saucers or dishes of water. A good soak for an hour or so can be beneficial, but waterlogging for days, or weeks, is detrimental to most plants.

DON'T use water from a hose that has been lying in the sun. The water will be warm, or even hot.

DON'T turn the tap on to full pressure when watering with a hose. A strong spurt of water can damage or uncover roots, with detrimental results.

DON'T just water the surface. Regular light spraying will result in the plant producing, and relying on, surface roots. If this frequent watering is then not possible for a period, the upper section of the pot dries out first, and the plant may not be able to cope. Aim at giving plants a thorough soak when watering is needed, rather than frequent light sprays.

Now, having looked at some of the pitfalls, let's take a positive look at watering.

Experience is undoubtedly the best teacher here, and you will find before too long that it is not difficult to know when a plant needs watering.

A reliable guide is to poke your finger into the potting mix. If it is dry and powdery as you scrape down a little, the plant almost certainly could benefit from some water. It is often important to actually scrape the potting mix in this way, as with several potting materials the upper surface can be deceiving, having a very dry appearance, while below the surface the mix is quite moist.

Other signs that suggest a plant could be dry include unnatural weeping of foliage tips, and leaves that look dry and curly.

Small manufactured aids for measuring the moisture content of soil mixes are available from garden suppliers, and may be of assistance if you are generally concerned about your ability to judge this, or if you are particularly concerned about a plant or plants in your collection.

Remember that different plant species have different needs for moisture. Some Australian plants grow best if kept fairly dry during the warmer months of the year, particularly those species that have adapted to these conditions through having grown naturally in low rainfall areas. This becomes a matter of particular importance if plants are being selected for grouping together in a large container.

Water should be applied gently, with a hose or watering can, until the potting mix is saturated. The plant will then absorb the moisture, while the container drains away the excess. This process could be repeated two or three times with small containers; with large tubs the hose could be allowed to run with a small trickle of water until the plant has been thoroughly soaked.

If the potting mix has not been pressed down correctly at the time of planting, or if the plant has been in the container for a long period, dry potting mix can leave the sides of the container, forming a ball. When this happens, water can run down between the soil and container and drain away without reaching the root area. If this happens, simply add additional potting mix, firming it down against the inside of the container with your fingers or a suitable gardening tool. Water well.

Although many Australian plants can survive on a minimum of water, once regular watering is commenced the plant often becomes accustomed to receiving this amount, and puts on new growth. It must then have continued watering for its survival.

It is not always easy to see when containers are too wet, and therefore it is a good idea to check from time to time that drainage holes are working adequately and are not clogged up. Sometimes, however, it is obvious that the soil is waterlogged. The top of the pot may contain a lush growth of moss or other small water-loving plants. It may become slimy or take on a sour smell. Re-potting may even be necessary. Check that you are not using too much peat moss or other moisture-retaining ingredient in your potting mix.

A highly successful method of watering, recently introduced, is known as trickle irrigation. This method is suitable for the home gardener, and involves the use of polythene pipe, from which small micro-tubes feed each individual plant with a very small trickle of water. In areas where limited water is available this method is ideal, as an absolute minimum of water is wasted. It is also extremely useful for gardeners who are planning a summer holiday, or for other reasons must be away from home for a period, since it can be used, in conjunction with a relatively inexpensive time switch, to turn the water on and off at selected times each day. One home gardener's kit available allows for forty micro tubes. Some could be used on container plants, while others may be placed in the vegetable garden or other selected areas.

If you are planning a holiday, or know that for a period you will not be able to water your plants regularly, avoid excessive watering or feeding in the preceding months. This will restrict the amount of lush new growth on the plants, and thus reduce the need for water. Pruning away any soft new growth will also reduce the moisture intake requirements of plants.

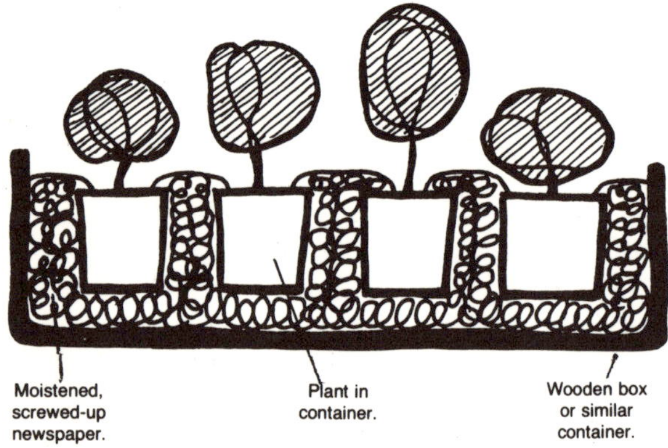

One method of storing containers during vacation.

If you are unable to secure the help of a neighbour or friend to water plants in your absence, and you do not have a trickle feed system, try to prevent the pots drying out as much as possible. Do not leave them in hot, open sunshine, or exposed to drying winds. They may if you wish be packed in boxes, and surrounded by moist peat moss, vermiculite or screwed up newspaper. A mulch placed on the top of the pots will prevent surface drying, but don't pack it tightly against the stems. If you want plants to benefit from any natural rainfall, be sure the mulch will allow the rain to penetrate.

Feeding

Container-grown plants should not be forced by artificial feeding, unless you wish to replace them each year or two after striving for maximum growth and flowering in that period. This can be done with some Australian plants, including the large golden everlasting daisy *Helichrysum bracteatum* 'Dargan Hill Monarch', Flannel Flowers — *Actinotus helianthi*, Kangaroo Paws — *Anigozanthos* species, and Fringe Lilies — *Thysanotus multiflorus*.

Excessive fertilizing can cause plants to become root bound, and species such as the Kangaroo Paws, which form extensive root systems, will need to be divided frequently.

On the other hand, plants grown in containers do not have access to the natural nutriments usually available in a garden, and therefore will possibly require some artificial feeding to maintain a healthy growth rate. Plants that are growing well are usually more attractive than those that are not, and in addition they are more resistant to disease and can cope better with garden pests.

As a general basic rule, if a plant is growing well it is neither necessary nor desirable to apply a fertilizer. If a plant is struggling, looking stunted or unhealthy, or failing to flower well, a fertilizer should be used.

Choose a cool morning or evening to apply the fertilizer, and use in accordance with the manufacturer's instructions.

Light top dressings of slow-release fertilizers can be applied at six-monthly intervals if desired. Care should be taken to ensure that the fertilizer is cultivated into the potting mix and then watered thoroughly.

Soluble fertilizers, which are dissolved or diluted in water before application, will usually promote a quick response in the plant. Their effectiveness is for a limited period only, as regular watering will leach out the soluble foods. Over-frequent use of these types, particularly if urea is the main component, can constitute force-feeding, and in some cases cause plant deaths. Liquid seaweed fertilizers do not produce this over-feeding problem, and most Australian plants respond well to their use. Best results are gained if the plants are not in a static growth stage.

Fertilizers in pill or tablet form are also now available, and may be suitable to your needs.

As a general rule, it would seem that short-term liquid fertilizers, or limited applications of a slow-release fertilizer, are the most suitable for maintaining healthy container-grown plants. In a garden quick growth is often desired, but this is not usually the case with plants in pots. Rather, a healthy and attractive plant is sought. Light fertilizing will usually achieve this, without causing the plant to double its size and become root-bound in the process.

Pruning

Some pruning of container-grown plants will almost certainly be desirable from time to time. Regular pinch pruning is, for many plants, the easiest and best method. Simply pinch out, with finger tips, the terminal growth on a branch. The branch will then no longer continue to grow in that direction. Side shoots will develop, and a generally more bushy plant results.

Spent flowers may be removed if desired, and the picking of a plant when in flower is another form of pruning.

Pruning should be carried out if a plant is re-potted, both to reduce the immediate demands on the root system, and to encourage subsequent new growth.

Immediate pruning of any dead or diseased areas of a plant should also be done.

Large container-grown shrubs will probably need pruning from time to time, and further information on methods of pruning will be found on page 43.

Pests and diseases
No pests or plant diseases affect container-grown plants that do not also affect plants in a garden. Reference should therefore be made to pages 43–4 for details of this aspect of cultivation.

The container-grown plant has many advantages in this regard. It is much easier to keep plants in pots, free from pests and diseases, than it is in the garden. Any diseased plant can be isolated from the rest, so that other plants are not infected, and problems within the soil can be kept to a minimum, particularly if sterilized potting mix is used.

Re-potting container-grown plants

If you are transplanting a plant from a small pot to a larger one, the procedure will be the same as that just described. It may however be desirable in some cases to re-pot a plant and return it to the same container. If a plant is not looking fresh and healthy, the addition of some fresh potting mix, plus a light pruning of the roots of the plant as well as the upper growth, can add new life and vigour. Re-potting can also be desirable if a container becomes infested with weeds such as couch, oxalis or sorrel, which are difficult to eradicate by any other means.

Procedure
1 Remove the plant from the container. Light tapping with a hammer or mallet can help in the case of large tubs. A large knife inserted around the edge of the tub will not harm the root system. Immersing the plant in water, or inserting a hose in the base drainage hole, can also help. With large tubs, the help of a second person may make the task much easier.
2 Reduce the root size by about 25 to 30 per cent. Fibrous roots can be removed with the fingers, but sharp secateurs should be used for the removal of any large roots. Tease out the outer roots in readiness for replanting.
3 Thoroughly wash the container, then rinse well.
4 Re-pot the plant, using the method described in the previous section, and taking care to maintain original soil level.
5 Water well, and lightly prune upper plant growth.

Selection of plants

To assist readers in selecting plants suitable for containers, a series of charts has been proposed, each listing 10–20 species. These are only a selection from many species that could be included under the various chart headings, but should at least provide a basis from which to work.

The comments given in the charts have been kept very brief, and aim simply to give an indication of the type of plant listed. Further reference should then be made to the alphabetical listing of species in Section 3 for more detailed descriptions concerning any species chosen.

Plants for pots of under 30 cm diameter
The plants listed here are all low, carpeting or clump-
forming species. They are excellent for small pots, and
are also useful in conjunction with other plants in
larger containers or planter boxes. Their presence in
large containers can help reduce weed growth and
provide a living mulch, thus reducing temperature
variation in the soil.

Chart 1   Plants for pots under 30 cm diameter

Botanical name	Common name	Flowering period	Comments
Claytonia australasica	White Purslane	Aug–April	A creeping and layering perennial, with fragrant white flowers.
Dampiera diversifolia		Sept–Feb	Prostrate species, with small leaves and deep blue flowers.
Frankenia pauciflora	Common Sea-heath	Mainly Nov–Feb	Dense matting species. Small greyish leaves, pink flowers.
Goodenia hederacea	Ivy Goodenia	Mainly Oct–Feb	A mat plant, with rounded leaves, and yellow to orange flowers.
Herpolirion novae-zealandiae	Sky Lily	Oct–Feb	A matting, grass-like plant, with white to pale blue star flowers.
Lechenaultia tubiflora	Heath Lechenaultia	Sept–Feb	Low, fine-foliaged plant. Cream, pink or red flowers.
Mazus pumilio	Swamp Mazus	Mainly Nov–April	A suckering mat plant, with mauve or white flowers.
Mentha diemenica	Slender Mint	Mainly Sept–Feb	A suckering plant with aromatic leaves and small mauve flowers.
Patersonia sericea	Silky Purple Flag	Sept–Dec	A coarse, grass-like clump, with deep purple-blue flowers.
Pratia pedunculata	Matted Pratia	Oct–April	A dense matting plant with white to blue flowers.
Pultenaea pedunculata	Matted Bush-pea	Sept–Dec	A spreading mat plant, with orange or yellow with red pea flowers.
Scleranthus biflorus	Knawel	—	A moss-like plant of bright light green.
Stylidium bulbiferum	Circus Trigger-plant	Sept–Dec	A tufting species, with red, pink or white flowers.
Viola betonicifolia	Showy Violet	Sept–Dec	A tufting perennial, with violet to purple flowers.
Viola sieberana	Tiny Violet	Most of year	A prostrate, matting plant, with small purple-blue and white flowers.
Wahlenbergia gloriosa	Royal Bluebell	Nov–Mar	A prostrate suckering species with deep bluish purple flowers.

above: Although well-known as a garden plant, the Waratah, *Telopea speciosissima* is not commonly grown in containers. These blooms are photographed on a plant grown in a tub of around 40 litre capacity.

right: A small plant suitable for a container or a small spot in the garden is the Silvery Daisy or Snow Daisy, *Celmisia asteliifolia*.

below: An Australian overseas. This delightful mat of *Pratia pedunculata* was photographed at the Strybing Aboretum, California USA. A very useful plant for gardens or containers.

Carefully selected rocks in combination with low, suckering form of *Dampiera linearis*, often sold as *Dampiera cuneata*.

Everlastings planted in gravel at the edge of a pathway. The golden yellow flowers are *Helichrysum bracteatum* Dargan Hill Monarch and the cream flowered shrub is another form of *Helichrysum bracteatum*.

Charts 2–9 Listing of plants according to flowering seasons

These charts list plants that will flower at specific times. There will be an overlap of flowering; some plants may flower, for example, in Winter to Spring, while others start in late Spring and continue through Summer. Seasonal conditions will affect the flowering period to some extent from year to year, and flowering will also be influenced by the general climatic conditions of the place where the plants are being cultivated. The charts should therefore be used as a guide only.

The plants listed as suitable for medium-sized containers of about 30-60 cm diameter may also be used in larger tubs or boxes if desired. They can be grown either individually or grouped with other plants. Similarly, species listed in Charts 2 to 9 are also suitable for inclusion in gardens.

A large number of plants flower during Spring, and therefore it is usually very easy to make a selection that will provide a display of flowers at this time of the year. Summer-flowering plants will be useful in areas of outdoor living. Plants around pools, barbecues or outdoor eating areas, whether grown in containers or in the garden, will usually be seen far more in the warmer months, when these areas receive their greatest use.

Autumn and Winter flowers are important in any garden, for their pleasing visual effect, and also as a continuing food supply for native birds and other garden creatures. Here again, many Australian plants do flower in these seasons, and the range is more than adequate for the needs of the average gardener. Plants flowering in the cooler months have value if placed where they can be viewed from within the house, particularly if the flowers attract birds, and much enjoyment can be gained from the garden even when adverse weather prevents outdoor activities.

Chart 2 Spring flowering plants for medium containers (30-60 cm diameter)

Botanical name	Common name	Flowering period	Comments
Acacia browniana		July–Oct	Low growing, with fern-like leaves and yellow globular flower-heads.
Actinodium cunninghamii	Albany Daisy	Aug–Jan	Low plant with white and red daisy-like flower-heads.
Baeckea ramosissima	Rosy Heath-myrtle	Aug–Nov	Small, spreading species with white to deep pink flowers.
Boronia mollis	Soft Boronia	Aug–Nov	Bushy shrub; soft foliage; bright pink star flowers.
Boronia molloyae	Tall Boronia	Oct–Jan	Has hairy, ferny leaves and pinkish-red bell flowers.
Boronia pinnata	Pinnate Boronia	Sept–Dec	Aromatic foliage, with bright pink star-shaped flowers.
Calectasia cyanea	Blue Tinsel Lily	Sept–Nov	Clumping perennial with blue to purple and yellow flowers.
Calytrix alpestris	Snow Myrtle	Aug–Dec	Attractive shrub; small leaves; white star-like flowers.
Chorizema cordatum	Heart-leaved Flame-pea	July–Dec	Small plant with colourful pea-flowers of orange, red bright pink and yellow.
Eremophila glabra	Tar Bush	June–Jan	Variable species. Orange to red tubular flowers.
Eriostemon spicatus	Pepper and Salt	June–Jan	Small narrow-leaved shrub. Deep pink to mauve star-like flowers.
Eriostemon verrucosus	Fairy Wax-flower	June–Nov	Warty leaves; pink to white star-like flowers.
Hibbertia fasciculata	Bundled Guinea-flower	June–Nov	Has fine leaves and yellow open-petalled flowers.
Hibbertia procumbens	Guinea-flower	Oct–Apr	A mat-forming species, with profuse bright yellow flowers.
Kunzea parvifolia — dwarf form	Violet Kunzea	Sept–Jan	Compact shrub with small leaves and mauve flower-heads.
Lechenaultia biloba	Blue Lechenaultia	July–Dec	Small shrub with spectacular blue flowers.
Melaleuca cordata		Sept–Dec	Open shrub; heart-shaped leaves; pink to red, globular flower-heads.
Micromyrtus ciliata	Fringed Heath-myrtle	May–Nov	A spreading shrub; profuse small, white to pink flowers.
Olearia ciliata	Fringed Daisy-bush	Mainly Oct–Jan	Dwarf shrub with pale to bright purple daisies.
Pimelea ferruginea		Mainly July–Oct	A dense shrub with shiny leaves and pink flower-heads.

Botanical name	Common name	Flowering period	Comments
Banksia baueri	Possum Banksia or Koala Banksia	July–Nov	Shrub with stiff serrated leaves and large, fluffy flower-heads.
Banksia caleyi	Caley's Banksia	Aug–Jan	Dense shrub; serrated leaves; pendant red to yellow flower-heads.
Banksia lemanniana		July–Dec	Dense shrub; serrated leaves; pendant yellow to yellow-green flower-heads.
Callistemon 'Reeves Pink'	—	Oct–Dec	A bushy shrub with pink bottlebrush flower-spikes.
Callistemon salignus	Willow Bottlebrush	Oct–Dec	Shrub to small tree; papery bark; white to deep pink flowers.
Chamelaucium floriferum	Walpole Wax	Aug–Nov	A compact shrub with white open-petalled flowers.
Darwinia fascicularis		Aug–Nov	Has narrow, aromatic foliage; cream to red flower-heads.
Eriostemon myoporoides	Long-leaf Waxflower	July–Dec	A hardy, bushy shrub with profuse white starry flowers.
Grevillea confertifolia	Grampians Grevillea	Aug–Nov	A variable species, with prostrate and upright forms. Mauve to pink flower-heads.
Hypocalymma robustum	Swan River Myrtle	July–Nov	Upright shrub with narrow leaves and clusters of showy pink flowers.
Leptospermum scoparium var *rotundifolium*	Round-leaved Tea-tree	Oct–Dec	Jervis Bay form; has bluish mauve-pink flowers.
Melaleuca decussata	Totem Poles	Sept–Jan	Dense shrub; greyish leaves; pale to deep mauve brushes.
Melaleuca fulgens	Scarlet Honey-myrtle	Sept–Dec	Has greyish leaves and scarlet to deep pink or salmon-pink brushes.
Melaleuca megacephala		Sept–Dec	Shrub with broad, thick leaves deep cream to yellow, globular flower-heads.
Petrophile serruriae		Oct–Dec	Shrub with arching branches; finely divided prickly leaves; clusters of pink to yellow flowers.
Prostanthera hirtula (prostrate form)	Hairy Mint-bush	Sept–Dec	Dense aromatic foliage; mauve to purple flowers.
Telopea speciosissima	NSW Waratah	Sept–Nov	An upright plant with spectacular red flower-heads.

Botanical name	Common name	Flowering period	Comments
Actinotus helianthi	Flannel Flower	Aug–Feb	Grey-green hairy leaves; soft white to cream daisy-like flower-heads.
Beaufortia purpurea		Sept–Apr	Has fine greyish-green leaves; purple-red globular flower-heads.
Beaufortia schaueri		Aug–Feb	Low spreading shrub with pink to purple, globular flower-heads.
Cheiranthera cyanea	Finger Flower	Oct–Jan	Slender-branched shrub with attractive deep blue flowers.
Dampiera linearis		Sept–Jan	Low suckering plant. Clustered flowers of deep blue with yellow centre.
Epacris longiflora	Fuchsia Heath	Mainly May-Jan	Has attractive red and white tubular flowers for most of year.
Helichrysum baxteri	Fringed, or White Everlasting	Oct–Jan	Low clumping species; white and yellow, daisy-like flower-heads.
Helichrysum bracteatum 'Dargan Hill Monarch'	Golden Everlasting	Most of year	Has soft, greyish foliage, and large golden papery flower-heads.
Helichrysum bracteatum 'Diamond Head'	Golden Everlasting	Most of year	A prostrate form, with golden papery flower-heads.
Helichrysum semipapposum	Clustered Everlasting	Mainly Oct–Feb	Greyish foliage; clusters of small golden yellow flower-heads.
Hibbertia obtusifolia		Aug–Feb	Prostrate or upright forms. Bright yellow flowers.
Hibbertia stellaris	Orange Stars	Mainly Oct–Jan	Has reddish stems; small scattered leaves; bright orange-yellow flowers.
Lechenaultia laricina		Oct–Feb	A dense low shrub with bright orange-red flowers.
Melaleuca pulchella	Claw Flower	Nov–Feb	Spreading shrub with mauve-pink claw-like flowers.
Melaleuca thymifolia	Thyme Honey-myrtle	Oct–Apr	Has greyish-green foliage and mauve to purple flowers.
Olearia frostii	Bogong Daisy-bush	Nov–Feb	Woolly, grey-green foliage; large mauve, pink or white daisy flowers.
Scholtzia involucrata		Throughout year	Spreading shrub. Pale pink tea-tree-like flowers.
Spyridium obcordatum		Sept–Jan	A compact, prostrate species. Dense heads of small cream flowers.

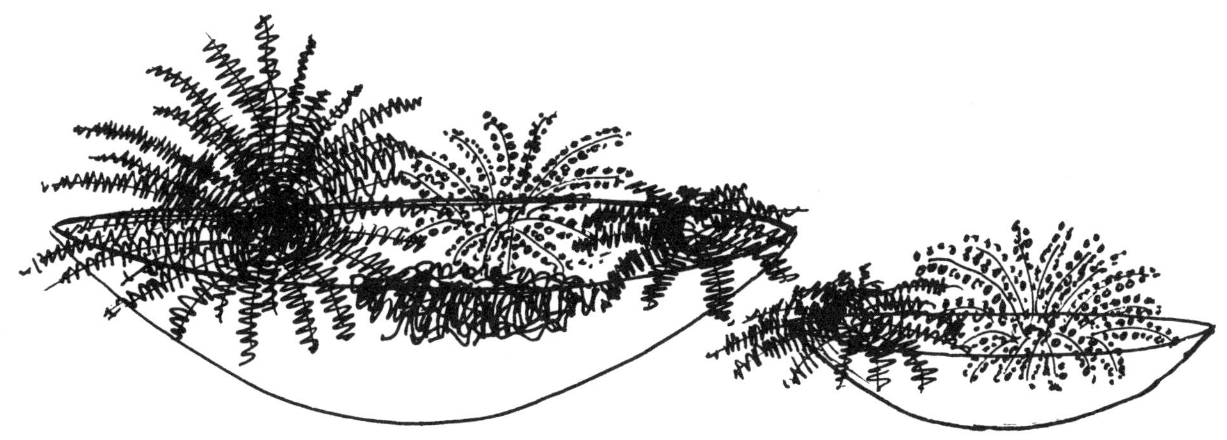

Chart 5   Summer flowering plants for large tubs (60 cm diameter or larger)

Botanical name	Common name	Flowering period	Comments
Acacia uncinata	Round-leaved Wattle	Mainly Sept–Mar	An open shrub with bright yellow globular flower-heads.
Baeckea virgata	Tall, or Twiggy Baeckea	Nov–Mar	An upright shrub. Profuse small white tea-tree-like flowers.
Banksia attenuata	Coast Banksia, Slender Banksia	Oct–Mar	Has stiff serrated leaves; bright yellow, cylindrical flower-heads.
Banksia baxteri	Bird's Nest Banksia	Nov–Mar	Has large triangular lobed leaves, and yellow-green dome-shaped flower-heads.
Callistemon viminalis	Weeping Bottlebrush	Mainly Nov–Mar	Pendulous branches. Bright red flower-spikes.
Calothamnus gibbosus		Nov–Feb	Has corky branches, pine-like leaves, and red flowers in one-sided spikes.
Darwinia lejostyla		Mainly Aug–Feb	Bushy small shrub with pinkish red bell-like flower-heads.
Eremaea beaufortioides	Round-leaved Eremaea	Sept–Feb	Has showy orange flower-heads.
Grevillea 'Robyn Gordon'		Most of year	Deeply lobed foliage; large terminal, bright red flower-heads.
Leptospermum epacridoideum		Mainly Dec–Feb	Shrub with dense foliage; white or rarely pinkish tea-tree flowers.
Melaleuca coccinea	Goldfields Bottlebrush	Nov–Feb	Has brilliant red brushes, produced on the old wood.
Melaleuca elliptica	Granite Honey-myrtle	Nov–Feb	A dense shrub with deep red flower brushes.
Melaleuca huegelii	Chenile Honey-myrtle	Nov–Jan	Has long, cream-white spikes of flower.
Melaleuca linariifolia	Snow in Summer	Nov–Feb	Small tree with soft papery bark and profuse white to cream terminal flower-heads.
Melaleuca nesophila	Showy Honey-myrtle	Dec–Mar	A relatively dense shrub; globular mauve-pink flower-heads.
Persoonia pinifolia	Pine-leaved Geebung	Mainly Dec–May	Has fine green foliage, and small yellow flowers in terminal spikes.
Scaevola striata	Royal Robe	Mainly Oct–Feb	A low suckering species, with mauve to rich bluish purple flowers.

14

Botanical name	Common name	Flowering period	Comments
Astroloma epacridis		Dec–Aug	A dense low shrub with small tubular pink and orange-red flowers.
Banksia laricina	Rose-fruited Banksia	April–Aug	Small, dense species, with globular yellow flower-heads and woody fruits.
Banksia violacea	Violet Banksia	Jan–July	Bushy species with small blue-green leaves and violet to deep purple flower-heads.
Bauera rubioides	Wiry Bauera	Throughout year	Variable shrub with white to pink open-petalled flowers.
Beaufortia sparsa	Swamp Bottlebrush, Gravel Bottlebrush	Dec–Apr	Has bright reddish-orange flower spikes.
Calytrix fraseri		Sept–May	Small open shrub. Flowers have bright pink-mauve to purple petals and golden stamens.
Correa 'Dusky Bells'		Mainly Mar–Sept	A low spreading shrub with pink bell-shaped flowers.
Crowea exalata	Small Crowea	Oct–June	Has aromatic foliage and waxy pink star-like flowers.
Epacris impressa (Bega)	Common Heath	Mainly Apr–Nov	This form, from Bega, NSW, has orange-red flowers.
Homoranthus darwinioides		Mainly Jan–July	A compact shrub with small leaves, and small pink yellow and green flowers.
Hypocalymma strictum		Dec–Apr	An upright shrub with narrow leaves and small pink flowers.
Platytheca verticillata	Platytheca	Mar–Dec	A dwarf open shrub with rich purple flowers.
Rhododendron lochae		Mainly Jan–Apr	Has shiny green leaves and clusters of waxy red bell-shaped flowers.
Thryptomene baeckeacea		Mainly Jan–July	Low shrub with arching branches; small mauve-pink tea-tree-like flowers.
Viola hederacea	Ivy-leaved Violet	Most of year	A spreading perennial herb with purple-blue and white flowers.

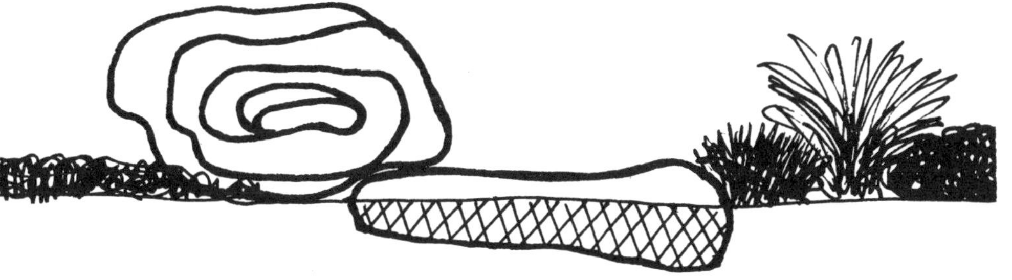

Chart 7   Autumn flowering plants for large tubs (60 cm diameter or larger)

Botanical name	Common name	Flowering period	Comments
Acacia iteaphylla	Gawler Range Wattle	Mar–Sept	Dense large shrub; bluish foliage; clusters of pale yellow flower-heads.
Banksia candolleana	Propellor Banksia	Mar–July	Has long, serrated leaves and orange, globular flower-heads.
Banksia marginata	Silver Banksia	Mar–Sept	Variable species. Pale to bright yellow, cylindrical flower-heads.
Banksia meisneri	Meisner's Banksia	Mar–Nov	Dense foliage; small narrow leaves; yellow flower-heads; ornamental seed cones.
Banksia ornata	Desert Banksia	Mar–Aug	A bushy species. Serrated leaves. Grey and yellow to brown flower-heads.
Banksia prionotes	Orange Banksia, Acorn Banksia	Feb–Aug	Highly ornamental flower-heads. Grey buds, opening to orange.
Grevillea x gaudichaudii		Mainly Sept–Apr	Prostrate plant with decorative foliage, and dark red to burgundy toothbrush flowers.
Grevillea 'Robyn Gordon'		Most of year	Deeply lobed foliage; large terminal, bright red flower-heads.
Hakea laurina	Pincushion Hakea	Mar–July	Large shrub to small tree. Pincushion-shaped heads of cream and red flowers.
Lambertia formosa	Mountain Devil, Honey Flower	Throughout year	A bushy shrub with pungent leaves. Clusters of orange to bright red flowers.
Leptospermum squarrosum	Peach Tea-tree	Feb–Apr	Bushy shrub with narrow leaves and white to deep pink flowers.
Melaleuca lateritia	Red Robin Bush	Mainly Nov–Apr	An open shrub with bright orange-red flower spikes on older wood.

Chart 8   Winter flowering plants for medium containers (30-60 cm diameter)

Botanical name	Common name	Flowering period	Comments
Acacia drummondii ssp. *affinis*		June–Sept	Low bushy plant; profuse bright yellow rod-shaped flower-heads.
Acacia leptospermoides		May–Oct	Small shrub with bluish foliage, and bright yellow globular flower-heads.
Astroloma ciliatum	Candle Cranberry-heath	Mainly May–Nov	Small dense shrub. Tubular flowers of red, greenish yellow and black.
Astroloma conostephioides	Flame Heath	May–Feb	A low shrub with scarlet tubular flowers.
Correa 'Mannii'		Mar–Sept	Has dark green leaves and red bell-shaped flowers.
Correa pulchella		Apr-Sept	A variable shrub with bright orange to vermilion flowers.
Correa reflexa	Common Correa	Mainly Mar–Nov	An extremely variable species. Pendulous bell-shaped flowers of cream, green, pink or red.
Epacris reclinata		June–Nov	A small shrub with small bright pink to red tubular flowers.
Grevillea brownii		Mainly May–Nov	A low-growing species with very bright red flowers.
Grevillea chrysophaea	Golden Grevillea	July–Nov	Has clusters of golden yellow flowers.
Grevillea glabella		Mainly June–Dec	Variable shrub with narrow green leaves. Flowers usually pink to red and cream.
Grevillea pilulifera		July–Nov	A small compact species. The small flowers are mainly cream.
Hovea pungens		Mainly July–Oct	An upright shrub with pungent leaves and bright purplish-blue pea-shaped flowers.
Lechenaultia formosa	Red Lechenaultia	Mainly Mar–Nov	A variable small species. Flowers can be yellow, orange, pink, magenta, scarlet or red.
Thryptomene saxicola	Rock Thryptomene	Mainly Apr–Oct	A spreading shrub with small aromatic leaves and clusters of pale to deep pink flowers.

Chart 9   Winter flowering plants for large tubs (60 cm diameter or larger)

Botanical name	Common name	Flowering period	Comments
Acacia boormanii	Snowy River Wattle	July–Oct	Has grey-green foliage and racemes of bright yellow flowers.
Acacia podalyriifolia	Silver Wattle	June–Oct	An attractive small tree with grey foliage and bright yellow globular flower-heads.
Acacia terminalis	Sunshine Wattle	Mar–July	Has dark green ferny leaves and yellow flower-heads.
Banksia brownii	Brown's Banksia	Feb–July	An erect shrub with reddish to golden brown flower-heads.
Banksia ericifolia	Heath-leaved Banksia	Apr–Nov	A bushy species with flower-heads of yellow, orange, deep red or cream.
Banksia marginata	Silver Banksia	Mar–Sept	A variable species. Has pale to bright yellow flower-heads
Banksia spinulosa	Hairpin Banksia	Mainly Mar–Aug	Variable species, with tall or dwarf forms. Flowers can be amber to yellow with red or black styles, or all gold.
Cassia nemophila	Desert Cassia	June–Nov	A bushy plant with silvery leaves and yellow flowers.
Darwinia citriodora	Lemon-scented Darwinia	Mainly Apr–Nov	A bushy shrub with aromatic leaves and and small flower-heads of yellow-green and red.
Eucalyptus caesia	Gungurru, or Gungunnu	June–Nov	Ornamental small tree. Flowers pink to red with gold.
Grevillea alpina	Cats Claw or Mountain Grevillea	June–Nov	Extremely variable species, with low-growing or tall forms. Flowers are white, pink, red, yellow or orange.
Grevillea baueri	Bauer's Grevillea	Mar–Nov	A hardy species, with flowers of pink, red and cream.
Grevillea diminuta		Mainly Jan–Aug	Has dark grey to green, oval leaves, and pendant clusters of red flowers.
Grevillea dimorpha	Flame Grevillea	Apr–Nov	Has dark green leaves and clusters of brilliant red flowers.
Grevillea floribunda		June–Jan	Flower colour is gold and green with short brown hairs giving an unusual rusty appearance.
Grevillea 'Poorinda Beauty'		June–Dec	A bushy plant with dense clusters of bright red to scarlet flowers.
Grevillea sericea	Pink Spider-flower	Most of year	A long-flowering species, with colour forms of white to mauve.
Hakea orthorrhyncha	Bird's Beak Hakea	Mainly July–Sept	An open shrub with stiff leaves. Bright red flowers are produced on older wood.
Templetonia retusa	Cockies Tongues	May–Oct	Has showy terminal clusters of pink to red pea-flowers.

Plants for medium to large containers in a very hot position

It is not always possible to place containers in a position that allows the most favourable conditions for plant growth. Often we have situations, such as on a patio at the front of a house, where we want to grow a plant in a container but realize that the area is in full sun for most of the day.

The construction of containers for use under these conditions can be a significant feature. For example, planter boxes made of wood will not conduct the heat through to the soil and plant roots as readily as will ceramic containers. A light-coloured exterior will reflect the sun's rays, while darker colours absorb more heat.

The watering of container-grown plants is also of prime importance if they are in a very hot position. Plants should not be watered while they are exposed to hot sunshine, even if they are seen to be wilting. All watering should be done very early in the morning or at least an hour after sunset.

For successful cultivation in very hot positions plants will need to be carefully selected, and the following list has been included to provide assistance in this regard.

Chart 10   Plants for medium to large containers in a very hot position

Botanical name	Common name	Flowering period	Comments
Acacia gracilifolia		Aug–Oct	An upright to spreading species with long narrow phyllodes and golden yellow flower-heads.
Acacia leptospermoides		May–Oct	Small shrub with bluish foliage and bright yellow globular flower-heads.
Banksia gardneri	Prostrate Banksia	Aug–Feb	Deeply lobed leaves; bronze to yellowish flower-heads.
Banksia meisneri	Meisner's Banksia	Mar–Nov	Has dense foliage with small narrow leaves, yellow flower-heads and ornamental seed cones.
Banksia petiolaris		Aug–Jan	Prostrate species, with serrated leaves, and flower-heads of grey and yellow.
Beaufortia squarrosa	Sand Bottlebrush	Sept–Apr	A large spreading shrub with flower-heads usually bright red.
Calothamnus sanguineus	Blood-red Net-bush	Oct–June	Low spreading shrub with dense pine-like leaves, and rich red flowers.
Chamelaucium uncinatum	Geraldton Wax	Aug–Jan	Various forms are available, with flower colours of reddish purple, mauve, pink or white.
Eremaea violacea	Violet Eremaea	Aug–Feb	A small shrub with flower-heads of purple and gold.
Eremophila maculata 'Aurea'	Native Fuchsia, or Spotted Emu-bush	June–Dec	A much-branched shrub. This form has yellow tubular flowers.
Grevillea lavandulacea	Lavender Grevillea	June–Nov	A variable species. Foliage is usually greyish, and flowers bright pink to red.
Hakea bucculenta	Red Pokers	July–Nov	An upright shrub with spectacular bright red flower spikes.
Lambertia ericifolia		Throughout year	Has showy custers of tubular orange-red flowers.
Petrophile biloba	Granite Petrophile	July–Sept	An upright shrub with stiff prickly leaves and flower clusters of pink and grey.
Phebalium bullatum	Desert Phebalium	Sept–Dec	Has small, scaly leaves, and bright yellow star-like flowers.
Prostanthera aspalathoides		Sept–Feb	A dense dwarf shrub with aromatic foliage, and flowers of red, orange, or yellow.
Regelia ciliata		Nov–Mar	Leaves are small and stem-hugging. The globular flower-heads are mauve to purple.
Regelia cymbifolia		Sept–Dec	An upright shrub with purplish-red flower-heads.
Verticordia monodelpha	Woolly Feather-flower	Nov–Dec	Has grey-green aromatic foliage and terminal clusters of pink woolly flowers.

Plants for medium to large containers in a shaded position

As with the previous section, it is sometimes necessary to choose container-plants for particular locations, and the careful selection of species is important.

When planting in a shaded position, we very often think first of ferns. The majority of ferns are highly suited to such conditions, and Chart 21 lists a selection suitable for container cultivation.

If however you are seeking plants other than ferns, to grow in a medium to large container in a shaded position, the following listing will assist you in finding suitable species.

Chart 11   Plants for medium to large containers in a shaded position

Botanical name	Common name	Flowering period	Comments
Banksia canei	Mountain Banksia	Oct–Feb	Has stiff, serrated leaves, and blue-grey buds opening to yellow-green flowers.
Bauera rubioides	Wiry Bauera	Most of year	A low shrub with open-petalled flowers of white to pink.
Bauera sessiliflora	Grampians Bauera	July–Dec	Has rose-purple to magenta flowers.
Boronia megastigma	Brown Boronia	July–Nov	A fragrant species, with various colour forms including greenish-yellow, burgundy and brown.
Boronia serrulata	Native Rose	Aug–Dec	Has fragrant, bright pink flowers.
Correa lawrenciana	Mountain Correa	Mar–Nov	A large shrub with leathery leaves and tubular flowers of cream to green, or red.
Correa reflexa	Common Correa	Mainly Mar–Nov	An extremely variable species. Has pendulous bell-shaped flowers of cream, green, pink or red.
Eriostemon myoporoides	Long-leaf Waxflower	July–Dec	A hardy, bushy shrub with profuse white starry flowers.
Eriostemon myoporoides 'Mountain Giant'		Sept–Apr	Similar to the above, but larger in most aspects.
Indigofera australis	Austral Indigo	Sept–Dec	An open shrub with fern-like grey-green leaves. Pale to bright lilac pea-flowers.
Olearia tomentosus	Toothed Daisy-bush	Usually Aug–Nov	Variable habit. Large daisy flowers, commonly white, or rarely pale mauve.
Phebalium lamprophyllum	Shiny Phebalium	Sept–Dec	Bushy shrub. Small, shiny, dark green leaves. White to cream flower clusters.
Prostanthera cuneata	Alpine Mint-bush	Oct–Mar	Dense shrub with aromatic dark green leaves and mainly white flowers.
Prostanthera lasianthos	Victorian Christmas-bush	Nov–Jan	A large shrub or small tree. Dark green leaves; dense heads of white flowers.
Prostanthera melissifolia	Balm Mint-bush	Oct–Jan	A compact shrub with strongly aromatic foliage and violet to deep lilac flowers.
Prostanthera walteri	Monkey Mint-bush	Mainly Nov–Feb	A spreading species, with dark green foliage and unusual green with purple flowers.
Pultenaea daphnoides	Large-leaved Bush-pea	Sept–Nov	Shrub with wedge-shaped leaves; pea-flowers mainly yellow.
Rhododendron lochae		Mainly Jan–Apr	Has shiny green leaves and clusters of waxy red bell-shaped flowers.
Spyridium parvifolium	Australian Dusty Miller	Sept–Feb	Low and tall forms available. Oval, crinkled leaves. Clusters of small white to cream flowers.
Westringia linifolia		Mainly Sept–Jan	Bushy species, with narrow leaves and scattered white to lilac flowers.

Foliage plants for medium to large containers

Many Australian plants have interesting and unusual foliage, and are cultivated primarily for this aspect. In the following chart the comments given for each individual plant refer mainly to the foliage. Other details, including flowering, will be found by reference to the Plant Descriptions in Section 3.

Chart 12 Foliage plants for medium to large containers

Botanical name	Common name	Flowering period	Comments
Acacia flexifolia	Bent-leaf Wattle	June–Oct	Has grey-green foliage and globular pale yellow flower-heads.
Callitris oblonga	Esk Cypress-pine		Dense upright conifer with bluish-green foliage.
Casuarina ramosissima		July–Nov	A spreading shrub with pine-like greyish foliage.
Grevillea brevicuspis		Aug–Nov	Has small, divided, prickly leaves and reddish stems. Profuse white to cream flowers.
Grevillea ilicifolia	Holly Grevillea	Mar–Nov	Variable, prostrate to medium shrub. Leaves often deeply lobed. Toothbrush flowers of cream, green and red.
Grevillea intricata		Aug–Nov	Finely lobed net-like leaves. Reddish stems.
Hakea victoriae	Royal Hakea	Aug–Oct	Has large, pungent, stem-clasping leaves, which colour with tones of cream to orange.
Homoranthus flavescens		Oct–Feb	A low plant with horizontal branches and greyish leaves.
Hypocalymma cordifolium		Sept–Nov	Small shrub with reddish stems. Round leaves, usually light green. Variegated form also.
Isopogon anethifolius	Cone-bush	Mainly Aug–Nov	An upright, branched shrub with finely divided leaves. Terminal yellow flower-heads.
Lasiopetalum behri	Pink Velvet-bush	Aug–Dec	Dense shrub with velvety stems and oblong greyish-green leaves. New growth is pinkish.
Leptospermum nitidum 'Copper Sheen'		Sept–Nov	Dense shrub with smooth dark leaves; new growth bright coppery red. Flowers lime-yellow.
Melaleuca diosmifolia		Oct–Dec	A stiff-branched shrub with crowded green leaves. Lime-green brushes.
Melaleuca incana	Grey Honey-myrtle	Sept–Dec	Weeping pendulous branches with soft grey-green leaves. Small yellow brushes.
Mirbelia dilatata		Sept–Nov	A much-branched shrub with wedge-shaped pungent leaves. Purple pea-shaped flowers.
Myoporum floribundum	Slender Myoporum	Nov–Jan	Graceful shrub with horizontal branches and very narrow drooping leaves. White flowers.
Olearia teretifolia (compact form)	Cypress Daisy-bush	Sept–Nov	Has dense dark green conifer-like foliage. Masses of small white daisy flowers.
Podocarpus lawrencei	Mountain Plum-pine		A dwarf conifer with ornamental dark green to grey-green leathery foliage.
Regelia velutina		Aug–Jan	An upright shrub with hairy, greyish leaves. Bright red flower spikes.

Fragrant plants for medium to large containers
The following chart includes Australian plants with perfumed flowers and some species with fragrant foliage. There is a further listing in Chart 29, and although that chart does include some trees and shrubs not generally suited to containers, there are several smaller plants that can be grown in pots.

Plants with fragrant foliage can give pleasure throughout the year, whereas those with perfumed flowers are fragrant only when in bloom. These are therefore ideally suited to container cultivation, as they can be moved to desired positions for the flowering period, then perhaps grown-on in another area during the non-flowering months.

Chart 13 Fragrant plants for medium to large containers

Botanical name	Common name	Flowering period	Comments
Backhousia citriodora	Lemon Ironwood, or Sweet Verbena Myrtle	Aug–Nov	Large shrub to tree. Living or dried leaves have a clear lemon fragrance.
Boronia anemonifolia	Sticky Boronia	Aug–Nov	Has strongly scented, small, green leaves. Abundant pink or white starry flowers.
Boronia megastigma	Brown Boronia	July–Nov	Renowned for its fragrance. Various colour forms include greenish-yellow, burgundy and brown.
Boronia purdieana		Aug–Nov	Small shrub. Greenish yellow bell-like flowers. Highly fragrant.
Boronia serrulata	Native Rose	Aug–Dec	Has fragrant, bright pink flowers.
Calytrix aurea		Sept–Feb	An upright shrub. Golden yellow starry flowers have a spicy fragrance.
Cymbidium madidum		Aug–Jan	Orchid, with racemes of fragrant yellow-green and brown flowers.
Darwinia citriodora	Lemon-scented Darwinia	Mainly Apr–Nov	Bushy shrub with aromatic leaves and small flower-heads of yellow-green and red.
Dendrobium falcorostrum	Beech Orchid	Aug–Nov	Orchid with fragrant white to cream flowers.
Herpolirion novae-zealandiae	Sky Lily	Oct–Feb	A matting, grass-like plant with white to pale blue star flowers.
Hymenosporum flavum	Native Frangipani	Oct–Dec	An upright tree with shiny dark green leaves and fragrant yellow flowers.
Indigofera australis	Austral Indigo	Sept–Dec	An open shrub with fern-like leaves and fragrant pale to bright lilac pea-flowers.
Jacksonia scoparia		Sept–Nov	An upright shrub, with greyish foliage, and profuse, fragrant, yellow to orange pea-flowers.
Kennedia glabrata		Nov–Dec	Prostrate creeper with clusters of perfumed, brick red pea-shaped flowers.
Lechenaultia floribunda		Sept–Jan	Low shrub. Various forms available. Blue flowers usually emit a delicate fragrance.
Prostanthera melissifolia	Balm Mint-bush	Oct–Jan	Compact shrub with strongly aromatic foliage and violet to deep lilac flowers.
Prostanthera rotundifolia	Round-leaf Mint-bush	Aug–Nov	Highly aromatic round to oval leaves. Mauve to purple, or pink, flowers.

Bird-attracting plants for medium to large containers

The presence of small native birds in a garden can be most enjoyable. If such birds are to be encouraged certain basic requirements will need to be provided, and these are discussed further with Chart 36.

Birds can be attracted to flowering plants in containers as readily as they will be to garden-grown specimens, although the total setting is of importance, and it is undoubtedly difficult to encourage birds to visit individual plants isolated from other garden areas. If, however, you live near a native garden area to which birds have been encouraged, even one bird-attracting plant in a container will result in their seeking it out as a source of food.

It is unfortunately not realistic to plant bird-attracting species and encourage native birds if you own a cat. This is particularly so of smaller container-grown plants, as they usually provide ideal opportunities for a cat to lie in wait, then pounce.

The following species can all be grown successfully in medium or large containers, although some will grow to large shrubs under garden conditions. Regular pruning will assist in maintaining smaller bushy plants, if desired. For pots or tubs of smaller size, low-growing *Correa* or *Epacris* species are highly recommended.

Chart 14 Bird attracting plants for medium to large containers

Botanical name	Common name	Flowering period	Comments
Banksia ericifolia	Heath-leaved Banksia	Apr–Nov	A bushy species, with flower-heads of yellow, orange, deep red or cream.
Banksia spinulosa	Hairpin Banksia	Mainly March–Aug	Variable species, with tall or dwarf forms. Flowers usually honey-coloured.
Brachysema aphyllum	Ribbon Pea	July–Oct	Unusual leafless species. Long bright red pea-shaped flowers.
Callistemon subulatus	Tonghi Bottlebrush	Oct–Dec	Shrub with crowded narrow leaves and deep red flower spikes.
Correa backhousiana		May–Nov	Oval, leathery green leaves; cream to pale green tubular flowers.
Correa lawrenciana	Mountain Correa	Mar–Nov	A large shrub with leathery leaves, and tubular flowers of cream to green, or red.
Correa 'Mannii'		Mar–Sept	Has dark green leaves and red bell-shaped flowers.
Epacris longiflora	Fuchsia Heath	May–Jan	Has attractive red and white tubular flowers for most of year.
Eucalyptus preissiana	Bell-fruited Mallee	Aug–Nov	A spreading small tree with clusters of bright yellow flowers.
Grevillea arenaria		June–Jan	Shrub with greyish leaves. Two forms available, flowers red or yellow-green.
Grevillea bipinnatifida	Fuchsia Grevillea or Grape Grevillea	Mainly Aug–Feb	Low shrub with large lobed leaves. Large pendant clusters of red flowers.
Grevillea 'Crosbie Morrison'		July–Nov	Spreading shrub with greyish foliage. Clusters of red to pink and cream flowers.
Grevillea longifolia	Fern-leaf Grevillea	Mainly June–Nov	Large shrub. Long, narrow, serrated leaves. Pink to red toothbrush flowers.
Grevillea mucronulata		Mainly Apr–Dec	Dense shrub with greenish flowers. Highly bird-attracting.
Grevillea 'Poorinda Constance'		Most of year	Much-branched shrub with clusters of red flowers.
Grevillea 'Poorinda Queen'		Mainly July–Dec	Dense shrub with apricot to pale orange flowers over a long period.
Grevillea speciosa	Red Spider-flower	Mainly June–Dec	Shrub with deep red to bright red wheel-like flower-heads.
Lambertia formosa	Mountain Devil, or Honey Flower	Throughout year	Bushy shrub with clusters of orange to bright red flowers.
Prostanthera microphylla	Small-leaf Mint-bush	Sept–Feb	Low shrub with small aromatic leaves and red or bluish-green tubular flowers.

Trailing plants suitable for containers

The design of some containers makes them very well suited to plants with a trailing habit. Trailing plants can also be used as ground-covers in large planters, in conjunction with taller shrubs or trees. Trailing plants can be used successfully in hanging baskets, and Chart 19 therefore also includes a number of species with a trailing habit.

The plants included in the following chart grow to varying sizes, and this factor should of course be considered in relation to the size of the container being used. Reference should be made to the Plant Description in Section 3 for further information on this aspect.

Chart 15   Trailing plants suitable for containers

Botanical name	Common name	Flowering period	Comments
Brachysema praemorsum		Mainly May–Feb	Has wedge-shaped leaves and pea-flowers, initially cream then ageing to red.
Dampiera cauloptera		July–Dec	Has winged stems and blue flowers borne in small clusters. Plants can sucker.
Dampiera diversifolia		Sept–Feb	Prostrate species, with small leaves and deep blue flowers.
Grevillea juniperina (prostrate forms)	Juniper Grevillea	July–Nov	Several prostrate forms are available, with prickly narrow leaves and flowers of buff, yellow or red.
Grevillea repens	Creeping Grevillea	Oct–Feb	Dense species, with holly-like leaves, often reddish. Deep red toothbrush flowers.
Grevillea thelemanniana (grey leaf form)	Spider-net Grevillea	Mainly May–Dec	This form has soft, hairy, greyish leaves and bright red flowers.
Hemiandra pungens	Snake Bush	Oct–Apr	Has narrow prickly leaves and mauve-pink flowers.
Hibbertia dentata	Trailing Guinea-flower	Mainly Aug–Dec	Has reddish stems, with toothed, shiny green leaves and yellow flowers.
Hoya australis		Sept–Nov	Has shiny, oval, dark green leaves and waxy white flowers.
Kennedia eximia		Aug–Dec	Leaves are oval, crinkled and dark green. Short racemes of dark red pea-shaped flowers.
Kennedia microphylla		Aug–Nov	Dense mat of small leaves, with deep brick red pea-shaped flowers.
Kennedia prostrata	Running Postman	Mainly Aug–Nov	Greyish green leaves; bright red with yellow pea-flowers.
Oxylobium tricuspidatum		Sept–Nov	Grey-green, wedge-shaped leaves. Pea-shaped flowers of orange and yellow with brown.
Scaevola aemula	Fairy Fan-flower	Sept–Feb	Light green, slightly hairy leaves. Flowers blue with yellow.
Scaevola phlebopetala	Royal Robe	Mainly Nov–May	Has wedge-shaped hairy leaves and deep purple with gold flowers.

Botanical name	Common name	Flowering period	Comments
Anigozanthos humilis	Cat's Paw	June–Dec	Strap-like leaves. Flower-heads vary from cream to yellow, orange, pink or red.
Anigozanthos manglesii	Red and Green Kangaroo Paw	June–Dec	Grey-green leaves. Red and green flower-heads.
Anigozanthos pulcherrimus	Golden Kangaroo Paw	Mainly Nov–Feb	Has large flower-stems, with golden yellow flower-heads.
Blancoa canescens	Winter Bell	June–Oct	Greyish hairy leaves; pink to red, hairy, tubular flowers.
Celmisia asteliifolia	Silver Daisy, or Snow Daisy	Dec–Mar	Strap-like leaves; daisy flowers of white with yellow centre.
Conostylis aculeata		Aug–Feb	Variable species, with strap-like leaves; clusters of yellow tubular flowers.
Conostylis candicans	Grey Cottonhead	July–Feb	Grey hairy leaves; clusters of densely hairy, tubular, yellow flowers.
Conostylis prolifera	Mat Cottonheads	Aug–Feb	Self-layering species; narrow leaves; hairy cream to yellow flowers.
Dryandra nivea	Couch Honeypot	July–Oct	Clumping or spreading plant. Long, decorative leaves; yellow and brown flower-heads.
Glischrocaryon behrii	Golden Pennants	Mainly Sept–Dec	Greyish green foliage. Clusters of small bright yellow flowers.
Helichrysum baxteri	Fringed or White Everlasting	Oct–Jan	Low clumping species; white and yellow daisy-like flower-heads.
Lomandra filiformis	Wattle Mat-rush	Sept–Dec	Narrow, grass-like leaves. Small cream to yellow flowers.
Orthrosanthus laxus	Morning Iris	Aug–Nov	Has narrow, strap-like leaves and pale to deep blue flowers.
Patersonia fragilis	Short Purple-flag	Oct–Feb	Has narrow rush-like leaves and purple flowers.
Sowerbaea juncea	Rush Lily, or Vanilla Lily	Oct–Dec	Grass-like foliage; globular clusters of fragrant mauve flowers.
Stylidium graminifolium	Grass Trigger-plant	Mainly Nov–Jan	Grass-like foliage; erect stems bearing many small pale to deep pink flowers.
Stypandra caespitosa	Tufted Lily	Mainly Oct–Feb	Greyish grass-like leaves. Flowers have blue petals and yellow stamens.
Thysanotus multiflorus	Fringe Lily	Nov–Mar	Has grass-like foliage, with dense heads of bright mauve flowers.

For the collector: rare or difficult-to-grow species suitable for containers

As mentioned in the introduction to container growing, this method of cultivation can often be used successfully to grow plants that are otherwise difficult to establish under garden conditions. Specialized soil mixes can be used for each individual plant, and drainage can be adjusted to suit specific requirements.

There are very many Australian plants that could at present qualify as 'rare', as so many species, not previously cultivated, are being introduced through nurseries and specialist collectors. The species included in this chart are all obtainable through Australian plant nurseries, although many are to date not commonly grown. Some have proved difficult to grow, while others are not readily obtainable because of propagation difficulties.

All have highly desirable horticultural features, and will give ample reward to those who seek them out and give them the little extra care required for successful cultivation.

Chart 17   For the collector: Rare or difficult-to-grow species suitable for containers

Botanical name	Common name	Flowering period	Comments
Calytrix fraseri		Sept–May	Small open shrub. Flowers have bright pink-mauve to purple petals and gold stamens.
Clianthus formosus	Sturt's Desert Pea	Mainly June–Mar	Prostrate species with hairy greyish leaves; spectacular red and black pea-flowers.
Conospermum amoenum	Blue Smoke-bush	Aug–Nov	Small shrub with pine-like leaves; small light blue flowers.
Conostylis bealiana		May–Sept	Tufting perennial with yellow to orange tubular flowers.
Darwinia meeboldii	Cranbrook Bell	Mainly Sept–Nov	Upright shrub; crowded small leaves; red or red and white bell-like flower-heads.
Diplolaena angustifolia	Yanchep Rose	July–Oct	Small shrub; pendant flower-heads of red to pale orange.
Dryandra proteoides	King Dryandra	Aug–Oct	Shrub with pungent, deeply lobed leaves. Flower-heads are yellow with brown bracts.
Eriostemon australasius		Aug–Nov	Upright shrub; greyish-green leaves; profuse mauve-pink waxy, star-like flowers.
Gossypium sturtianum	Sturt's Desert Rose	Oct–Feb	Shrub with oval blue to greyish leaves; pink to purple flowers.
Grevillea flexuosa	Tangled Grevillea	Mainly Sept–Mar	A spreading, low shrub with deeply lobed greyish leaves and delicate bright pink flower-heads.
Grevillea insignis		Mainly Aug–Nov	An open shrub with grey-green holly-like leaves; clusters of pink waxy flowers.
Grevillea intricata		Aug–Nov	Has finely lobed, net-like leaves, and reddish stems. Cream flower-spikes.
Grevillea quercifolia	Oak-leaf Grevillea	Aug–Nov	Has grey-green prickly leaves and deep pink to purple flowers.
Hibbertia stellaris	Orange Stars	Mainly Oct–Jan	Has reddish stems, small scattered leaves and bright orange-yellow flowers.
Hypocalymma puniceum	Large Myrtle	Nov–Apr	Spreading shrub with short narrow leaves and pink to reddish flowers.
Isopogon latifolius		Oct–Nov	Shrub with long, flat, light green leaves; large deep purple to pink flower-heads.
Pimelea spectabilis		Mainly Sept–Nov	A shrub with narrow grey-green leaves and profuse white flower-heads.
Pultenaea subalpina	Rosy Bush-pea	Mainly Sept–Dec	Compact shrub with small narrow leaves and pink to purple pea-flowers.
Verticordia densiflora		Mainly Nov–Feb	Small shrub with narrow grey-green aromatic leaves and clusters of white to pink feathery flowers.

Grouping of plants in containers

It is not always necessary or desirable to grow plants on the basis of one plant per container. Many containers are ideally suited to the planting of two or more plants, and similarly, a number of plant species are suited to cultivation in association with others. Small matting plants such as *Pratia pedunculata* can provide an attractive ground-cover beneath taller plants, and can be used even in small to medium containers.

Consideration must be given to the root area required by different plant species, and this is of equal importance to the upper growth, if the plants are to grow successfully together. Plants also have varying requirements in regard to moisture, fertilizers and tolerance of sun or shade, and these aspects can also affect the successful cultivation of species grouped together in one container.

Plants can be grouped on the basis of flower, foliage combinations or growth habit and form. It is even quite possible to obtain pleasing combinations in all respects, with some careful thought. To achieve this goal a knowledge of the plants being chosen is essential. Specialist nurseries can usually provide the necessary information relating to specific plants if you are unsure. Flowering period is important if the plants are being chosen on the basis of flower. You may seek plants that flower at different times, to provide an extended period of beauty, or plan for a combination of flowers to give a striking display at a particular time.

A successful and satisfying combination of species will be achieved with careful planning, and can be well worth the effort involved.

The following chart lists a selection of species that have been found to combine well with other plants in containers. These are only a very small number of species, out of a possibility of many hundreds that could be used in this way. The chart is designed to give a starting point only in regard to plant groupings, and experienced growers will undoubtedly find many other species equally desirable for this purpose.

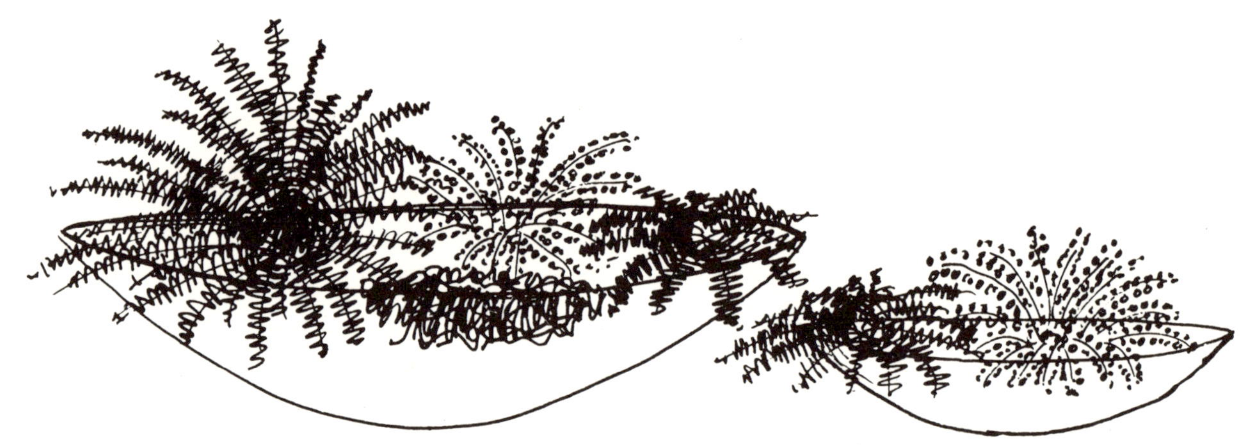

A pleasing combination of rocks and the tufting foliage of *Dianella tasmanica*.

A small garden area featuring dwarf plants on either side of a gravel pathway. The species have been chosen to provide flower throughout the year. *Helichrysum bracteatum* Diamond Head, the yellow everlasting, forms an attractive colour combination with the mauve *Patersonia occidentalis*.

left: A gravel area at the side of a driveway, planted with two species of Kangaroo Paws. The red is *Anigozanthos rufus*, and the yellow *A.pulcherrimus*.

above: Plants such as *Helichrysum apiculatum* are useful for softening, yet defining, the edges of pathways.

below: The Fish-bone Fern, *Nephrolepis cordifolia*, is used to advantage here beside an informal pathway.

Botanical name	Common name	Flowering period	Comments
A *Acacia drummondii* ssp. *affinis*		May–Sept	A low bushy plant, with profuse bright yellow flower-heads.
WITH *Brachysema praemorsum*		Mainly May–Feb	Prostrate to low species, with cream pea flowers ageing to red.
B *Actinotus helianthi*	Flannel Flower	Aug–Feb	Grows to 1.5 m high, and has creamy white flowers, tipped with green.
WITH *Dampiera linearis*		Sept–Jan	A low suckering species, with deep blue flowers.
C *Anigozanthos rufus*	Red Kangaroo Paw	Sept–Feb	A clump-forming plant, with deep red flowers on stalks of up to 1.5 m high.
WITH *Hibbertia procumbens*	Guinea-flower	Oct–Apr	A matting species, with profuse bright yellow flowers.
D *Blandfordia grandiflora* (or *B. nobilis*) WITH	Christmas Bells	Nov–Jan	Has grass-like leaves, and orange and yellow bell-shaped flowers.
Pratia pedunculata (or *P. erecta*)		Oct–Apr Sept–Feb	Dense ground-covers, with small blue or white flowers.
E *Correa reflexa* (or *C.* 'Mannii', or *C. pulchella*) WITH	Common Correa	Mainly Mar–Nov	Small shrub, with tubular flowers of cream, green, pink or red.
Spyridium cinereum	Tiny Spyridium	Sept–Apr	A prostrate species, grown mainly for its small, greyish, wedge-shaped leaves.
F *Dampiera diversifolia*		Sept–Feb	Prostrate species, with deep blue flowers.
WITH *Epacris longiflora*	Fuchsia Heath	Mainly May–Jan	Small shrub, with red and white tubular flowers.
G *Eriostemon verrucosus* (white flowered form) WITH	Fairy Waxflower	June–Nov	Small shrub, with white starry flowers.
Grevillea brownii		May–Nov	Low spreading plant, with clusters of very bright red flowers.
H *Helichrysum baxteri*	Fringed or White Everlasting	Mainly Oct–Jan	A low clump-forming species, with yellow and white daisy-like flower-heads.
WITH *Goodenia geniculata*	Bent Goodenia	Oct–Mar	A dense mat-plant, with bright yellow flowers.
I *Melaleuca thymifolia*	Thyme Honey-myrtle	Oct–Apr	Small compact shrub with mauve to purple flowers.
WITH *Viola hederacea*	Ivy-leaved Violet	Mainly Sept–Mar	Low spreading plant, with purple-blue and white flowers.
J *Rhododendron lochae*		Mainly Jan–Apr	Shrub, with oval, smooth, shiny leaves, and waxy red bell-shaped flowers.
WITH *Scleranthus biflorus*	Knawel	—	A moss-like plant, with bright green foliage.
K *Xanthorrhoea australis*	Austral Grass-tree	—	An attractive clump of slender grass-like leaves.
WITH *Astroloma humifusum*	Cranberry Heath	Mar–Oct	Ground-covering species, with grey-green leaves, bright red flowers, and succulent green berries.

Hanging baskets

There is much interest at present in the cultivation of plants in hanging baskets. With this interest has come an awareness that many plant species are particularly attractive when grown in this way, and there has been a corresponding increase in the range of hanging baskets and plant hangers obtainable.

For many years ferns have been grown in hanging baskets, with the main type of container being a wire frame into which sphagnum moss is placed to support the potting mix and root system. The hanger was similarly a bent piece of wire, and the attractiveness of the unit relied almost solely on the plant.

Today we see a wide range of containers designed as hanging baskets, made from plastic, metal, timber, tree fern fibre or ceramics. Much thought and creativity is also given to the hangers.

Baskets Aesthetic values vary greatly with individual taste, but there are some functional aspects that are worthy of consideration.

Hanging baskets are likely to dry out more quickly than other containers, and this aspect is accentuated by the use of unglazed ceramic pots. If unglazed ceramic containers are used, a lining of black plastic can help to retain moisture. There must be drainage holes in the base of this lining. Weight is another important consideration if ceramic pots are used, and the roof structure, the hook and the hanger must be easily adequate to support the weight of the pot and contents.

Plastic containers have the advantage of being very light, but they must be strong enough to support the plant and potting mix. Avoid containers that are supported by the hanger passing through small holes in the plastic without supporting the base of the pot. Plastic will break down after a period of time and become brittle. Pots of light colours seem the most susceptible in this regard.

Tree fern fibre can dry out very quickly, and this also applies to wire framed baskets lined with moss, or the fibre liners available commercially for this purpose. This aspect must be watched carefully if baskets are to be hung in an exposed position.

Metal is an efficient conductor of heat, and heat from the sun, or excessive cold, will be readily transmitted to the root systems of plants in metal containers.

For hanging baskets in relatively open or exposed positions, containers of timber, plastic or glazed ceramics would appear to be the most suitable.

Further details regarding different types of plant containers will be found on page 2.

Hangers Hangers must be strong enough to support the weight of the hanging basket, plus the potting mix and the plant. The material should also be relatively durable, although most fibres will break down in time. Ropes from natural fibres such as sisal can rot when they are continually moist, and exposure to sunshine and water will damage synthetic fibres.

Macrame hangers are currently widely used, and as

well as being attractive, the use of multiple fibres gives them added strength. Wire and chain suspensions are also used successfully.

Hangers should always be selected with regard to the suitability of their design. As mentioned above in relation to plastic containers, some containers are adequately supported by a hanger attached at the top, but others need support under the base of the pot.

A hanger can be simply something that holds up the basket, or it can be an attractive feature of the total unit. To achieve a pleasing combination it is vital that the hanger be selected or constructed to blend with the container, so that each will complement the other.

Hooks It may seem trivial to discuss hooks for hanging baskets, but if you have a valued plant or container, lack of attention to this aspect can result in disaster. It is rarely adequate to use a large-size nail or a cupboard hook to support hanging baskets. A range of hooks is now manufactured specifically for this purpose, and these are available from hardware stores and nurseries.

Swivel hooks allow for plants to be turned easily, in order that they can receive equal sunlight on all sides.

Many of the hooks available are marked with the weight they will adequately support. This eliminates all need for guesswork in this regard, and it is only necessary for the completed hanging basket to be weighed to enable a suitable hook to be purchased.

Make sure that the plant has been recently watered, to ensure that the maximum weight is recorded.

The structure into which a hook is placed is also an important factor. If it is going into a wall or ceiling of plaster or other soft material, be sure the hook is attached through to the wooden frame.

Plants The selection of plants for a hanging basket will depend to a major extent on the position of the basket. In addition to climatic considerations, which are of utmost importance, the position from which the hanging basket will be seen is also vital. If the container is to hang only about a metre from ground level and be viewed from above, a wide range of plants suitable for small and medium containers can be used. The majority of hanging baskets seem to be held at or above eye level, and therefore are best suited to spreading or trailing plant species.

The size of the container will affect the suitability of species, and the smaller the container, the smaller will be the range of plants that may be grown successfully in it.

The following chart gives a selection of Australian plants suitable for hanging baskets. As with most other sections, it is a selection only, of tried species, and undoubtedly there are many more that would be equally suited to the purpose.

Care of indoor plants

Only a limited amount of work has been done with the growing of Australian plants indoors. Experiments have been carried out with a number of species, mainly from the tropical rain forest areas of Queensland, and several have proved to be most successful.

Information in earlier chapters about containers and potting applies also to indoor plants.

It is not possible to state hard-and-fast rules regarding the maintenance of plants indoors, as conditions inside each house vary greatly. The amount of natural or artificial light available will affect a plant's growth, as will the temperature of the room in which it is located. The temperature may be constant, or may reach a peak for certain hours of the day or evening, then drop considerably during the night. Smoke or oil-heater fumes can also affect plants.

Chart 19   Plants suitable for hanging baskets

Botanical name	Common name	Flowering period	Comments
Chorizema diversifolium		Sept–Oct	Of light twining or trailing habit, with multicoloured pea-flowers, mainly orange.
Dampiera diversifolia		Sept–Feb	Has small leaves, and deep blue flowers.
Dampiera linearis	Common Dampiera	Mainly Sept–Jan	A suckering species, with terminal clusters of blue flowers. Several forms available.
Darwinia camptostylis		Sept–Dec	Prostrate, with cascading branches; small clusters of cream to pink flowers.
Eutaxia microphylla		Sept–Nov	Low spreading shrub; narrow grey-green leaves; profuse pea-flowers, mainly yellow.
Goodenia lanata	Trailing Goodenia	Oct–Mar	Prostrate, with dark green toothed leaves, and bright yellow flowers.
Grevillea x gaudichaudii		Mainly Sept–Apr	Prostrate, with decorative foliage, and dark red to burgundy toothbrush flowers.
Grevillea nudiflora		July–Dec	Trailing species, with bright red flowers on stems which extend beyond the foliage.
Hibbertia empetrifolia	Guinea-flower	Aug–Nov	Spreading plant, with small leaves, and masses of yellow open-petalled flowers.
Kennedia microphylla		Aug–Nov	Dense mat of small leaves; deep brick-red pea-flowers.
Lechenaultia formosa	Red Lechenaultia	Mainly Mar–Nov	A variable small species. Flowers can be yellow, orange, pink, magenta, scarlet or red.
Myoporum parvifolium	Creeping Myoporum	Nov–Mar	Has narrow leaves, and small white or rarely pale pink flowers.
Oxylobium tricuspidatum		Sept–Nov	Has grey-green, wedge-shaped leaves. Pea-flowers of orange and yellow with brown.
Pultenaea pedunculata	Matted Bush-pea	Sept–Dec	Spreading mat plant, with orange or yellow with red pea-flowers.
Scaevola microphylla		Mainly Oct–Jan	A low carpeting plant, with small leaves; profuse small pale blue fan-shaped flowers.
Tetratheca ciliata	Pink Bells	July–Dec	A small clumping species, with oval leaves and pendant pink or white flowers.
Thomasia grandiflora		Aug-Nov	A spreading species. Leaves have a crinkled edge. Flowers are pendant and pink to mauve.

All these points will be relevant, and while in a garden or glasshouse we aim to provide conditions to suit the plants, the situation here is vastly different. In most cases we are not able, nor do we wish, to change conditions within a house to suit the needs of our plants, therefore we will be seeking plants that can tolerate the conditions we have chosen for our way of life. It will therefore be largely a matter of experimenting in each individual house.

The basic needs of a plant, as expressed in earlier chapters, remain the same. Plants also have a basic need for light, which can be supplied from natural or artificial sources. If you wish to consider artificial lighting for indoor plants, the electricity authority in your capital city will be able to offer guidance. Plants are also adapted to receiving natural moisture intake through their leaves, and if your house is one with a very dry atmosphere, a bowl of water in the vicinity of indoor plants can assist their growth.

Leaves of plants, fern fronds and so on can become very dusty indoors, and therefore should be wiped over regularly with a damp cloth or sponge. The addition of white oil will help to combat any scale pests. Apart from improving the appearance of the foliage, this allows the plant to breathe naturally through the leaves.

Most plants will benefit from a few hours outside, every few weeks, and if possible during light rain. Try to select a time when the difference in temperature from indoors to outdoors is not too great.

Some Australian plant species grown indoors have a limited life span as indoor plants, for example *Schleffera actinophylla* and *Stenocarpus sinuatus*. This also applies to introduced species such as the Rubber Plant, *Ficus elastica*. Some will eventually grow too large and need transplanting elsewhere.

A combination of indoor and outdoor gardening provides one of the best solutions for those who do not necessarily want the same plant indoors for an indefinite period. A wide range of plants will tolerate a period indoors, ranging from a few days to several weeks. By this means container-grown plants can be brought to a place where they can be seen and admired at their best, then later returned to their regular position outdoors.

If plants have been inside for some time, it will be desirable to place them in a sheltered position outdoors for a few days, to allow for 'hardening off' before they are fully exposed to wind or hot sunshine.

Among plants commonly grown outdoors, then brought inside for a period, are potted Christmas trees. Introduced conifers are widely used for this purpose. Suitable Australian native species are the White Cypress Pine, *Callitris columellaris*, Mountain Plum Pine, *Podocarpus lawrencei*, or Heath-leaved Banksia, *Banksia ericifolia*. Several other species would also be suitable, depending on the extent to which you wish to retain a Christmas tree of traditional appearance.

The following chart lists a selection of Australian plant species that have been grown with success indoors. Many other species can be grown indoors but to succeed in this area, attention must always be given to the basic needs of a plant. These are for an adequate and balanced availability of nutriment, moisture, air and light.

Flowering periods have not been given in this chart, as plants would be unlikely to flower when grown indoors.

Chart 20   Plants suitable for indoor containers

Botanical name	Common name	Comments
Brachychiton populneus	Kurrajong	Ultimately a tree. Has decorative, simple or lobed leaves.
Brachychiton rupestre	Bottle Tree	Slow growing tree; has a bottle-shaped trunk, and decorative narrow foliage.
Cardwellia sublima		From tropical rainforests. Has large, shiny, lobed leaves.
Castanospermum australe	Black Bean	Ultimately a tree. Has large shiny, dark green leaves composed of many small leaflets.
Cissus antarctica	Kangaroo Vine	A climber, with shiny, dark green toothed leaves.
Cordyline stricta		An erect, palm-like plant, with racemes of small white to purple flowers.
Grevillea robusta	Silky Oak	Ultimately a large tree. Has attractive, large, deeply divided leaves.
Lepidozamia peroffskyana		Slow-growing cycad, with deeply lobed, shiny foliage.
Nothofagus cunninghamii	Myrtle Beech	A slow-growing tree, with many smooth, shiny, oval leaves and reddish to bronze new growth.
Schefflera actinophylla	Umbrella tree	Has large, shiny leaves, radiating like the spokes of a wheel.
Stenocarpus sinuatus	Firewheel Tree	Ultimately a tree. Leaves are large, and shiny dark green. Orange to red flowers in wheel-like formation.

Ferns suitable for containers

A large number of ferns are ideally suited to container cultivation, both indoors and outdoors.

Over-watering is possibly one of the most common causes of failure, and many ferns will not tolerate excessive moisture, as is the case when a container is left for long periods in a saucer or dish filled with water. Some protection from wind is also desirable if ferns are to be grown in a confined area, and a through-draft can be damaging, particularly to new fronds.

Ferns may be grown individually in a container or grouped together. *Blechnum fluviatile* and *B. penna-marina* are ideal small ground-covers that can be grown at the base of taller species. Many ferns can also be combined successfully with other plants, provided that they all have similar cultivation requirements. Species of *Boronia, Patersonia* and *Viola* are among those suitable in this regard.

The ferns listed in this chart can also be grown under normal garden conditions, with the exception of *Platycerium bifurcatum*, the Elkhorn, which is commonly grown on slabs of tree fern or timber. Ferns can be planted in comparatively small spaces, and as they are tolerant of shaded conditions, they can be of considerable value in small-area gardens.

Chart 21   Ferns suitable for containers

Botanical name	Common name	Comments
Adiantum aethiopicum	Common Maidenhair Fern	A well-known fern, with delicate fronds.
Asplenium australasius	Bird's-nest Fern	Has large, erect, radiating fronds.
Asplenium bulbiferum	Mother Spleenwort	Has soft, much-divided fronds, with young plants produced at frond tips.
Asplenium simplicifrons		Similar to A. nidus, but has shorter and narrower fronds.
Blechnum fluviatile	Ray Water-fern	A spreading, prostrate fern, with pale green fronds.
Blechnum minus	Soft Water-fern	Has semi-weeping, deeply divided fronds. New growth often bronze or pinkish.
Blechnum nudum	Fishbone Water-fern	A hardy species, with fishbone-shaped fronds.
Blechnum penna-marina	Alpine Water-fern	A hardy matting species, with small fishbone-like fronds.
Blechnum wattsii	Hard Water-fern	Has dark green, leathery, deeply divided fronds. New growth can have reddish tonings.
Cyathea cooperi		A comparatively quick-growing, and decorative tree-fern.
Cyathea rebeccae		Tree-fern with arching, shiny, dark green fronds.
Dicksonia antarctica	Soft Tree-fern	Tree-fern with large arching fronds.
Dicksonia youngiae		Tree-fern, usually quick-growing whilst young. Has a slender trunk.
Doodia aspera	Prickly Rasp-fern	Spreading fern, with erect fishbone-shaped fronds. New growth pink to red.
Doodia media	Common Rasp-fern	Similar to D. aspera. New growth can be purplish red.
Lastreopsis shepherdii	Shiny Shield-fern	Has shiny arching fronds.
Nephrolepis cordifolia	Fishbone Fern	Well-known in cultivation. Spreads by runners.
Pellaea falcata	Sickle Fern	Spreads by creeping rhizomes. Fronds are of fishbone shape.
Platycerium bifurcatum	Elkhorn	A commonly grown epiphytic fern.
Polystichum proliferum	Mother Shield-fern	Has arching, dark green, divided fronds, and produces young plants at the frond tips.
Pyrrosia rupestris	Rock Felt-fern	Spreads by creeping rhizomes. Has strap-like fronds covered with soft hairs.
Todea barbara	King Fern	Develops a short, broad trunk, and can have multiple heads of fronds.

Orchids suitable for containers

Orchids are commonly divided into two major categories. Species which under natural conditions grow in the ground are classified as terrestrial, whilst epiphytes are those which are usually found growing on other plants such as trees or tree-fern trunks.

Plants from both groups are suitable for growing in containers, and in fact this method of cultivation is both the most commonly used and the most successful. Terrestrial species can be provided with the necessary care and protection when in pots, as containers can be moved in accordance with seasonal requirements. It is also easier to cope with slugs and snails, which present a major problem with garden-grown plants. Most epiphytic orchids can be grown in containers of potting mix, or can be attached to supporting structures such as slabs of timber or tree-fern. Specially prepared potting mixes are obtainable for the growing of both terrestrial and epiphytic species.

There are over 600 species of Australian native orchids. Many are not widely available and are cultivated only by collectors and enthusiasts, whilst others can require specialised conditions for cultivation, such as provided by a heated glasshouse. There are however a number of species that are obtainable from nurseries, and that have proved successful in cultivation, and it is from these that the following chart has been compiled.

Chart 22   Orchids suitable for containers

Botanical name	Common name	Flowering period	Comments
Chiloglottis trapeziformis	Broad-lip Bird Orchid	Sept–Nov	A terrestrial species, with purple and green flowers.
Corybas diemenicus	Slaty Helmet-orchid	June–Oct	A terrestrial orchid, with unusual, purplish helmet-shaped flowers.
Corybas dilatatus	Veined Helmet-orchid	June–Oct	Similar to *C. diemenicus*.
Cymbidium madidum		Aug–Jan	Has racemes of fragrant yellow-green and brown flowers.
Dendrobium x *delicatum*		Aug–Oct	A hardy natural hybrid. Epiphytic. Has racemes of white or cream flowers.
Dendrobium falcorostrum	Beech Orchid	Aug–Nov	Has fragant white to cream flowers.
Dendrobium x *gracilimum*		Sept–Oct	A natural hybrid, with small fragrant, white or yellow flowers.
Dendrobium kingianum	Pink Rock-orchid	Aug–Nov	A commonly cultivated epiphytic. Flowers are usually pink, but can be white or purple.
Dendrobium speciosum	Rock Orchid	July–Nov	A hardy epiphytic species. Has fragrant white, cream or yellow flowers, in outstanding racemes.
Diuris longifolia	Wallflower Orchid or Donkey Orchid	July–Nov	A terrestrial orchid, with distinctively shaped flowers of yellow or brown and yellow.
Diuris maculata	Leopard Orchid	July–Nov	Similar to *D. longifolia*. Petals have many dark brown spots.
Liparis reflexa	Yellow Rock-orchid	Mar–May	A terrestrial species, with small pale greenish-white to yellow-green flowers.
Pterostylis concinna	Trim Greenhood	May–Oct	A terrestrial orchid. Flowers are green and white striped with brown markings.
Pterostylis curta	Blunt Greenhood	July–Oct	Flowers are mainly green, with red and brown markings.
Pterostylis nutans	Nodding Greenhood	July–Nov	A distinctive greenhood, with nodding, translucent green flowers.
Pterostylis pedunculata	Maroonhood	July–Nov	Flowers have green and white stripes with a maroon or reddish brown hood.

Bonsai

Bonsai is a specialized form of container growing, which until recent years has only been rarely used in association with Australian plants. By regular root pruning, careful pruning of branchlets, and in some cases wiring of the foliage, trees that would normally grow to many metres high are cultivated in containers of small size. Correct watering and fertilizing are essential, and plants are also re-potted as necessary, to maintain healthy growth. Bonsai plants are normally grown outdoors, and are brought inside for a few days at a time.

It is not intended to cover fully the methods of bonsai cultivation, but rather to mention some of the Australian plant species that are suitable for this specialized form of horticulture.

Australian plants can now be seen at most bonsai exhibitions. Eucalypts were possibly the first group to receive attention from bonsai enthusiasts. Many species have decorative trunks, such as the smooth white trunks of *Eucalyptus citriodora* or *E. maculata*, and these are ideally suited to bonsai culture. The Iron-bark, *E. sideroxylon*, has thick, black, furrowed bark, while *E. spathulata* has a smooth, brown shiny trunk. Those species with a mallee habit of growth also have much potential. Some of these eucalypts normally grow to very large trees, and therefore are not described in this book, nor are they regarded as suitable for small garden areas, or general container cultivation. Other publications are obtainable that will provide further information on the large range of *Eucalyptus* species.

Melaleucas, leptospermums and callistemons are members of the Myrtaceae family, as are the eucalypts, and many of these are also highly suited to bonsai culture. A highly decorative, papery bark is found, particularly on a number of *Melaleuca* species. Other interesting features include fine or fragrant foliage, foliage colour varying from grey to bronze, or a weeping or otherwise attractive growth habit.

Rough or corky bark is found on a number of Australian plants, and this can be a highly ornamental feature of bonsai specimens.

The foliage of plants such as *Casuarina* species, commonly known as She Oaks, or the *Callitris*, or Native Cypress-pines, has encouraged bonsai growers to cultivate these particular plants.

Despite early thinking that the roots of Australian plants would not tolerate treatment such as is necessary for bonsai cultivation, it is now realized that this is not so, and many of our native plants can be very successfully grown in this way.

The use of Australian plants for bonsai cultivation has only recently received wide acceptance, and consequently the range of species being tried is increasing all the time.

It is not necessary to use species that have already been found suitable, and it may be more rewarding to try a plant species that has not been previously cultivated by bonsai enthusiasts.

Anyone interested in this aspect of horticulture is urged to go along to a bonsai specialists' meeting, or to obtain one of the excellent detailed publications on bonsai cultivation. After obtaining a knowledge of the basic principles and practices you will be ready to seek out appropriate Australian plants, and share in the pleasure of bonsai cultivation, using our own native flora.

Small Area Gardens

The term 'Small Area Gardens' can be interpreted in two separate ways, and is in fact intended to cover both areas — gardens on a small block of land, and small gardens within a larger total area.

We will basically be looking at the former situation in this book, but it is hoped that the information will be of assistance to anyone planning a small garden area.

Planning is a most important stage with any garden, but never is it more important than with a small-area garden. There will be room only for a limited number of plants, and each plant will be of considerable significance in the overall picture. Your planning may take a little while to formulate. You may buy a book or two, or borrow from a local library or from friends. Spend a little time browsing and taking notes. Visit other gardens, then draft out a sketch plan. Go along then to your local plant nursery and have a chat with the people there. They are in most cases very willing to discuss your particular needs and advise you whether the plants you have noted down are going to be suitable. Don't feel you need to know all the answers before you visit a nursery. Ask your friends about nurseries they have found to be helpful and reliable, then go to a recommended supplier and seek his advice. If there is a local group of the Society for Growing Australian Plants where you live, you can get helpful advice by going to meetings and talking to members.

Don't feel that because you have only a small garden it is not worth doing anything with. This is far from true, with even the smallest area. Treat it as a challenge, if you like, determine that it is going to be attractive, enjoyable and functional, and you will undoubtedly find there is much pleasure to be gained in a limited garden space, without a lot of the frustrations of caring for larger gardens.

Basic planning

It is most important to think through the overall needs of whoever lives in the house, and their relationship to the garden area. What are you going to do in your garden? What are the demands?

Do you enjoy gardening?

Do you enjoy outdoor living — barbecues and so on?

Do you have children who need areas for play?

Do you want areas where you can sit and relax, simply observing and enjoying nature?

Do you need areas for drying clothes?

Do you want to grow your own vegetables?

Do you need a service area for an incinerator, tools and the like?

Try to work out these priorities, and it will help as you begin to plan.

The planning of a garden can be an exciting exercise as you seek to visualize the finished product. It is recommended that a plan be drawn, to scale, in a workable size that is easy to read. This can be done by using the following steps.

1 Start with an outline of the house and any other buildings. If you have an original builder's plan of your house, this can be used to trace the outline. It will have the scale noted on the plan. Alternatively, you will have to make the necessary measurements. Mark doors and windows, as these will be important when planning access to or outlook from the house.
2 Mark in boundaries of the property, and the North, South, East and West aspects.
3 Mark in drains (stormwater and sewerage), water supply pipes, electricity and telephone wires.
4 Mark in any other fixtures.
5 Mark in any existing plants you wish to retain.

At this stage you may find it valuable to use a sheet of drafting paper, or tracing paper, with the main plan. Fix the drafting sheet securely to the main plan, using adhesive tape on one side. Planning steps and ideas can be placed on the drafting sheet until an overall picture is gained, then transferred to the main plan later if you wish. Several layers of drafting paper can be used

above: The reddish new growth of *Acacia glaucoptera* adds to the beauty of this wattle. A sculptural effect is provided by the weath-ered red gum log.

right: A small garden area, showing diversity in foliage and plant form.

below: A simple and informal seating area.

top left: Inspiration for small pools and bog gardens can be gained from areas such as this delightful natural pool at Lake Mountain, Victoria.

above: Trunks such as those of the *Melaleuca* seen here add both beauty and an illusion of greater space to a small area.

top right: A small but colourful garden area featuring low-growing plants.

right: Casuarinas are noted mainly for their fine foliage. The female flowers can be decorative also, particularly when back-lit by sunlight.

left: Crowea exalata is a hardy dwarf plant, and highly recommended for gardens or container cultivation.

top left: Jasminum suavissimum can be grown as a
climber or a ground cover.
The white flowers are
highly fragrant.

above: A quick-growing
climber from WA, is Har-
denbergia comptoniana.

left: A decorative feature of
many Australian plants is
the new foliage growth.
Colourful bronze tips are
provided by Banksia mar-
ginata.

together as planning proceeds, and it is also relatively easy to discard an unwanted sheet if a major alteration to the design becomes desirable.

6 Mark in proposed traffic areas, paths, driveways. (Don't forget the electricity, water and gas meters, or the oil supply tank, and the need for these to be reached with ease.)
7 Plan outdoor living areas such as patios, barbecues, paved areas and informal seating spots.
8 If you want a pool or pond, decide where it is to go.
9 Consider the natural or proposed contours of the land. If you are going to incorporate any rock outcrops or large logs, locate these on the plan. Plan areas for the planting of shrubs or trees, and open areas such as lawns.
10 Choose plants suitable for specific areas. Start with trees and shrubs, working down towards mat plants. Mark these in on the plan, or overlay.

Let's look at a few of these steps in more detail.

Step 3: Underground drains and overhead wires
It is not always easy to know the location of underground drains, but if this information is available it is wise to include it in planning. Most gardeners are familiar with the havoc that can be created by an introduced willow if it is planted too close to any pipes into which the roots can gain the smallest point of entry. Although Australian plants do not share the reputation of the willow, it is still considered unwise to plant any large, moisture loving species close to underground drains. Similar consideration should be given when planting beneath overhead wires. It is relatively simple to select plants that will not interfere with the wires, but it can be difficult and costly to remove large trees or shrubs at a later date.

Step 6: Traffic areas, paths and driveways.
So often we are confronted with insufficient room to alight from cars, because of many differing obstructions in a garden. It is time well spent to allow half an hour to measure the space necessary for you to manoeuvre your vehicle. Allow adequate access to doors, boot and engine compartment. If you have a small car, don't overlook the possibility that a larger vehicle may at some future time be using the space allocated.

Service pathways should take the most direct route. This does not mean that paths must be straight, creating harsh visual lines; they can be softly curved to give a less formal effect. Once again, allow ample width.

Step 7: Outdoor living areas
When planning outdoor living and paved areas, try to make them blend with the house and garden. Use materials that complement rather than contrast with the surroundings. This is most applicable to small gardens. By blending there is an illusion of greater space, whereas contrast often has the opposite effect, giving an enclosed appearance. It is certainly worth trying very hard to achieve the illusion of a larger-than-true area.

An outdoor living area does not have to be large. A path that leads to a widened area, with a few logs or boulders for seats, can be a place for many hours of enjoyment. An outdoor eating spot for a small family or group of people only needs to be slightly larger than the size of a small table. If it's quiet relaxation and involvement with nature you seek, a pool with its reflections and beauty will add much to such an area. It will also encourage the birds, which can be absolutely fascinating to watch. Honey-eaters will feed on the nectar-producing plants such as banksias, callistemons, grevilleas and melaleucas, and other small birds, such as robins, wrens and silver-eyes, will catch insects that are attracted by flowering plants. Butterflies may come to feed on helichrysums, pimeleas and other plants. Here is relaxation and enjoyment, as well as an educational experience.

Step 9: Coping with contours
In many new gardens there can be the problem of treating embankments, particularly where the house is built on a concrete slab. There are several materials that can be used, including railway sleepers, treated pine logs, tree trunks, boulders, bricks and bluestone pitchers. It is important here, again, to select materials that will blend with the surroundings. In a small garden, retaining walls can be overwhelming in appearance, making outdoor areas look minute, but by careful blending of materials and plants they can add beauty, as well as providing a necessary function. A browse through some of the landscaping books available can provide ideas and inspiration. You may also need to pay specific attention to drainage in such a situation.

Step 10: The use of plants
Plants can be used in specific ways to help create pleasant surroundings. If too many contrasting species are used a disjunctive appearance can result. This is very applicable to small gardens, where simplicity is often the best treatment. We can learn greatly in this regard from the principles of small Japanese gardens, noting their use of plants and other landscaping materials.

A major concern of many home gardeners is the need to create privacy or screen out unsightly areas. It is easy initially to screen out such areas by planting a few quick-growing plants such as wattles or gums. In many cases, however, in a few years time the main foliage is on the upper branches of the tree, leaving bare trunks, and the areas you wished to screen are plainly visible. The best method of preventing this is by careful selection of plant species. A group of plants may be used, with mature heights managing from 0.5 m to whatever height is desired. Usually three height layers is sufficient. This will result in a dense cover from ground level, and avoids the necessity of trying to establish young bushy plants under the trunks of established tall trees, which can be quite difficult.

When planting in gardens of small area, care must

be exercised in regard to the mature size of any trees planted, and also to the number of tall trees and shrubs chosen. Consideration should be given to the effect such planting will have within the garden boundaries, and also to the effect plants will have on neighbouring properties.

Dense tall planting on a northern boundary will restrict the sunshine in any area, and similarly, dense tall planting on a southern boundary will result in a restriction of sunlight to the neighbouring property.

Large trees should not be planted too close to a house or other structure such as, an in-ground swimming pool or patio. Problems may be caused by the extensive root systems, and if it later becomes necessary to remove the plant, the removal of a large tree from within a confined area can be very costly.

Dense planting of tall shrubs or trees close to buildings can also present a problem, in that the plants can create excessively dry soil conditions, resulting in structural cracking. Again, these aspects should be considered in regard to neighbouring buildings, as well as to your own property.

As can be seen from the charts, there are many different types of plants suitable for small gardens. Undoubtedly an important aspect is the flowering time. By careful thought there can be flowers throughout the year.

Trunks, bark, foliage and seed capsules are also an important feature of plants, and these aspects should not be overlooked when selecting suitable species. A further dimension of enjoyment can be added by fragrance, species noted for this aspect will be found in the charts provided.

It cannot be over-emphasized that the soil conditions and climatic aspect should be our guide in the choice of plants for specific locations. So often we blame the plant species if it dies, while in reality it is because we did not select a suitable position for its growth. It we do not have the conditions for a desired plant species, it is sometimes possible to undertake landscape works that will improve the situation; often a more suitable alternative is to grow the plant in a container.

Garden construction and planting

The following steps are recommended as a guideline for garden construction.

1 Decide on the area to be constructed. In many cases it is better to concentrate on one small area at a time. This will enable easier and more effective control of weed growth, and the experience gained can lead to the use of improved methods in subsequent areas of construction. Mark any plants that are to be retained, so they will not be damaged when work is carried out.
2 Remove all rubbish. Eradicate and remove weed growth or unwanted plants.
3 Install any necessary drains to improve the drainage.
4 Mark out areas, as planned, for paths, pools, planting and lawn areas.
5 Undertake the levelling or contouring for paths, pools, planting, lawn and other areas. Construct or allow for areas such as patios, outdoor living areas and service areas.
6 Prepare the soil for planting and mulching.
7 Place boulders, large logs, garden sculpture and so on in permanent position.
8 Plant and mulch.

Some of these steps will be simple, while others are major tasks.

Amplification of construction steps
1 If you have original native vegetation, the *marking of plants* is really necessary, especially if there are any small plants such as lilies and orchids. These can be difficult to re-establish, which makes it even more important to retain them if possible.
2 *Weed control* is covered later under Garden Maintenance, but if it is possible to remove any rubbish and all or most of the weeds at the time of construction, the task of maintenance will be greatly reduced. It is also very much easier to eradicate weeds before planting than when they are growing among established plants.

Most weeds can be removed by hand cultivation. This is probably one of the best methods of removing creeping weeds such as the various types of couch, kikuyu, creeping bent and sorrel. It is very important to make sure that all creeping stems or stolons are removed. The alternative is to use chemical sprays, some of which have the effect of sterilizing the soil for up to three months. These can also damage the roots of other existing plants, so it is important to read all labels carefully.

Rotary hoeing can actually assist the spread of creeping grasses, chopping the roots into small pieces, each of which can grow into a new plant. Rotary hoeing also tends to create soil particles that are too fine and readily compacted. This does not allow adequate aeration of the soil and drainage.

It is recommended that the area be left fallow for a few weeks after weeding to allow for any regrowth and further eradication.
3 *Drainage.* Many Australian plants require well drained soils. If you have light soils such as sandy loam or gravels there is probably no need for extra drainage, but perhaps you have heavy soil, such as clay-loam,

Drainage can be improved by the raising of planting areas.
  A — Flat natural soil level.
  B — Mounding completed, showing original soil level and drainage channels.
  C — Planned final development.

which is prone to waterlogging. There are alternative ways of overcoming this situation.

(a) The surface can be contoured with spoon drains. This type of drain can blend well with the garden and take away any excess surface moisture.

(b) Drainage can be improved by raising planting areas, using soil from where paths will be located or from pool areas, or soil brought in specifically for this purpose (see comments on Step 6). To grow many of the plants from well drained, deep, sandy soil areas, it is desirable and in some cases necessary that beds be built up above the natural soil level.

(c) Underground artificial drains can be incorporated, using appropriate materials such as unglazed terracotta pipes and screenings, or one of the many specially produced plastic pipes, in conjuction with coarse sand.

4 *Transfer of plans from paper to the garden.* In marking out the proposed areas at full scale, you may find there is need for alteration to some aspects. Now is the time to do this if it is necessary.

5 *Levelling and contouring.* Many gardens will probably not require this preparation, and if contouring of the soil is overdone in a small area it could spoil the

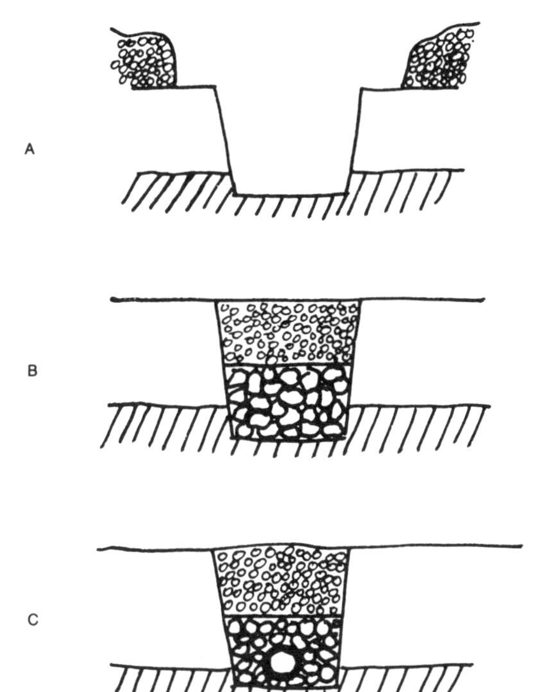

Underground drains.
  A — Dig channel down into clay subsoil.
  B — Rubble drain, constructed by partly filling channel with coarse rock or rubble. Back-fill to original level with topsoil.
  C — Agricultural pipe drain, constructed by placing agricultural pipe near base of channel, and filling as in B.

whole concept of your garden. Remember that simplicity is often the best approach.

It is a good idea to prepare pathways first, followed by pools, if any, and finally garden contouring. Mention has been made of raising garden beds, under Step 3, Drainage. Soil can be brought in to build up the level of planting areas. It is best however to use local soils if possible. With soils from other areas, it is imperative that they be thoroughly mixed with the local soil, as this will provide better conditions for the development of strong roots, rather than to encourage the growth of surface roots in the new soil while not penetrating into the natural garden soil.

An alternative for the specialist grower who wishes to plant difficult-to-grow species from sandy areas such as in Western Australia, is to create an artificial sandhill or mound in the garden. This may consist of (a) pure sand (varying types); (b) 1 part coarse sand, 1 part good quality loam; (c) 1 part scoria gravel, 1 part good quality loam, 1 part sandy loam; (d) 1 part scoria gravel, 1 part coarse sand, 2 parts good quality loam.

There are other alternatives, and a great deal depends on personal preferences. Growing plants in pots or tubs is often the most successful method for some of the more difficult garden species.

Note: Before any soil is brought into a garden it is wise to find out whether it is contaminated with any diseases that could cause damage to plants. One dangerous disease is Cinnamon Fungus, *Phytophthora cinnamomi*, to which many Australian and introduced plants are susceptible. This is a fungal disease that attacks plant roots, and to date there is no method of totally eradicating it from an area once introduced; so any efforts to prevent its introduction are strongly recommended. Sterilized soil can be purchased, and sterilization will eliminate the risks of this and other fungal diseases.

6 *Preparation for planting*
(a) Cultivation of the soil to a depth of about 25-30 cm, with the use of a spade, is recommended. This method is preferable to rotary hoeing, as the latter can leave a hard-pan base, which may create drainage problems. Rotary hoeing can also break the soil into very fine particles, which in dry weather results in compaction detrimental to plant growth.
(b) If the soil is very heavy and difficult to break up, the addition of gypsum will help to improve the friability. Gypsum should be incorporated into the soil, not just left lying on the surface. Application rate is 1–1.5 kg per square metre.
(c) If possible, leave the soil fallow for a few weeks. There is the possibility of germination of weeds, and these can be easily controlled by light cultivation with a hoe or similar tool. This will make your task easier after planting.
(d) Mulching can be a valuable asset to the life and growth of garden plants, as well as being a considerable labour-saving aid. There are however many considerations which should be noted to avoid some pitfalls. Some mulches are applied before planting is undertaken, so it is suggested that section 8(b) on this subject be read before any planting is commenced.

7 *Use of rocks and logs.* The need for simplicity must be emphasized when using boulders or other sculptured materials in small gardens. A small number of large boulders can create a much more natural and pleasing visual effect, if used well, than lots of small rocks. Next time you are in the bush, observe some of the rock outcrops. We can learn a great deal from nature regarding the relationship of plants, rocks, logs, mulches and so on. When considering the use of rocks and logs, the aspect of ease of maintenance should be borne in mind, as it should throughout all stages of planning. Rocks or logs can look very attractive, but if unwisely used can be a disadvantage when mowing or weeding.

8 (a) *Planting.* Before planting, areas can be drenched with a suitable fungicide to combat the spread of any soil fungus that might be present. Further information on this subject will be found under Diseases, page 44.

For a natural appearance it is usually necessary to partly bury rocks or boulders.

A suggested planting technique is as follows:
(i) Water plants well, about twelve hours before planting.
(ii) Dig the planting hole, approximately twice as wide as it is deep.

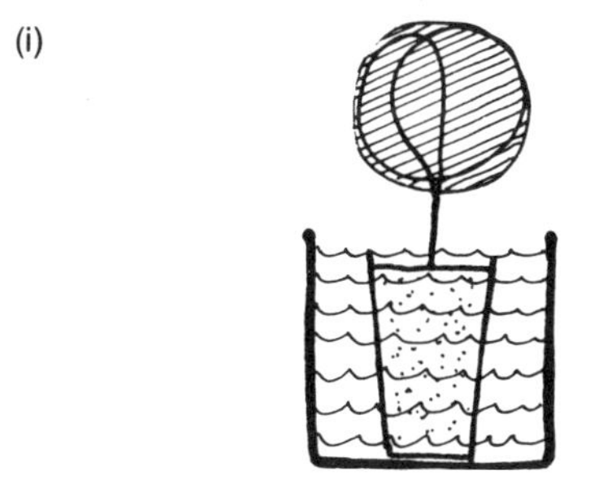

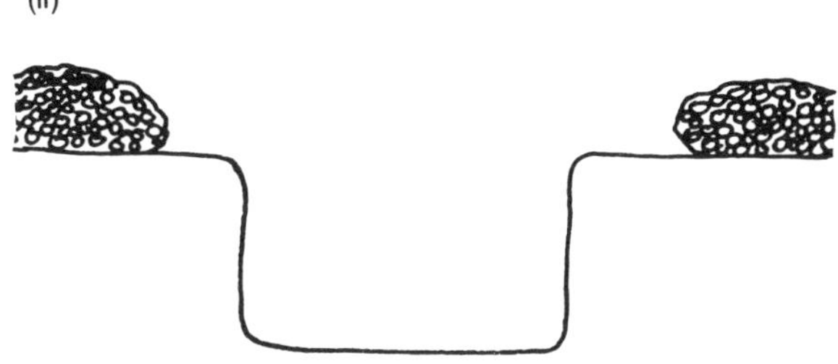

(iii) If the soil is dry, pour water into the hole and allow to drain.

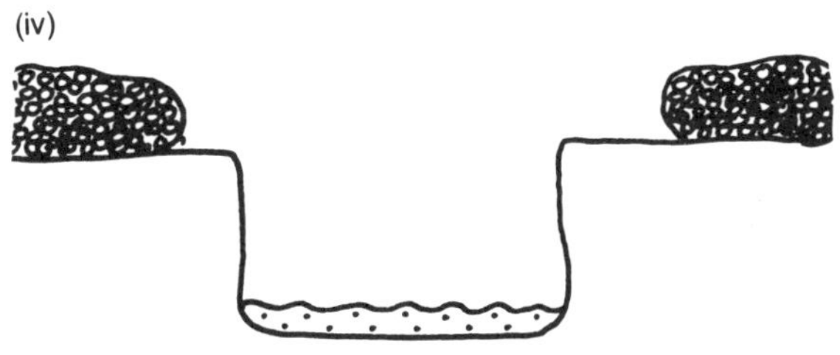

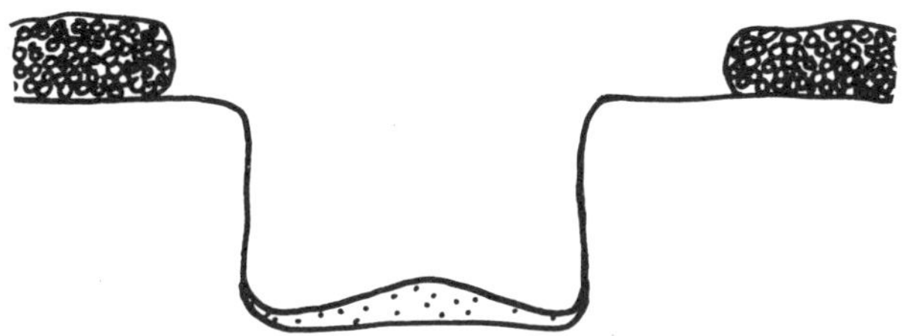

(iv) Mix a small amount of a slow release fertilizer evenly through the soil at the base of the hole. Mound the soil slightly to allow plant roots to point down.
(v) Remove the plant carefully from the container. Plants may be tipped from containers with sloping sides (A) or from plastic bags (B). Straight-sided tins should be cut with tinsnips to avoid root damage to the plants (C).

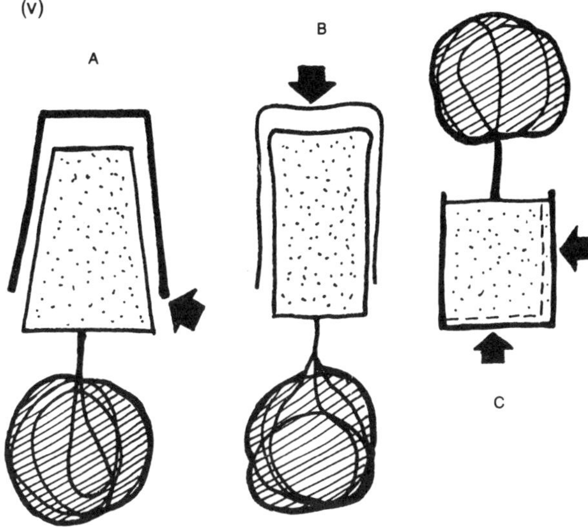

(vi) Inspect the roots of the plant for curling. Straighten roots if necessary, and prune with secaturs any that are excessively long. Lightly loosen exterior soil so the roots can readily penetrate the garden soil. If possible do not break the main ball of soil, as this could damage roots.

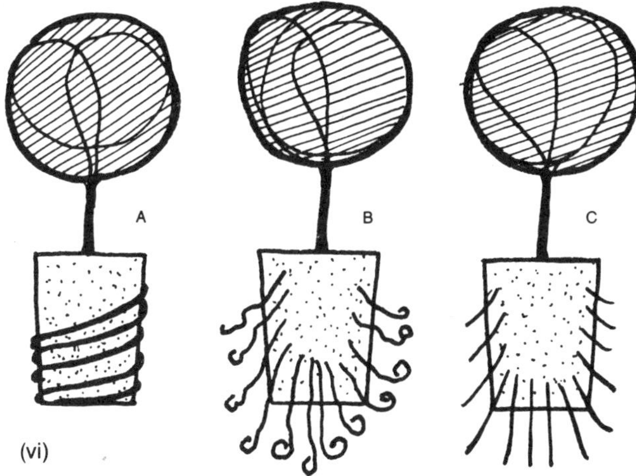

A — Coiled roots.
B — Roots after untangling.
C — Ready to plant, broken and crooked roots pruned off.

(vii) Place plant in hole, maintaining the same surface level as that of the original plant container. Spread roots evenly.

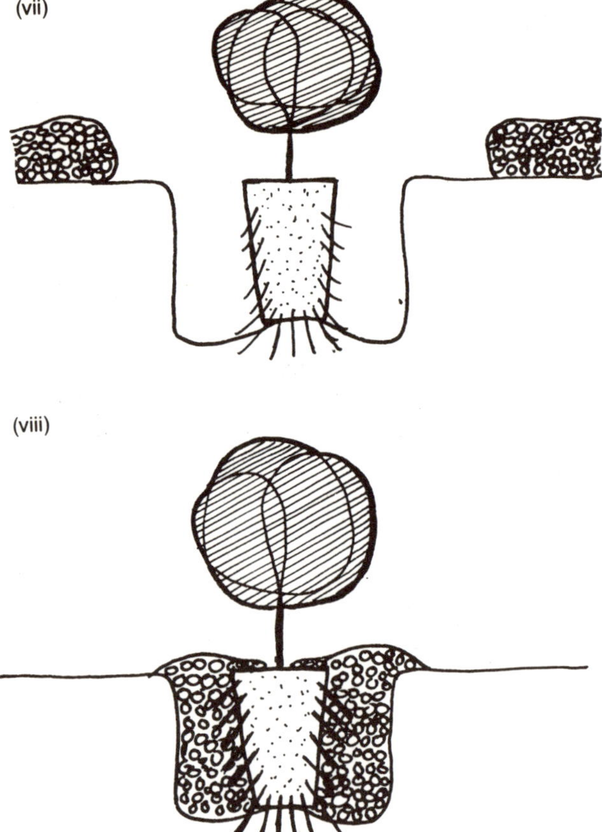

(viii) Backfill the hole with soil, and firm it around the plant.

(ix) Water well, with one bucket (about 10 litres) of water. The addition to the water of a fungicide, a root stimulant and a seaweed-base fertilizer can be beneficial in helping to establish young plants.

(x) It is not usually necessary to stake young plants, and they develop stronger trunks and root systems when not staked. For further information on staking, see page 45.

8 (b) *Mulching*. There are many benefits to be gained by mulching, but hazards can also be encountered if care is not taken in the choice of mulching materials and their application.

The three main benefits from mulching are:
(i) conservation of moisture during hot or dry weather;
(ii) maintenance of a fairly constant temperature in the root area;
(iii) reduction of weed growth.

Undoubtedly one of the best mulches is provided by low ground-cover plants. There are many Australian species useful for this purpose, and a selection is contained in Chart 23.

Many other materials can also be used. Some of these are readily available, and others may be obtained commercially. One major hazard is that often organic mulches are placed too close to the stems and trunks of plants. This can result in the death of a plant, especially if the mulch is moist for most of the time. A common sight is grass clippings piled around trunks; this should be discouraged. One of the areas of a plant with greatest susceptibility to disease is just above and below ground level. It is most important to leave this area free of organic mulches. Sand, gravel and screenings do not have the same adverse effect, because they allow well-drained conditions.

Do not place organic mulches right against the stems or trunks of plants.

Some confusion exists over the terms tan bark and pine bark. Tan bark is from acacia and eucalypt trees, and in the past was readily available. With the use of chemicals in the leather tanning process, true tan bark is now rarely obtainable. Pine bark is peeled from pine trees that have been logged, and is generally much coarser in its initial state than tan bark. There are now various grades available, so that one may choose from a coarse to a very fine pine bark.

Hardwood mulches of sawdust or wood shavings are generally better than softwood types. Care must be exercised in the choice of any softwood material. Never use a mulch of timber that has been treated with preservatives (e.g. treated pine), as the chemicals used have toxic properties. It is usually easiest to spread sawdust or wood-shaving mulches before planting.

Newspaper may be used underneath mulch material to help eliminate the initial germination of weeds. It is placed on the soil, 3-6 sheets thick, making sure that it is overlapping, then covered with the mulch.

Mulching chart

Mulch	Durability	Moisture Permeability	Moisture Retention	Weed Reduction	Temperature Control	Depth	Comments
Coarse sand	Excellent	Excellent	Very good	Good	Excellent	5–7.5 cm	Highly recommended, but sandy materials are excellent for seed germination so weeds should not be allowed to set seed. They do not adversely affect plants if placed next to stems and trunks, but should be kept to a depth of 5 cm around trunks. Very durable, but also expensive.
Gravel	Excellent	Excellent	Very good	Good	Excellent	5–7.5 cm	
Screenings	Excellent	Excellent	Very good	Very good	Excellent	5–7.5 cm	
Fine sand	Excellent	Poor when dry	Very good	Good	Excellent	5–7.5 cm	The main problem is that water will run off when the sand is dry.
Hardwood sawdust	Fair	Good (poor when dry)	Excellent	Excellent	Excellent	5–25 cm	Good, but breaks down and will need replenishing. Plants can become deficient in nitrogen, which can be corrected by application of blood-and-bone. Do not place mulch against trunks of plants.
Hardwood wood shavings	Good	Good (poor when dry)	Excellent	Excellent	Excellent	5–25 cm	It is recommended that the surface be covered with a thin layer of coarse sand. This prevents mulch from blowing away, and allows water to penetrate more readily.
Hardwood chips	Very good	Good	Excellent	Excellent	Excellent	5 cm	Highly recommended, but not readily available.
Bush litter and material from mulch shredder, including eucalypt bark	Very good	Good	Excellent	Excellent	Excellent	5–10 cm	Excellent, but will need some replenishing as material breaks down. If gathered from the bush, collect only from areas known to be free from Cinnamon Fungus.
Softwood, shavings or chips	Fair	Good	Excellent	Very good	Excellent	5–7.5 cm	Commonly creates a nitrogen deficiency when breaking down.
Pine bark	Very good	Good	Excellent	Very good	Excellent	5–7.5 cm	A good mulch. Should be used with care if close to plants.
Tan bark	Very good	Good	Excellent	Very good	Excellent	5–7.5 cm	Excellent, but rarely obtainable.
Coffee bean husks	Fair	Good	Excellent	Very good	Excellent	5 cm	Good, but can become messy as the husks break down. Best incorporated with the soil.
Peanut shells	Good	Good	Excellent	Good	Excellent	5–7.5 cm	Very good.
Mushroom compost	Fair	Good (poor when dry)	Excellent	Very good	Excellent	5–7.5 cm	Very good, but do not place near trunks of plants. Best incorporated with soil.
Straw or hay	Fair	Good (poor when dry)	Excellent	Very good, but often contains much seed	Excellent	5–10 cm	Very good. Ideal for embankments. The main problem is the germination of seed from grain crops and weeds.
Pine needles	Good	Fair (poor when dry)	Good	Excellent	Very good	5–10 cm	A fair mulch. Not recommended, as penetration of moisture is very slow.
Grass clippings, lawn shavings	Short	Good (poor when dry)	Excellent	Excellent	Very good (green clippings create heat)	5–10 cm	Good, but do not stack around trunks. Mainly valuable for incorporation with soil.
Compost	Short	Good (poor when dry)	Excellent	Excellent	Excellent	5–10 cm	Excellent, but will need replenishing as material breaks down. Mainly valuable for incorporation with soil.
Plastic sheeting	Very good	Poor	Excellent	Excellent initially	Fair	—	Not recommended, as it can help create sour soil in poorly drained areas. Plastic can be used on embankments and other sloping areas, in combination with a covering such as boulders, pine bark, etc.; but if holed, or as it breaks down, weed regeneration occurs, and this can become a major problem.

In some cases mulches will need to be replenished, so this aspect will become part of a maintenance program. As plants grow, they can provide organic matter such as leaves and twigs, which is valuable either as mulch or for use in composting.

In areas of heavy frost it is not wise to use organic mulches such as sawdust, pine bark or grass clippings.

There are three recommended alternatives for use in frost prone areas.

(i) Mulch with coarse sand, gravel, screenings or similar material.

(ii) Leave the ground around plants bare and uncultivated.

(iii) Use frost-hardy matting and ground-cover plants.

The mulching chart is provided as a guide to the various types of mulch at present available.

Maintenance

Regardless of the size of a garden, there is always a need for maintenance. The amount required really depends on personal taste. Some people like a very tidy garden, others prefer a more natural appearance. There is no such thing as a maintenance-free garden, but the need for maintenance can be reduced by careful initial planning and by choosing plants suitable for the garden.

Maintenance can be divided into seven main categories:

1 Watering;
2 Fertilizing;
3 Pruning;
4 Pest and Disease Control;
5 Weed Control;
6 Replanting, and the addition of extra mulching; and
7 Staking.

1 Watering

It is not wise to over-water Australian plants. This is particularly true during hot weather. Many of our plants grow naturally in areas of low or negligible summer rainfall. These have not adapted to receiving excess moisture during hot periods, and continually wet root systems often kill them. Species from rain forest areas have adapted to quite different conditions, and this emphasizes the importance of getting information about a plant's requirements, rather than simply digging a hole, planting it and expecting it to grow.

Another problem is that with moisture, high temperatures and soils that are not very well drained, there is a high possibility of rapid spread of fungal diseases, which will attack root systems.

You can tell when plants should be watered simply by placing a finger in the soil. If it is moist, there is usually no need for watering, provided that the previous watering has been thorough. When watering, the root area should be thoroughly soaked. Do not sprinkle lightly, as this will only help to increase surface roots, resulting in the need for constant watering to keep the plant alive. Deep soaking will encourage the roots to go deeper, and seek their own supply of moisture. This will result in much hardier plants, less likely to require regular watering.

If planting can be carried out during autumn, it is likely that the plants will have developed a good root system by the next summer, sufficient to procure most of the water needed. Young plants need to be kept constantly moist, but not wet, while becoming established.

It is recommended that watering be done during cool weather, if at all possible. This decreases the risk of promoting the spread of fungal disease. If it is necessary to water during warm periods, avoid spraying the foliage.

As mentioned earlier in regard to garden planning, if plants that are likely to require hand watering can be grouped together, this area of maintenance can be kept to a minimum.

2 Fertilizing

A golden rule for fertilizing is that if plants are growing well there is generally no need to apply fertilizer.

A healthy and vigorous plant is best able to cope with pests or disease, and fertilizers can be useful for maintaining healthy vigour.

For general maintenance purposes, plants will usually respond well to light applications of a slow-release fertilizer, such as blood-and-bone. This should be lightly cultivated into the soil or mulch, then watered in thoroughly. Water-soluble fertilizers should not be used regularly, but in some cases nitrogen-deficient plants respond well to a light application. Seaweed-based fertilizers have proved highly satisfactory for Australian plants, but liquid fertilizers containing urea are not recommended.

If plants are over-fed there is a tendency to promote foliage growth at the expense of the roots. In windy and storm-prone areas there is then the problem of plants being top-heavy, with a resulting breaking off of branches or uprooting. It is often a desire to have plants that grow quickly, and many Australian plants fit naturally into this category. Those that do not develop too quickly in the first few years, however, usually become stronger and more capable of withstanding harsh winds and storms.

There are some species that respond well to regular light applications of fertilizer. These include callistemons and melaleucas. Fertilizers should not be used to force early growth, but can promote flowering once plants become established.

3   Pruning

Nearly all Australian plants respond well to judicious pruning; many in fact need pruning, to promote healthy growth. This particularly applies to old plants. In the bush, plants get constant pruning from animals such as kangaroos, wallabies, emus, koalas, possums and the introduced rabbits. Chewing insects and caterpillars also prune plants by chewing out growth tips.

We may wish to prune garden plants for a variety of reasons. They may be spreading further than desired, or growing too tall; we may seek a bushier plant; or a branch or branches may be diseased or dead. If the latter is the case, pruning should be carried out as soon as possible.

The recommended time for general garden pruning is after the main flowering has finished, otherwise you may be removing branches that will provide the next season's flowers. Cutting flowers for decoration also provides pruning for the plant.

One of the best pruning methods is called tip-pruning. This can be done at any time of the year. Simply pinch out the growth tips. This provides lateral growth, or the development of side branches from leaf axils, thus giving a denser plant. (See illustration below.)

It is of paramount importance when pruning to use sharp, clean tools. Blunt tools can damage the sap wood, thus leading to the entry of disease. It is wise to clean the pruning saw or secateurs regularly by soaking them for a short time in disinfectant. This reduces the risk of spreading plant disease. It is particularly wise to do this after pruning any dead or diseased material.

Tip pruning promotes bushy growth.
A — Before pruning.
B — After new growth.

One of the main aims in pruning evergreen plants is to remove excess growth without visible evidence that pruning has occurred. The art is acquired through experience. Choose randomly placed branches, rather than just hacking back over the whole plant. A poorly pruned plant, with a harsh outline, or pieces of branch still protruding from the main stem or trunk, is not only unattractive: it can be dangerous, and it can allow the entry of disease and pests. If plants are pruned off close to the main stem, this allows new sap wood to quickly grow over and seal the wound.

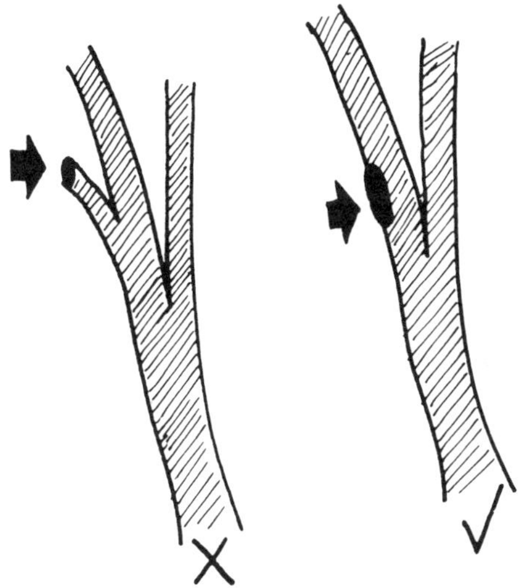

Pruning procedure.
Always cut as closely as possible to the trunk. Stubs are dangerous and can allow the entry of disease and pests.

On branches of over 2 cm diameter it is recommended that the cut be painted with a suitable pruning wound sealant.

Large trees require careful study before any major pruning, and this may be a task best left to a professional tree surgeon. The home gardener should however feel quite confident about light pruning of any small to medium sized Australian shrubs. The plants will almost certainly respond well to light pruning, even in the hands of an inexperienced gardener.

Do not burn prunings, unless they are diseased. Leaves can be added to the compost bin, or prunings can be cut or broken up and used as a mulch.

4   (a)   Pest control

Introducing Australian plants to your garden will usually lead to the presence of many native birds. These birds will help control most of the common garden pests.

Silvereyes, thornbills and pardalotes will help control scale. Wattlebirds, butcher-birds and cuckoo shrikes will enjoy many of the caterpillars usually found on plants, while wrens, robins, and many of the honey-eating birds will devour small insects.

By planting Australian plants, you can try to create a natural balance in your garden, where nature keeps things under control. There may from time to time be outbreaks of some pest that the birds cannot control; this is discussed later. If you want the birds to be part of your garden, it is necessary for a supply of insects, as well as nectar, to be available for them. The use of pesticides and insecticides will diminish the food supply for the birds, and in some cases there may be a build-up of poison in the birds if they eat the sprayed insects. This leads to the death or sterility of the birds, and unfortunately is a situation that often occurs.

Some of the major pests, most likely to attack Australian plants, are listed below. Many of these can be easily controlled by simply squashing them between the fingers or underfoot, which is a little messy perhaps, but safe and effective. Watch out for the hairy caterpillars, as they can irritate the skin; it is best to break off the infested leaf, then squash them underfoot. The alternative methods of control suggested here are of low toxicity to birds, and break down readily.

(i) *Scale.* Sap-sucking insects, protected by an outer cover. Usually found on leaves and young branches. Control by using white oil. Apply on a cool day, as damage to foliage can occur during hot weather.

(ii) *Aphids.* Small sap-sucking insects, found on young growth tips. Control with a pyrethrum-based contact spray.

(iii) *Leaf-eating caterpillars.* These can be controlled by a carbaryl-based spray.

(iv) *Borers.* Borers usually attack firm branches, or stems at least one year old. Most holes observed in trunks are exit holes, made by the adult. The most readily observed borers are those that protect their entrance by a sawdust mantle, which can surround the branch. A few drops of fly spray, ammonia, bleach or turpentine should be squirted into the hole. An old hypodermic needle is ideal for this purpose. After a short time the caterpillar, if still there, will emerge and can be killed. Alternatively, the hole can be plugged immediately after treatment. If the borer's hole is not too long, or twisted, a piece of wire may be inserted, with a view to killing the offender. This is not always successful.

(v) *Gall insects.* Some plants are prone to attacks of galls, caused by various insects. These can be in the form of reddish lumps on leaves, or brown woody clusters on branches, as often seen in wattles. There is no guaranteed method of controlling such infestation, apart from burning affected leaves or branches.

4 *(b) Diseases*

The most common diseases that affect Australian plants are of the fungal type. As well as attacking root systems, plant tissue above the ground can be affected, and death can result.

The Cinnamon Fungus, *Phytophthora cinnamomi*, is a minute organism that attacks Australian plants, as well as introduced species. Plants very often die following the destruction of their small feeder roots by this fungus. An effective method of eradicating this disease has yet to be found, so positive action to prevent its introduction, as well as the introduction of other diseases, can be most worthwhile.

(i) Before planting, the soil can be drenched with a suitable chemical to combat fungal disease.

(ii) Planting areas should be very well drained. If this is not possible, choose plants that grow naturally in waterlogged soils, since they are usually more resistant to fungal disease than plants from drier areas.

(iii) Healthy plants with vigorous root systems should be selected. If possible, it is best to buy plants that have been grown in a mix sterilized to eliminate disease. A light application of a complete slow-release fertilizer, incorporated in the soil at the base of the planting hole, will stimulate initial growth of the plant and enable it to cope more successfully with any disease attack.

(iv) A regular maintenance program that includes light applications of fertilizer where necessary will maintain vigour in plants, and enable them to be more disease-resistant. Pruning and burning any diseased plant material is also important.

(v) If plants die for no apparent reason, it is recommended that the soil be drenched with a fungicide before replanting. Your nurseryman will be able to suggest a suitable product for this purpose. Unfortunately it is not possible to readily identify the presence of diseases such as Cinnamon Fungus, as this can only be positively done in a laboratory.

Fungus diseases such as moulds and powdery mildew attack plant foliage. Species with hairy leaves and stems, or soft flowers that are retained on the bushes, are among the most susceptible, and attacks are usually noticed during periods of humidity when there is a minimum of air movement. Lack of air movement can be a problem in this regard, in small gardens, or with container-grown plants in confined spaces. Control can usually be achieved by the use of copper-based or benomyl sprays.

Sooty mould grows in the exudate of the scale insects. If the scale is controlled, this will eliminate any sooty mould.

5 *Weed control*

The sooner weeds are removed, the less likelihood there is of their flowering and seeding then germinating to be a greater problem later. Do not allow weeds to grow near young plants, as they will severely inhibit the plant's development.

If there are many young weed seedlings, a light cultivation with a hoe on a warm sunny day is usually very effective. Most weeds are easily controlled manually in a small garden, using a hand-fork or small spade. With creeping weeds, such as species of couch, bent, sorrel or oxalis, control can be more difficult. These weeds should never be allowed to spread among the roots of garden plants, as they will become entwined, making their removal almost impossible without damage to the other plants. If possible, elimination of these weeds before planting is the most satisfactory course of action, even if it is necessary to delay planting for some time for this purpose. Constant vigilance is then necessary to ensure that new plants do not creep in underneath fences, or germinate in the garden from seed blown in. Plants added to a garden should always be checked for weeds before planting.

If poisons are necessary in an established garden, it is recommended that products that do not sterilize the soil be used. These chemicals affect the chlorophyll in plants, so it is important that the spray should not come in contact with the stems or foliage of garden plants.

Mulching can be important in the control and elimination of weeds, and further information on this aspect will be found under Garden Construction.

6 Replanting

In an established garden there is often the need for plants to be removed and replaced by younger plants. It may be that a plant has died, or been broken by wind or accidentally. It could also be that the plant has been found unsuitable for the position chosen, or having grown successfully for a period, has now lost all vigour.

When young plants are introduced in an already mature garden there are often difficulties associated with a lack of light, created by the established plants, together with very dry soil matted with roots. Under such conditions it is difficult to produce healthy strong plants unless some assistance is given. The following steps are therefore recommended.

(a) Choose plant species that are likely to grow successfully under the conditions available. It is very probable that the plant will grow at a slower rate, and when fully grown will be smaller than it would if it did not have to compete with the established plants. It is reasonable therefore to allow for this in choosing a species of suitable size.

(b) If the area has dense overhead shade, thin out branches to allow sunshine and rain to penetrate.

(c) Dig the soil to a spade's depth. Break it up thoroughly and incorporate gypsum if desired.

(d) Water thoroughly, until penetration is down to the full depth of digging.

(e) Leave fallow for several days and repeat watering.

(f) Incorporate through the soil some peat moss, vermiculite or well-decomposed organic material such as compost or leaves, until the soil is friable.

(g) Incorporate some blood-and-bone into the soil, at the rate of approximately 30 g per square metre.

(h) If the soil is dry, water until moist but not wet.

(i) Carry out planting as described on pages 38-40.

For several months after planting it will be necessary to keep the young plants moist, as competition from the established shrubs will make it difficult for the young roots to obtain necessary moisture. When watering, soak plants thoroughly to encourage the roots to extend deeper in search of moisture.

7 Staking

Most plants do not need stakes to support them as they grow. Usually plants will develop with greater strength if they do not have to rely on some form of support. There are, however, occasions when staking is necessary, and certain rules should be adhered to so that staking will be of benefit and not detrimental to growth.

(a) When placing a stake in the ground, care must be taken to avoid damage to existing roots. It should therefore be placed at a distance from the trunk (see illustration). If staking is done at the time of planting, the stake should be put in place before backfilling the hole with soil, again to avoid root damage. If it is placed too close to a plant, abrasion between the trunk and the stake can occur, resulting in wounding of the trunk.

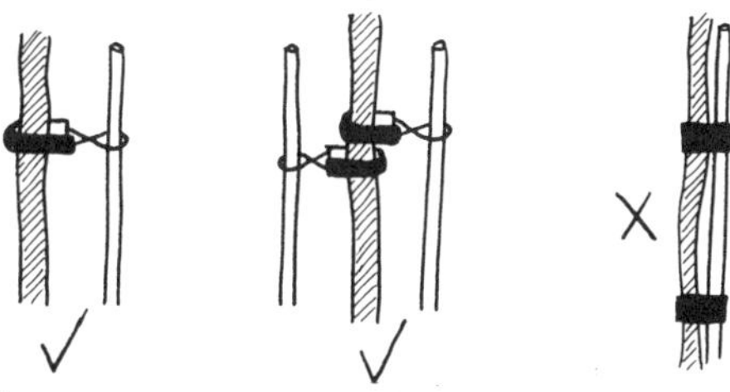

Staking.
A — Recommended single tie. Note protective material used.
B — Recommended double tie.
C — Incorrect staking. This method does not allow for any movement of the plant.

(b) For large plants, multiple staking or guying may be necessary (see illustration).

(c) Always use a coarse material for tying the plant, such as cloth, panty hose or thick string. If using wire or fine string, a protective outer coating such as water hose should be used (see illustration).

(d) Never tie the plants tightly, but always allow for some movement of the trunk. If this is done, the plant will be better able to support itself when the stake is removed.

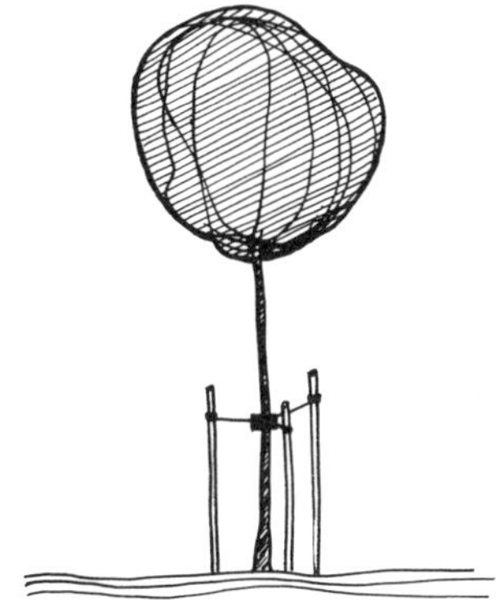

Recommended staking for large plants, where necessary. This method is especially suitable in areas of strong winds.

Selection of plants

The following charts are designed to assist with the selection of plants for small gardens. As with the charts provided for container cultivation, a brief comment only has been made regarding each species, to give some indication of its horticultural value. More detailed information will be found regarding each plant on the page indicated in the chart.

Before referring to the charts, the section on the Use of Plants, page 35, may provide assistance and avoid costly errors in planning.

The charts give only a selection of plants for specific areas within small gardens. There are many more species that could be included under each of the headings.

A separate chart has not been given for shrubs of small to medium size, suitable for locations that are well drained and that receive filtered sunlight or full sun for portion of the day. A very wide range of Australian plants can be grown in these conditions, and selection for such a position can therefore be based on other features of desirability. Reference to Charts 2–9 will provide listings of many suitable plants according to their flowering period; plants may be chosen on the basis of growth habit, foliage, fruits, bird attraction etc. by reference to other charts provided.

The selection of plants is one of the most important aspects of any garden planning, and the extra time involved in making a careful and correct choice is usually well rewarded.

Chart 23　Low ground-cover plants (See also Charts 1, 15, 19)

Botanical name	Common name	Flowering period	Comments
Acacia aculeatissima	Thin-leaf Wattle	June–Nov	Low spreading species with prickly foliage; pale to bright yellow flower-heads.
Acacia pravissima 'Golden Carpet'		Aug–Oct	A wide-spreading, prostrate form. Profuse yellow flower-heads.
Asterolasia trymalioides	Alpine Star-bush	Oct–Jan	Low shrub; dark green, shiny leaves; small yellow star-like flowers.
Brachysema sericeum		July–Jan	A variable, prostrate to low shrub; pea-shaped flowers of cream or yellow-green.
Correa decumbens		Nov–Feb	A low spreading shrub with erect narrow tubular flowers of red with green tip.
Correa 'Dusky Bells'		Mainly Mar–Sept	A low, spreading shrub with pink bell-shaped flowers.
Dampiera diversifolia		Sept–Feb	Prostrate species with small leaves and deep blue flowers.
Dampiera rosmarinifolia	Rosemary Dampiera	Aug–Nov	A suckering species with small narrow leaves; dense spikes of flowers, usually blue.
Dodonaea procumbens	Trailing Hop-bush	Spasmodic	A low spreading shrub with wedge-shaped leaves and decorative reddish hops.
Goodenia geniculata	Bent Goodenia	Mainly Oct–Mar	A matting plant with dark green leaves and bright yellow flowers.
Goodenia hederacea var *alpestris*	Ivy Goodenia	Mainly Oct–Feb	An excellent matting plant with rounded and toothed leaves; yellow to orange flowers.
Grevillea acanthifolia		Sept–Mar	Low spreading plant with deeply lobed, prickly leaves; pink to mauve toothbrush flowers.
Grevillea aquifolium (prostrate form)	Variable Prickly Grevillea	Mainly Sept–Feb	A variable species, including prostrate forms. Holly-like leaves; green and red toothbrush flowers.
Grevillea tridentifera (prostrate form)		Aug–Nov	A large, dense, spreading species. Finely divided, light green leaves, clusters of cream flowers.
Halgania cyanea	Rough Halgania	Mainly Sept–Feb	A low shrub; can sucker. Has small, rough leaves and small open-petalled blue flowers.
Helichrysum apiculatum	Common Everlasting	Sept–Feb	A spreading species with hairy foliage and clusters of bright yellow flower-heads.
Kunzea pomifera	Muntries	Sept–Nov	Dense spreading plant with small light green leaves. Clusters of white to cream flowers, followed by bluish berries.
Leptospermum 'Horizontalis'		Oct–Dec	Dense, spreading shrub with horizontal branches. Has prickly foliage, and profuse white flowers.
Leptospermum humifusum		Sept–Nov	Variable, spreading, dwarf shrub; small white flowers.
Myoporum parvifolium	Creeping Myoporum	Nov–Mar	Has narrow leaves and small white or rarely pale pink flowers.
Spyridium cinereum	Tiny Spyridium	Usually Sept–Apr	Prostrate species with small greyish leaves. White to cream flowers.
Thomasia petalocalyx	Paper-flower	Oct–Dec	Low shrub with dense, hairy foliage. Pendant mauve-pink flowers.

47

Botanical name	Common name	Flowering period	Comments
Anigozanthos flavidus	Tall Kangaroo Paw	Oct–Feb	Has long, green, strap-like leaves. Flower stalks up to 3 m high; various colour forms available.
Anigozanthos rufus	Red Kangaroo Paw	Sept–Feb	Not as vigorous as *A. flavidus*. The woolly stems and tubular flowers are deep red.
Anigozanthos viridis	Green Kangaroo Paw	July–Dec	Has narrow, dark green leaves, and woolly yellow-green to emerald flowers.
Brachyscome multifida	Cut-leaf Daisy	Mainly Aug–Mar	Has dense, dark green, fine foliage; profuse bluish, pink or white daisy flowers.
Conostylis setigera	Bristly Cottonhead	Aug–Dec	Has narrow hairy leaves, with cream to yellow flowers borne on short stems.
Danthonia pallida	Silver-top Wallaby Grass	Oct–Dec	A graceful fine-foliaged grass. Slender flower-stalks bear small flowers with red anthers.
Diplarrena moraea	Butterfly Flag	Nov–Jan	Has long, strap-like leaves and white flowers.
Dryandra drummondii		Mainly Feb–May	Has long, deeply lobed, bluish green leaves and brownish-yellow flower-heads.
Gahnia sieberana	Red-fruit Saw Sedge	Sept–Dec	Has long, sharp-edged, narrow leaves; cream and brown flower-spikes borne on long stems.
Orthrosanthus multiflorus	Morning Flag	Aug–Nov	Has flat, grass-like leaves and blue flowers.
Patersonia occidentalis	Purple Flags	Oct–Feb	Leaves are flat and grass-like. Flowers are purple and yellow.
Poa caespitosa	Snow Grass	Oct–Feb	Soft greyish-green grass. Flower-heads often have purple tonings.
Restio tetraphyllus	Tassel-cord Rush	Mainly Sept–Dec	A decorative rush with small tassel-like clusters of brown to reddish flowers.
Stypandra glauca	Nodding Blue-lily	Mainly Sept–Nov	Has blue-green, grass-like leaves; flowers have blue petals with yellow stamens.
Tetratheca thymifolia		Aug–Dec	A clumping perennial, with hairy stems and leaves; pendant pink flowers.
Themeda australis	Kangaroo Grass	Oct–Jan	A dense tussock grass. The very small flowers have colourful anthers.

Chart 25 Shrubs for well-drained and sunny positions (See also Chart 10)

Botanical name	Common name	Flowering period	Comments
Acacia acinacea	Gold-dust Wattle	Aug–Dec	A spreading shrub with deep gold globular flower-heads.
Acacia buxifolia	Box-leaf Wattle	July–Dec	A hardy shrub with grey-green leathery foliage; profuse yellow globular flower-heads.
Atriplex rhagodioides	Silver Salt-bush		Has silvery-grey foliage.
Baeckea astarteoides		Mainly Oct–Jan	A small shrub with arching branches and small leaves. Small pink tea-tree-like flowers.
Beaufortia decussata		Mainly Jan–Apr	A medium shrub with crowded oval leaves and deep red flower spikes.
Brachysema lanceolatum	Dark Bush-pea	Mainly June–Oct	Foliage is dark green above, silvery below; pea-shaped flowers are dark to bright red.
Calothamnus villosus	Silky Net-bush	Sept–Feb	Has hairy, pine-like foliage and bright red one-sided flower spikes.
Calytrix tetragona	Common Fringe-myrtle	Aug–Nov	Shrub with small narrow leaves and white to pink starry flowers.
Cassia artemisioides	Silver Cassia	Mainly June–Dec	A bushy shrub with silvery, divided leaves; yellow bell-like flowers in clusters.
Dillwynia sericea	Showy Parrot-pea	Sept–Dec	An upright shrub with short narrow leaves and massed spikes of orange to yellow pea flowers.
Gompholobium ecostatum	Dwarf Wedge-pea	Sept–Jan	A small open shrub with hairy bluish-green leaves and apricot to orange-red pea flowers.
Grevillea acerosa		Aug–Dec	A small dense shrub with prickly fine leaves and small cream woolly flowers.
Grevillea banksii	Banks' Grevillea	Mainly July–Nov	A shrub with greyish-green divided leaves and large bright red flower-heads.
Grevillea lanigera	Woolly Grevillea	Aug–Jan	Bushy plant with narrow greyish-green, hairy leaves; clusters of red and cream flowers.
Grevillea lavandulacea	Lavender Grevillea	June–Nov	A most variable species; foliage usually greyish; profuse clusters of bright pink to red flowers.
Hakea obtusa		June–Oct	An upright shrub with oval leaves and white to cream flowers, which deepen to pink or red.
Hibiscus heterophyllus		Mainly Oct–Feb	Shrub with slightly prickly stems and leaves; flowers white with dark red to purple markings.
Hypocalymma angustifolium	White Myrtle	June–Dec	Low shrub with small narrow leaves; clusters of white flowers, which deepen to pink.
Melaleuca nematophylla	Wiry Honey-myrtle	Mainly Aug–Nov	A shrub with needle-like leaves and globular mauve-pink and gold flower-heads.
Phebalium squamulosum ssp *ozothamnoides*		Oct–Jan	Bushy shrub with smooth blunt leaves and small bright yellow flower clusters.
Swainsonia galegifolia	Darling Pea	Oct–Feb	An open-branched shrub with soft greyish-green fern-like leaves and multi-coloured pea flowers.
Verticordia plumosa		Sept–Dec	Small shrub with aromatic grey-green leaves and clusters of small mauve-pink feathery flowers.

Botanical name	Common name	Flowering period	Comments
Acacia elongata	Slender Wattle	Aug–Oct	Large, upright, open shrub; bright yellow globular flower-heads.
Blechnum minus	Soft Water-fern	—	Has semi-weeping, deeply divided fronds. New growth often bronze or pinkish.
Blechnum nudum	Fishbone Water-fern	—	A hardy species with fishbone-shaped fronds.
Callistemon citrinus	Crimson Bottlebrush	Mainly Sept–Dec; also Mar–Apr	A variable species with bright red bottlebrush flower-heads.
Callistemon pallidus	Lemon Bottlebrush	Sept–Jan	Dense shrub; grey-green to dark green leaves; cream to yellow brushes.
Goodenia humilis	Swamp Goodenia	Mainly Oct–Mar	A dense matting plant with bright yellow flowers.
Hakea nodosa	Yellow Hakea	Mainly Feb–May	Shrub with narrow pine-like leaves and strongly scented cream to yellow flowers.
Kunzea parvifolia	Violet Kunzea	Sept–Jan	Open shrub with very small narrow leaves and mauve to magenta flower-heads.
Leptospermum lanigerum	Woolly Tea-tree	Mainly Nov–Jan	Dense shrub with small grey to green leaves and white flowers.
Leptospermum phylicoides	Burgan	Nov–Feb	Large shrub to small tree; narrow leaves; white to pale pink flowers.
Melaleuca decussata	Totem Poles	Sept–Jan	Dense shrub; greyish leaves; pale to deep mauve brushes.
Melaleuca ericifolia	Swamp Paper-bark	Oct–Nov	An upright shrub to small tree; crowded fine leaves; small cream brushes.
Melaleuca gibbosa	Slender Honey-myrtle	Oct–Jan	Small to medium shrub with lilac to mauve flower-heads.
Melaleuca spathulata		Oct–Dec	Initially an upright plant, spreading with maturity. Deep pink globular flower-heads.
Melaleuca thymifolia	Thyme Honey-myrtle	Oct–Apr	Has greyish-green foliage and mauve to purple flowers.
Melaleuca violacea		Mainly Sept–Oct	Usually a flat-topped shrub, with greyish-green leaves and purple to violet clusters of flower.
Ranunculus collinus	Strawberry Buttercup	Nov–Jan	A prostrate plant; suckering; has shiny lobed leaves, bright yellow flowers.
Scaevola hookeri	Creeping Fan-flower	Nov–Mar	A mat plant with small shiny leaves and profuse small white to mauve flowers.

above: Sturt's Desert Pea, *Clianthus formosus*, is an extremely showy Australian plant. Here it is seen with the Yellow Kangaroo Paw, *Anigozanthos pulcherrimus*.

top right: An attractive upright plant, useful for very narrow areas is *Cordyline stricta*.

right: Melaleuca incana is attractive in both form and flower, and is renowned for its soft grey foliage.

below: Leptospermum lanigerum, the Woolly Tea-tree is one of the species attractive to butterflies, moths, and other insects.

above: This Australian annual, *Helipterum roseum*, is ideal for massed planting.

left: One of the many forms of *Correa reflexa*. Plants vary in habit, and also flower colour. Flowering times also vary to cover a major portion of the year.

bottom left: The flower-spikes of *Banksia ericifolia* can be up to 25 cm long. They are eagerly sought by honey-eating birds.

centre: There are various forms of *Grevillea lavandulacea*, and this one from Tanunda, SA, is a small compact bush with greyish foliage and bright red flowers.

above: Callistemon viminalis 'Captain Cook' is a comparatively low-growing bottlebrush, with bright red flowers.

right: *Callistemon* 'Reeves Pink' is an attractive cultivar, with soft pink brushes.

bottom right: A showy display of mauve to bluish purple flowers is provided by the low groundcovering *Scaevola striata*.

The double-flowered form of *Eriostemon verrucosus* is an excellent tub or garden species. It provides a showy display of flowers over a long period.

The Common Heath, *Epacris impressa*, can be white, pink or red. This form from Bega NSW is particularly attractive.

Pandorea jasminoides is a relatively quick-growing climber, and produces an attractive display of large pale pink flowers.

Chart 27 Plants for shaded areas (See also Charts 11 and 21)

Botanical name	Common name	Flowering period	Comments
Acacia alata	Winged Wattle	Sept–Nov	Shrub with unusual winged branchlets; cream to deep yellow globular flower-heads.
Acacia terminalis	Sunshine Wattle	Mar–July	A showy wattle with dark green ferny leaves and yellow flower-heads in racemes.
Asterolasia asteriscophora	Lemon Star-bush	Sept–Nov	A slender shrub with hairy, blunt leaves and lemon yellow star-shaped flowers.
Baeckea virgata	Tall Baeckea, or Twiggy Baeckea	Nov–Mar	An upright shrub. Profuse small white tea-tree-like flowers.
Boronia crenulata		July–Dec	Small shrub with aromatic leaves and pink flowers.
Boronia fraseri	Fraser's Boronia	Aug–Nov	Bushy shrub with smooth ferny leaves and open-petalled pink flowers.
Boronia heterophylla	Red Boronia	Aug–Nov	An upright bushy shrub with reddish-pink bell-like flowers.
Correa baeuerlenii	Chef's Cap Correa	Mar–Aug	A rounded shrub with unique green tubular flowers resembling a chef's cap.
Gompholobium huegelii	Common Wedge-pea	Sept–Feb	Small open branched shrub with bluish-green foliage, and pale to bright yellow pea-flowers.
Goodenia elongata	Lanky Goodenia	Oct–Mar	Spreading mat-plant, bearing bright yellow flowers on upright stems.
Grevillea buxifolia	Grey Spider-flower	Mainly July–Dec	Shrub with oval hairy leaves and rusty brown new growth. Usually grey and brown flower-heads.
Hovea elliptica	Tree Hovea	Aug–Oct	An upright shrub with olive green leaves, and blue-purple pea-shaped flowers.
Hovea heterophylla	Common Hovea	Aug–Oct	Dwarf shrub with clusters of pale bluish-purple pea-flowers.
Lomatia polymorpha	Mountain Lomatia	Dec–Feb	Shrub with narrow leaves, sometimes lobed; clusters of cream flowers above the foliage.
Olearia iodochroa	Violet Daisy-bush	Sept–Nov	Rounded shrub with shiny dark green oval leaves and violet daisy flowers.
Pomaderris lanigera	Woolly Pomaderris	Mainly Sept–Nov	Upright shrub with woolly foliage and small yellow flowers in dense clusters.
Prostanthera ovalifolia	Oval-leaf Mint-bush	Mainly Sept–Dec	The most commonly grown Australian Mint-bush. Flowers usually purple.
Prostanthera rotundifolia	Round-leaf Mint-bush	Aug–Nov	Variable species. Mauve to purple or pink flowers.
Thysanotus tuberosus	Common Fringe-lily	Oct–Jan	Small perennial with grass-like leaves. Has mauve to rose-purple flowers.
Viola hederacea	Ivy-leaved Violet	Most of year	A spreading perennial herb with purple-blue and white flowers.
Xanthosia rotundifolia	Southern Cross	Mainly Aug–Nov	A perennial herb with broad toothed leaves and cream flowers.

Chart 28 Foliage plants for the garden (See also Chart 12)

Botanical name	Common name	Flowering period	Comments
Acacia glaucoptera	Clay Wattle	Aug–Nov	A spreading shrub with flat, winged, blue-green foliage and reddish new growth.
Acacia vestita	Hairy Wattle	Sept–Oct	Dense shrub with pendulous branches and hairy, grey-green foliage.
Baeckea linifolia	Weeping Baeckea	Dec–Mar	Slender shrub with pendulous branches and small leaves; new growth is reddish.
Banksia dryandroides	Dryandra-leaved Banksia	Jan–Aug	Small to medium shrub with shiny dark green, deeply serrated leaves.
Bossiaea linophylla		July–Nov	Shrub with narrow, dark green leaves. A form with bronze-red foliage is available.
Callitris columellaris	White Cypress-pine		Upright conifer with dark green foliage and pendulous branchlets.
Calocephalus brownii	Cushion Bush	Sept–Feb	Dense plant with silvery stems and leaves.
Casuarina microstachya		Aug–Oct	A much-branched shrub with slightly greyish typical she-oak foliage.
Dryandra nivea	Couch Honeypot	July–Oct	A clumping or spreading plant. Long decorative leaves; yellow and brown flower-heads.
Eucalyptus kruseana	Book-leaf Mallee	Mainly Mar–Aug	A spreading species with oval blue-grey leaves and yellow flowers.
Eupomatia laurina	Copper Laurel or Bolwarra	Sept–Mar	Shrub to small tree. Has smooth shiny leaves with green to purple tonings.
Grevillea endlicherana	Spindly Grevillea	Mainly June–Dec	Usually an upright shrub, with narrow grey leaves and white to pale pink flowers.
Grevillea johnsonii		June–Nov	Dense shrub with fine, divided, dark green leaves on reddish stems. Pink to red flowers.
Grevillea steiglitziana	Brisbane Ranges Grevillea	June–Nov	A spreading shrub with dark green prickly lobed leaves. Red and green toothbrush flowers.
Hakea undulata		July–Sept	Upright shrub. Has oval leaves with wavy toothed margins. White to cream flowers.
Homoranthus flavescens		Oct–Feb	Low spreading shrub with horizontal branches; small greyish-green leaves; clusters of small yellow flowers.
Melaleuca micromera		Aug–Sept	Shrub with conifer-like foliage and globular yellow flower-heads.
Melaleuca seriata		Nov–Jan	An upright species with narrow silvery-grey leaves. Pink flower-heads.
Prostanthera incana		Aug–Nov	Bushy shrub with soft, hairy, grey-green leaves. Flowers usually lavender-blue.
Pultenaea subternata		Sept–Dec	Small shrub with pendulous branchlets and oval greyish-green leaves.
Rhagodia spinescens	Hedge Saltbush	Irregular	A dense spreading plant with greyish, hairy, triangular leaves.
Symphionema montanum		Oct-Jan	Compact dwarf shrub with light green divided leaves. Small white flowers.

52

Botanical name	Common name	Flowering period	Comments
Acacia leprosa	Cinnamon Wattle	Aug–Sept	Small tree, often with weeping habit. Aromatic foliage.
Acacia redolens		Aug–Oct	Spreading shrub. The greyish green foliage has a distinctive sweet fragrance.
Acacia suaveolens	Sweet Wattle	Apr–Oct	A spreading shrub with bluish-green foliage. Sweetly scented, cream to pale yellow flower-heads.
Boronia megastigma	Brown Boronia	July–Nov	Renowed for its fragrance. Various colour forms include greenish-yellow, burgundy and brown.
Darwinia diosmoides		Apr–Jan	Dense bushy shrub with small, delightfully aromatic leaves.
Dichopogon strictus	Chocolate Lily	Oct–Dec	Grass-like perennial. The purple flowers have a chocolate or caramel-like fragrance.
Hardenbergia comptoniana	Native Lilac	Sept–Nov	Quick growing climber. Has racemes of bluish purple to mauve, fragrant, pea flowers.
Hymenosporum flavum	Native Frangipani	Oct–Dec	An upright tree with shiny dark green leaves and fragrant yellow flowers.
Jacksonia scoparia		Sept–Nov	Upright shrub; greyish foliage; profuse, fragrant, yellow to orange pea flowers.
Jasminum suavissimum	Sweet Jasmine	Mainly Oct–Feb	A light climber with clusters of highly fragrant white flowers.
Leptospermum petersonii	Lemon-scented Tea-tree	Dec–Feb	Large shrub with smooth narrow, green, lemon-scented leaves. White to cream flowers.
Mentha diemenica	Slender Mint	Mainly Sept–Feb	A suckering plant with aromatic leaves and small mauve flowers.
Plectranthus argentatus		Mainly Sept–Apr	Dense rounded shrub with aromatic toothed foliage. The small pale blue flowers have a spicy fragrance.
Prostanthera incisa		Sept–Nov	Spreading shrub with strongly aromatic, oval, toothed leaves. Flowers usually purple.
Prostanthera violacea		Aug–Dec	Dense, much-branched shrub. Has very small, oval, aromatic leaves. Violet flowers.
Pultenaea graveolens	Scented Bush-pea	Oct–Nov	Compact shrub with pendulous branchlets. The small narrow leaves have a spicy aroma.

Botanical name	Common name	Flowering period	Comments
Billardiera longiflora	Purple Apple-berry	Aug–Dec	Light climber with greenish yellow tubular flowers, followed by deep bluish purple berries.
Ceratopetalum gummiferum	NSW Christmas Bush	Oct–Nov	Small tree. After flowering the calyces enlarge and become red.
Coprosma quadrifida	Prickly Currant-bush	Sept–Nov	Light shrub with small white flowers, followed by shiny reddish berries.
Cyathodes juniperina	Crimson Berry	Aug–Jan	Member of heath family. Small white tubular flowers, followed by pale to deep pink berries.
Dianella tasmanica	Tasman Flax-lily	Sept–Feb	Clumping plant. Blue star-shaped flowers, followed by shiny, oblong, bluish fruits.
Dodonaea adenophora		Dec–Mar	Shrub with aromatic foliage. Minute flowers followed by decorative reddish hops.
Dodonaea boroniifolia	Hairy Hop-bush	Sporadic	A bushy shrub with fern-like leaves; minute flowers, followed by showy green, pink to red hops.
Elaeocarpus reticulatus	Blueberry Ash	Oct–Nov	Small tree. Has white flowers, followed by dark blue berries.
Eucalyptus erythrocorys	Illyarrie	Mainly Feb–May	A small upright tree. Flower buds have bright red caps; yellow flowers, followed by large woody fruits.
Eucalyptus forrestiana	Fuchsia Gum, or Forest Marlock	Mainly Dec–July	Small bushy tree with decorative pendant buds and fruits.
Eucalyptus tetraptera	Square-fruited Mallee	Mainly Sept–Jan	A spreading shrub with thick leathery leaves. Large pink to red buds and fruits.
Eucalyptus torquata	Coral Gum	Mainly Sept–Feb	A small tree. Decorative ridged buds and fruits; pink to red flowers.
Myoporum debile	Sprawling Myoporum	Sporadic	A matting plant with small white to pink flowers, followed by pink to reddish berries.
Pittosporum phillyraeoides	Butter-bush	Sept–Nov	An upright shrub to small tree with pendulous branches. Yellow scented flowers, followed by yellow fruits.
Polyscias sambucifolius	Elderberry Panax	Sept–Dec	An upright species with pinnate olive-green leaves. Small greenish flowers, followed by bluish berries.
Syzygium coolminianum		Nov–Jan	Dense small tree; shiny leaves; purple to bluish berries.

Botanical name	Common name	Flowering period	Comments
Billardiera bignoniacea	Orange Bell Climber	Mainly Sept–Mar	A light twiner with pendant tubular flowers of orange and greenish yellow.
Billardiera cymosa	Sweet Apple-berry	Mainly Aug–Dec	A light climber. Has tubular flowers, followed by oblong berries.
Billardiera longiflora	Purple Apple-berry	Aug–Dec	Light climber with greenish yellow tubular flowers, followed by deep bluish purple berries.
Billardiera ringens	Chapman Creeper	Mainly Aug–Mar	A light climber with clusters of flowers, initially orange, then deepening to red.
Billardiera scandens	Common Apple-berry	Sporadic	Light twining plant. Tubular greenish yellow flowers are followed by green berries.
Chorizema diversifolium		Sept–Oct	Of light twining or trailing habit, with multicoloured pea flowers, mainly orange.
Clematis aristata	Austral Clematis	Aug–Mar	A vigorous climber with creamy white star-like flowers, followed by fluffy seed-heads.
Clematis microphylla	Small-leaved Clematis	Aug–Mar	Quick growing. Has greenish-cream star-like flowers, followed by fluffy seed-heads.
Hardenbergia comptoniana	Native Lilac	Sept–Nov	Quick growing. Has racemes of bluish purple to mauve, fragrant pea flowers.
Hardenbergia violacea	False Sarsaparilla, or Purple Coral-pea	July–Oct	A vigorous climber or trailer with dark green leaves and racemes of mauve to purple pea flowers.
Hibbertia dentata	Trailing Guinea-flower	Mainly Aug–Dec	A climbing or trailing plant with reddish stems, shiny toothed leaves, and yellow open-petalled flowers.
Hibbertia scandens	Climbing Guinea-flower	Sporadic	Climber with long trailing stems, shiny leaves and yellow flowers.
Jasminum suavissimum	Sweet Jasmine	Mainly Oct–Feb	A light climber with clusters of highly fragrant, white flowers.
Kennedia beckxiana		Mainly Aug–Dec	Strong climber with bluish-green leaves; bright red with green pea-shaped flowers.
Pandorea jasminoides	Bower Climber	Mainly Dec–Mar	A vigorous climber with shiny dark green leaves and trumpet-like white to pink flowers.
Pandorea pandorana	Wonga Vine	Mainly July–Nov	A strong climber with variable foliage and tubular cream to brown flowers.
Passiflora cinnabarina	Red Passion-flower	Mainly Sept–Dec	Usually vigorous. Has large, 3-lobed, dark green leaves, and bright coppery-red flowers.
Sollya heterophylla	Bluebell Creeper	Mainly Sept–Feb	A dense climber with bright green leaves. Flowers can be blue, pink or white.
Sollya parviflora		Sept–Feb	Similar to *S.heterophylla*. Has small clusters of deep blue flowers.

Botanical name	Common name	Flowering period	Comments
Acacia howittii	Sticky Wattle	Sept–Nov	A graceful plant with pendulous branches; pale yellow flower-heads.
Acacia spectabilis	White Stem, or Glory Wattle	Aug–Oct	Has glaucous fern-like leaves; clusters of golden yellow flower-heads.
Agonis juniperina	Juniper Myrtle	Feb–Mar also Aug–Nov	Upright plant; branchlets often pendulous. Leaves narrow. Clusters of small white flowers.
Angophora hispida	Dwarf Apple	Nov–Feb	Has grey-green leaves, attractive buds and cream flowers.
Callistemon salignus	Willow Bottlebrush	Oct–Dec	Shrub to small tree; papery bark; white to deep pink flowers.
Callistemon viminalis	Weeping Bottlebrush	Mainly Nov–Mar	Has pendulous branches and bright red flower-spikes.
Eucalyptus burdettiana	Burdett Gum	Jan–Mar	Has light canopy of foliage and clusters of yellow-green flowers.
Eucalyptus crenulata	Silver Gum	Sept–Dec	Dense greyish-green foliage, with clusters of small white flowers.
Eucalyptus macrandra	Long-flowered Marlock	Mainly Dec–Mar	Has a smooth trunk, bright green leaves and large clusters of yellow-green flowers.
Eucalyptus spathulata	Swamp Mallet	June–Nov	Has a smooth reddish-brown trunk, narrow dark green leaves, and clusters of small cream flowers.
Hakea salicifolia	Willow Hakea	July–Nov	A quick-growing shrub with smooth long leaves. Has clusters of small white to cream flowers.
Hymenosporum flavum	Native Frangipani	Oct–Dec	An upright tree with shiny dark green leaves and fragrant yellow flowers.
Leptospermum phylicoides	Burgan	Nov–Feb	A large shrub to small tree, with narrow leaves and white to pale pink flowers.
Melaleuca armillaris	Bracelet Honey-myrtle	Aug–Jan	A large shrub with narrow, dark green leaves and cream flower-spikes.
Melaleuca linariifolia	Snow in Summer	Nov–Feb	A small tree with soft papery bark and profuse white to cream flowers.

For an effective screen, plants of various height groupings should be planted simultaneously.

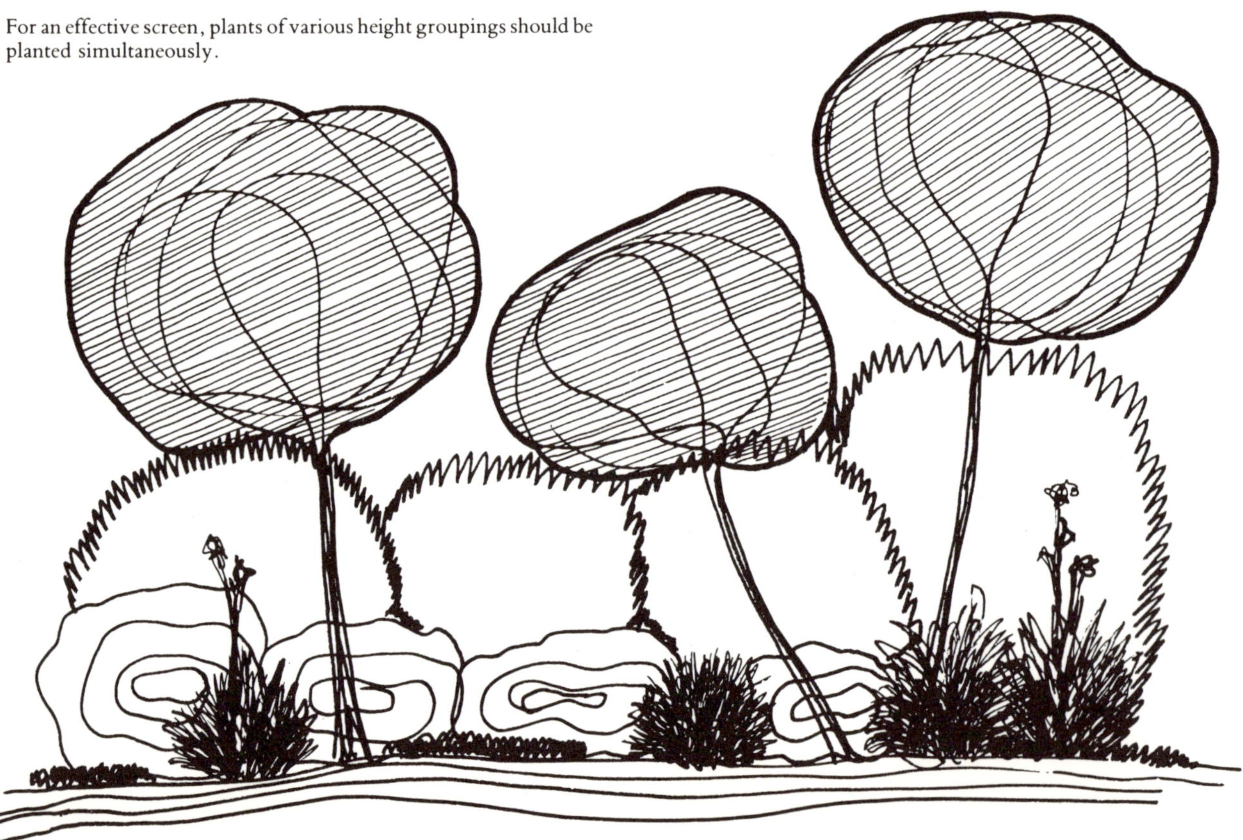

Chart 33   Quick-growing screen plants

Botanical name	Common name	Flowering period	Comments
Acacia cultriformis	Knife-leaf Wattle	Aug–Oct	Has dense foliage, with triangular grey-green phyllodes. Racemes of golden yellow flower-heads.
Acacia fimbriata	Fringed Wattle	Aug–Oct	Upright to spreading; with racemes of deep cream to yellow, globular flower-heads.
Acacia howittii	Sticky Wattle	Sept–Nov	Graceful plant with pendulous branches. Pale yellow flower-heads.
Acacia iteaphylla	Gawler Range Wattle	Mar–Sept	Dense large shrub; bluish foliage; clusters of pale yellow flower-heads.
Acacia longifolia	Sallow Wattle, or Sydney Golden Wattle	July–Oct	A fast growing tree. Has bright yellow, rod-like flower heads.
Acacia pravissima	Ovens Wattle	Aug–Oct	Dense large shrub with triangular phyllodes and racemes of bright yellow globular flower-heads.
Acacia retinodes	Wirilda	Mainly Nov–May	A quick-growing, variable species. Lemon-yellow flower-heads, produced over a long period.
Eucalyptus lehmannii	Bushy Yate	Mainly July–Dec	Has dense canopy of deep green leaves. Large green to yellow-green flower-heads.
Goodia lotifolia	Golden Tip	Sept–Dec	A bushy plant with clover-like foliage and yellow pea-flowers.
Grevillea glabrata		Sept–Jan	A dense shrub with grey-green lobed leaves and white to cream flowers.
Grevillea rosmarinifolia	Rosemary Grevillea	June–Dec	A very dense shrub with narrow leaves, slightly prickly. Pink to red with cream flowers.
Hakea elliptica	Oval-leaf Hakea	Oct–Feb	Has oval leaves and rusty brown new growth. Flowers are white to cream.
Hakea petiolaris	Sea Urchins	May–July	Upright species; oval grey to green leaves. Flower-heads are pincushion shape, and cream to cream and purple.
Hakea salicifolia	Willow Hakea	July–Nov	Quick-growing shrub with smooth, long leaves. Clusters of small white to cream flowers.
Kunzea recurva var *montana*		Sept–Nov	Upright shrub with small, soft leaves. Globular yellow flower-heads.
Leptospermum flavescens	Tantoon	Sept–Dec	Large, many-branched shrub with prolific white to cream flowers.
Leptospermum lanigerum	Woolly Tea-tree	Mainly Nov–Jan	Dense shrub with small grey to green leaves and white flowers.
Leptospermum phylicoides	Burgan	Nov–Feb	Large shrub to small tree, with narrow leaves and white to pale pink flowers.
Melaleuca armillaris	Bracelet Honey-myrtle	Aug–Jan	A large shrub with narrow dark green leaves and cream flower spikes.
Olearia phlogopappa	Dusty Daisy-bush	July–Nov	An upright shrub with greyish-green hairy leaves and daisy flowers.
Westringia fruticosa	Coast Rosemary	Mainly Sept–Oct	A hardy dense shrub. Flowers are white with purple markings.

Botanical name	Common name	Flowering period	Comments
Acacia boormanii	Snowy River Wattle	July–Oct	Has grey-green foliage and racemes of bright yellow flowers.
Callistemon 'Mauve Mist'		Oct–Dec	A hardy bottlebrush with mauve flower spikes.
Correa baeuerlenii	Chef's Cap Correa	Mar–Aug	A rounded shrub with unique green tubular flowers resembling a chef's cap.
Grevillea 'Clearview David'		Mainly July–Nov	Has narrow, dark green, prickly leaves and clusters of vivid red and white flowers.
Grevillea miqueliana	Oval-leaf Grevillea	Mainly June–Nov	Has oval, hairy leaves and pendulous clusters of orange-red to bright red flowers.
Grevillea pinaster		Mainly June–Dec	Soft narrow leaves, with loose pendant clusters of bright red flowers.
Grevillea 'Poorinda Firebird'		Mainly June–Dec	Leaves are narrow and dark green; clusters of bright red flowers.
Grevillea victoriae var *tenuinervis*		Mainly Sept–Jan	Has soft, narrow, light green leaves and pendant clusters of red flowers.
Kunzea ericifolia		Sept–Nov	Has soft, small, narrow leaves and globular yellow flower-heads.
Mirbelia oxyloboides	Mountain Mirbelia	Oct–Dec	Leaves are narrow and dark green. Profuse yellow and red pea-shaped flowers.
Prostanthera stricta		Sept–Oct	Has soft hairy leaves and deep purple flower clusters.
Regelia ciliata		Nov–Mar	Leaves are small and stem-hugging; flower-heads mauve to purple.
Thomasia macrocarpa		Sept–Nov	Has hairy, greyish foliage and mauve-pink starry flowers in clusters.
Westringia glabra	Violet Westringia	Mainly Aug–Dec	A long-flowering species with lilac coloured flattened, tubular flowers.

Plants for narrow garden beds

Very often small gardens contain planting areas that are quite narrow, and although plants are desired, perhaps to screen a fence or other structure, the choice is restricted to species that will not spread widely, or that can be successfully pruned to a narrow upright habit. Such situations often exist between a path or driveway and the dividing fence, or at the side of dwellings or other buildings.

As well as considering the size, it is important to consider the needs of any plant chosen. A location adjacent to a building can often be beneath overhanging eaves, where plants will receive little or no natural rainfall. Similarly, plants grown in a narrow area between buildings or fences may be in total shade for most of the year.

Pruning is a valuable asset to the cultivation of plants in restricted areas. Regular light pruning will maintain bushy growth, yet limit the size of the plant. Pruning can also be used effectively to train a shrub or small tree onto a trunk. This is particularly useful in narrow areas adjacent to pathways. If all or some of the lower branches are pruned away the trunk will occupy a minimum of space in the garden, yet there can still remain an overhead canopy of foliage.

The following chart lists a selection of plants that are naturally of upright habit, or that can be successfully trained to grow in this manner.

Chart 35   Plants for narrow garden beds

Botanical name	Common name	Flowering period	Comments
Anigozanthos flavidus	Tall Kangaroo Paw	Oct–Feb	A clump-forming plant with long strap-like leaves. Flower stalks to 3 m high. Various colour forms available.
Anigozanthos rufus	Red Kangaroo Paw	Sept–Feb	Not as vigorous as *A. flavidus.* The woolly stems and tubular flowers are deep red.
Baeckea virgata	Tall Baeckea, or Twiggy Baeckea	Nov–Mar	An upright shrub with profuse small white tea-tree-like flowers.
Boronia heterophylla	Red Boronia	Aug–Nov	An upright bushy shrub with reddish pink bell-like flowers.
Callitris oblonga	Esk Cypress-pine		Dense upright conifer with bluish-green foliage.
Calytrix tetragona	Common Fringe-myrtle	Aug–Nov	Shrub with small narrow leaves and white to pink starry flowers.
Cordyline stricta		Sept–Dec	An erect palm-like plant with racemes of small white to purple flowers.
Correa schlechtendalii		Nov–Apr	An upright bushy plant with dark green leaves and tubular pendant flowers of red with green.
Dianella tasmanica	Tasman Flax-lily	Sept–Feb	A clumping plant with blue star-shaped flowers, followed by shiny, oblong, bluish fruits.
Epacris impressa	Common Heath	Apr–Nov	A small plant of 1–2 m high. Flowers can be white ,or various shades of pink to red.
Epacris reclinata		June–Nov	Small shrub to 1.5 m high. Bright pink to red tubular flowers.
Isopogon anethifolius	Cone-bush	Mainly Aug–Nov	An upright, branched shrub with finely divided leaves. Terminal yellow flower-heads.
Jacksonia scoparia		Sept–Nov	Upright shrub with greyish foliage; profuse, fragrant, yellow to orange pea-flowers.
Melaleuca micromera		Aug–Sept	Shrub with conifer-like foliage and globular yellow flower-heads.
Melaleuca seriata		Nov–Jan	An upright species with narrow silvery-grey leaves; pink flower-heads.
Melaleuca spathulata		Oct–Dec	Initially an upright plant, spreading with maturity unless pruned. Deep pink globular flower-heads.
Patersonia occidentalis	Purple-flag	Oct–Feb	A clump-forming plant with flat grass-like leaves. Flowers are purple and yellow.
Templetonia retusa	Cockies Tongues	May–Oct	Has showy terminal clusters of pink to red pea-flowers.
Tetratheca thymifolia		Aug–Dec	A clumping perennial with hairy stems and leaves; pendant pink flowers.

Botanical name	Common name	Flowering period	Comments
Acacia paradoxa	Hedge Wattle	Aug–Nov	A dense thorny plant with profuse golden globular flower-heads.
Acacia verticillata	Prickly Moses	July–Nov	Of open habit. Flower-heads are pale yellow and rod-shaped.
Grevillea juniperina	Juniper Grevillea	July–Nov	Has narrow, dark green, prickly leaves and dense clusters of yellow to orange-red flowers.
Grevillea phanerophlebia		July–Oct	A spreading shrub with pungent trilobed leaves and white to cream flowers.
Grevillea 'Pink Pearl'		Mainly July–Oct	Has short, narrow, pungent leaves and clusters of bright pink flowers.
Grevillea triloba		July–Nov	A dense shrub with variable, lobed, light green leaves. Dense clusters of white flowers.
Hakea costata		Aug–Nov	Leaves are crowded, narrow and prickly. Has clusters of small white to cream flowers.
Hakea rostrata	Beaked Hakea, or Turkey Gobbler	Sept–Nov	An open shrub with prickly pine-like leaves and sweetly scented white flowers.
Hakea sericea	Silky Hakea	Mainly Apr–Sept	Has short, pungent leaves; flowers of white or various shades of pink.
Hakea suaveolens	Sweet-scented Hakea	Mainly Apr–June	Has smooth, deeply lobed, pungent leaves and sweetly scented white to cream flower-heads.
Prostanthera spinosa	Spiny Mint-bush	Sept–Mar	A variable spreading species with small oval leaves and narrow spines. Lilac to lavender flowers, also white.

Attracting birds to native gardens

There is immense enjoyment to be gained through the presence of native birds in a garden. The visual experience is fascinating and captivating, and many hours can be spent watching the small birds moving from plant to plant.

The honey-eaters, with their long narrow beaks, hover as they probe into each flower, seeking out the nectar, while small insect-eating birds such as the thornbills, robins and wrens search for any aphids, thrip or other insects that might be on or around the plants.

It is an ever-changing activity, and as the seasons come and go, the birds in a garden will also be different, as some species move on and others arrive for a period.

As well as being able to watch these wonderful creatures at close range, their various calls will provide an even further dimension of pleasure within a garden.

For birds to remain within a particular area, three basic requirements must be met. These are food, water and shelter.

The most satisfactory method of supplying food needs is by growing suitable plants. This gives a natural food supply, rather than the artificial forms of feeding such as is provided by bird-feeders, and a careful selection of plants will maintain a food supply at all times of the year.

Water is an essential requirement, particularly of small birds. It can be provided by a pond or other garden structure, or by a simple bowl that is regularly cleaned and kept full.

Shelter plants are necessary if birds are to remain within a garden area for longer than just food gathering visits. Bushy plants will give the birds a sense of security, and shrubs with pungent leaves or spines will also offer some protection against predators such as the domestic cat.

There are publications available on bird identification and the attracting of native birds to gardens, and these are recommended to anyone with a particular interest in this topic.

For the gardener who wishes to grow Australian plants to encourage some of our beautiful birds, the following chart has been provided. The plants listed are all rich in nectar production, and therefore will attract many of the honey-eaters. In addition the nectar attracts small insects, which in turn bring birds of the insect-eating group, as well as supplementing the diet of the honey-eaters. Seed-eating birds such as rosellas are not readily attracted to small gardens, unless the garden is adjacent to a larger area of trees and shrubs.

Chart 14 lists a number of bird-attracting species for container cultivation, and these plants are also suitable for garden planting.

Botanical name	Common name	Flowering period	Comments
Banksia spinulosa	Hairpin Banksia	Mainly Mar–Aug	Variable species, with tall or dwarf forms. Flowers can be amber to yellow, with red or black styles, or all gold.
Beaufortia orbifolia	Ravensthorpe Bottlebrush	Nov–July	Has grey-green oval leaves and flowers of lime green and red.
Callistemon 'Harkness'		Mainly Sept–Feb	A large shrub with masses of bright red flower-spikes.
Calothamnus quadrifidus	Common Net-bush	Mainly Oct–Mar	Variable species with narrow grey to grey-green leaves and bright red flower-spikes.
Calothamnus rupestris	Cliff Net-bush	Aug–Nov	Bushy species with dense, pine-like leaves. Rich red flowers.
Correa schlechtendalii		Nov–Apr	An upright bushy plant with dark green leaves and tubular pendant flowers of red with green.
Epacris impressa	Common Heath	Mainly Apr–Nov	Small plant with tubular flowers of white, pink or red.
Eucalyptus lehmannii	Bushy Yate	Mainly July–Dec	Dense small tree with large clusters of green to yellow-green flowers.
Eucalyptus leucoxylon	Yellow Gum	Mainly Mar–Dec	Low-growing forms recommended. Profuse flowers of white to deep pink.
Eucalyptus polybractea	Blue-leaf Mallee	Mar–Oct	Has narrow, bluish-green foliage; clusters of small white to cream flowers.
Grevillea aquifolium	Variable Prickly Grevillea	Mainly Sept–Feb	Variable species with holly-like foliage. Green and red toothbrush flowers.
Grevillea hookerana	Toothbrush Grevillea	Mainly Aug–Dec	Several forms of this species. Fern-like leaves, with toothbrush flowers, usually bright red.
Grevillea jephcottii	Green Grevillea	Most of year	A dense shrub with hairy light green foliage and pale greenish flowers.
Grevillea shiressii		July–Dec	A dense shrub with long olive-green leaves and bluish-green flowers.
Hakea multilineata	Grass-leaf Hakea	Mar–Oct	A large upright shrub with long narrow leaves and pink to red flower-heads.
Homoranthus darwinioides		Mainly Jan–July	A compact shrub with minute succulent bluish-green leaves. Small pink, yellow and green flowers.
Kunzea baxteri	Baxter's Kunzea	Mainly May–Oct	A shrub to small tree, with short oblong leaves and bright red flower-spikes with gold tips.
Melaleuca hypericifolia	Hillock Bush	Mainly Sept–Feb	A dense shrub with pendulous branches and orange-red flower-spikes.
Melaleuca wilsonii	Violet Honey-myrtle	Mainly Sept–Oct	An open to dense shrub; narrow dull-green leaves; lilac to reddish pink flower clusters.
Prostanthera chlorantha	Green Mint-bush	Mainly Aug–Mar	Low spreading shrub with minute aromatic leaves and pale green tubular flowers.

Butterfly-attracting plants

Over recent years there has been an increasing interest in the topic of butterflies within a garden, and a quest for information about plant species that attract these creatures.

For those who have grown butterfly-attracting plants, there will be no need to expand on the beauty and enjoyment to be gained during the flowering period.

It is not uncommon to see ten, twenty or more butterflies feeding on even a small plant in full bloom, whether in a container or in a garden. It is a quiet and unobtrusive scene, and you may walk by without even noticing them, but if you pause for a moment, you will observe a fascinating scene of intense activity, as these small creatures flit from flower to flower probing for food.

Chart 38   Butterfly-attracting plants

Botanical name	Common name	Flowering period	Comments
Actinotus helianthi	Flannel Flower	Aug–Feb	Grey-green hairy leaves; soft white to cream daisy-like flower-heads.
Asterolasia trymalioides	Alpine Star-bush	Oct–Jan	Low shrub with dark green shiny leaves; small yellow star-like flowers.
Calytrix alpestris	Snow Myrtle	Aug–Dec	Attractive shrub with small leaves and white star-like flowers.
Dillwynia sericea	Showy Parrot-pea	Sept–Dec	An upright shrub with short narrow leaves and massed spikes of orange to yellow pea flowers.
Helichrysum apiculatum	Common Everlasting	Sept–Feb	A spreading species, with hairy foliage and clusters of bright yellow flower-heads.
Helichrysum baxteri	Fringed, or White Everlasting	Oct–Jan	Low clumping species; daisy-like flower-heads of white and yellow.
Helichrysum bracteatum	Golden Everlasting	Mainly Sept–Feb	Has large, golden, papery flower-heads.
Hypocalymma strictum		Dec–Apr	An upright shrub with narrow leaves and small pink flowers.
Jacksonia scoparia		Sept–Nov	An upright shrub with greyish-green foliage and fragrant yellow to orange pea flowers.
Leptospermum 'Horizontalis'		Oct–Dec	Dense spreading shrub with horizontal branches. Has prickly foliage and profuse white flowers.
Olearia ciliata	Fringed Daisy-bush	Mainly Oct–Jan	Dwarf shrub with pale to bright purple daisies.
Pimelea ferruginea		Mainly July–Oct	A dense shrub with shiny leaves and pink flower-heads.
Pimelea spectabilis		Mainly Sept–Nov	A shrub with narrow grey-green leaves and profuse white flower-heads.
Pratia pedunculata	Matted Pratia	Oct–Apr	A dense matting plant with white to blue flowers.
Pultenaea pedunculata	Matted Bush-pea	Sept–Dec	A spreading mat plant with orange or yellow with red pea flowers.
Scaevola hookeri	Creeping Fan-flower	Nov–Mar	A mat plant with small shiny leaves and profuse small white to mauve flowers.
Scaevola striata	Royal Robe	Mainly Oct–Feb	A low suckering species with mauve to rich bluish-purple flowers.
Sowerbaea juncea	Rush Lily, or Vanilla Lily	Oct–Dec	Has grass-like foliage and globular clusters of fragrant mauve flowers.
Thysanotus multiflorus	Fringe Lily	Nov–Mar	Has grass-like foliage, with dense heads of bright mauve flowers.

Aquatic plants

Water can be an important feature of any garden, and small areas are no exception. Even a shallow pond can give attractive reflections and be a focal feature in an area. If birds are to remain in a garden the provision of water is essential, and this can be supplied by a small pond.

A number of Australian plants have adapted to growing in water or in permanently wet soils. These can be useful for growing in ornamental ponds, or for functional planting in areas of poor drainage.

It is worthy of mention here that most ferns should not be regarded as aquatic plants, and in fact many will die if planted in wet, boggy conditions. Conversely, some of the species listed in the following chart will also grow successfully in drier conditions, and their requirements are included in the Plant Descriptions that follow in Section 3.

Chart 39   Aquatic plants

Botanical name	Common name	Flowering period	Comments
Alisma plantago-aquatica	Water Plantain	Nov–Mar	Has a basal clump of broad leaves and many small, pale pink flowers produced on a tall stem.
Azolla filiculoides	Pacific Azolla, or Red Azolla	—	A free-floating fern with reddish foliage colouration.
Claytonia australasica	White Purslane	Aug–Apr	A creeping and layering perennial with fragrant white flowers.
Lemna minor	Common Duckweed	—	A free-floating species with oval to round bright green leaves.
Ludwigia peploides	Clove Strip, or Water Primrose	Oct–Apr	Has small bright yellow buttercup-like flowers.
Marsilea drummondii	Common Nardoo	—	A perennial aquatic fern with clover-like leaves.
Myriophyllum propinquum	Water-milfoil	Sept–Apr	Has bright green conifer-like branchlets and small white or pink flowers.
Ranunculus collinus	Strawberry Buttercup	Nov–Jan	A prostrate plant; suckering. Has shiny lobed leaves and bright yellow flowers.
Restio tetraphyllus	Tassel-cord Rush	Mainly Sept–Dec	A decorative rush with small tassel-like clusters of brown to reddish flowers.
Triglochin procera	Water Ribbons	Mainly Sept–Apr	Has long strap-like leaves and small green to reddish flowers.
Triglochin striata	Streaked Arrow-grass	Mainly Sept–Apr	Has rush-like or slightly flattened leaves and small flowers borne on an erect stem.
Utricularia gibba		Sept–Mar	A bladderwort with leaves submerged. Profuse small yellow flowers displayed above the water.
Vallisneria spiralis	Ribbon Weed, or Eel Grass	Nov–June	Has long, flat, ribbon-like leaves.
Villarsia reniformis	Running Marsh-flower	Sept–Mar	Has oval to kidney-shaped leaves and bright yellow flowers on a tall branched stem.

Plants suitable for coastal conditions

In Australia there seems to be a constant demand for native plants that will grow well in coastal areas. A large number of Australians live in coastal regions, while others have land or holiday houses beside the sea for recreational purposes. In these areas there is usually a need for screening plants, and also for trees and shrubs to act as windbreaks. Many Australian plants have been found highly suitable for such purposes, and we now tend to look first to our native species for fulfilling these needs.

Throughout the Plant Descriptions in Section 3, the code of C2 has been used to mark those species that will grow under exposed coastal conditions. Such plants are highly tolerant of salt–laden winds, and can be used to form the basic first line of protection. Even with these plants, however, some protection in the initial stages of growth can help them to become established more quickly. Plants should not be rigidly staked, nor totally protected from winds, or they may be unable to cope when exposure does take place. Screens made of dried plant material, light tea-tree stakes or hessian-type fabric are ideal, as they give some protection while allowing a degree of penetration by wind or salt spray.

Plants listed as being suitable for exposed coastal conditions are not always unaffected by adverse climatic conditions. New foliage growth is often burnt by salt-laden winds, but although growth may be slowed down, this usually makes the plant bushier, in a similar manner to that achieved by pruning.

Species marked as C1 in the descriptions in Section 3 need some protection if in coastal situations. They can be grown successfully in the protection of other plants, or if given some shelter by buildings or fences.

A selection of hardy, ornamental plants has been chosen for the following chart. These are species that could form the basis of a native garden influenced by coastal conditions. Further plants could be selected from the other species marked as suitable in Section 3.

Chart 40　Plants suitable for coastal areas

Botanical name	Common name	Flowering period	Comments
Acacia longifolia var *sophorae*	Sallow Wattle	July–Oct	Fast-growing tree. Has bright yellow rod-like flower-heads.
Banksia ericifolia	Heath-leaved Banksia	Apr–Nov	A bushy species, with flower-heads of yellow, orange, deep red or cream.
Banksia marginata	Silver Banksia	Mar–Sept	Variable species. Pale to bright yellow cylindrical flower-heads.
Callistemon pallidus	Lemon Bottlebrush	Sept–Jan	Dense shrub; grey-green to dark green leaves; cream to yellow brushes.
Callistemon viminalis	Weeping Bottlebrush	Mainly Nov–Mar	Has pendulous branches and bright red flower-spikes.
Calocephalus brownii	Cushion Bush	Sept–Feb	A dense plant with silvery stems and leaves.
Calothamnus sanguineus	Blood-red Net-bush	Oct–June	Low spreading shrub with dense pine-like leaves and rich red flowers.
Chamelaucium floriferum	Walpole Wax	Aug–Nov	A compact shrub with white open-petalled flowers.
Correa alba	White Correa	Mainly Nov–May	Dense shrub with oval leaves. White starry flowers.
Correa backhousiana		May–Nov	Dense shrub with oval leathery green leaves; cream to pale green tubular flowers.
Darwinia fascicularis		Aug–Nov	Has narrow, aromatic foliage; flower-heads cream to red.
Eucalyptus lehmannii	Bushy Yate	Mainly July–Dec	Dense small tree with large clusters of green to yellow-green flowers.
Eucalyptus leucoxylon	Yellow Gum	Mainly Mar–Dec	Low-growing coastal forms recommended. Profuse flowers of white to deep pink.
Hibbertia scandens	Climbing Guinea-flower	Sporadic	Climber with long trailing stems, shiny leaves and yellow flowers.
Kunzea pomifera	Muntries	Sept–Nov	Dense spreading plant with small light green leaves. Clusters of white to cream flowers, followed by bluish berries.
Leptospermum 'Horizontalis'		Oct–Dec	Dense spreading shrub with horizontal branches; prickly foliage; profuse white flowers.
Leptospermum squarrosum	Peach Tea-tree	Feb–Apr	Bushy shrub with narrow leaves and white to deep pink flowers.
Melaleuca lanceolata	Moonah	Oct–Feb	Small tree with dark, hard-barked trunk. Profuse small white to cream brushes.
Melaleuca nesophila	Showy Honey-myrtle	Dec–Mar	A relatively dense shrub; globular mauve-pink flower-heads.
Myoporum parvifolium	Creeping Myoporum	Nov–Mar	Mat plant. Has narrow leaves and small white or rarely pale pink flowers.
Pimelea ferruginea		Mainly July–Oct	A dense shrub with shiny leaves and pink flower-heads.
Regelia velutina		Aug–Jan	An upright shrub with hairy, greyish leaves. Bright red flower-spikes.
Templetonia retusa	Cockies Tongues	May–Oct	Has showy terminal clusters of pink to red pea-flowers.

Annual species, or plants with a limited lifespan in cultivation

There are comparatively few Australian plants recognized as 'annuals', or plants that complete their entire life-cycle within a year. Such plants, although not long-lived, usually present a spectacular display of flowers when at their peak, and are considered well worth growing for this purpose.

Some of the plants listed in the following chart are generally regarded as having a limited life-span, although they are not annuals. *Actinotus helianthii*, the Flannel Flower, does tend to die out over a period, but it sets seed readily, and will either self-sow naturally or the seed can be gathered and re-sown. The *Anigozanthos* species included present a showy display when in flower, and the vigour of these plants can be prolonged by regular applications of fertilizer. Following the flowering period, plants can be lifted and divided, and this process often gives new life; otherwise they can die back. *Helichrysum* species grow readily from cuttings, and as the older plants can tend to become unattractive after a period of years, they can be replaced by fresh young plants. The *Lechenaultia* species listed are renowned for their spectacular flowering, but are not generally regarded as long-lived, for a number of reasons. Here again, plants strike readily from cuttings, and new plants can replace the old. The *Helipterum, Kennedia* and *Trachymene* species listed all set seed readily.

Not all gardeners will be attracted to annuals or plants with a limited life span, but for those who are, there is a colourful reward.

Chart 41 Annual species, or plants with a limited lifespan in cultivation

Botanical name	Common name	Flowering period	Comments
Actinotus helianthi	Flannel Flower	Aug–Feb	Has grey-green hairy leaves and soft white to cream daisy-like flower-heads.
Anigozanthos humilis	Cat's Paw	June–Dec	Has strap-like leaves. Flower-heads vary from cream to yellow, orange, pink or red.
Anigozanthos manglesii	Red and Green Kangaroo Paw	June–Dec	Has grey-green leaves. Flower-heads are red and green. ,
Anigozanthos viridis	Green Kangaroo Paw	July–Dec	Leaves are narrow and dark green; flower-heads yellow-green to emerald green.
Helichrysum baxteri	Fringed, or White Everlasting	Oct–Jan	Low clumping species with white and yellow daisy-like flower-heads.
Helichrysum bracteatum	Golden Everlasting	Most of year	Has large golden papery flower-heads.
Helipterum manglesii	Pink Everlasting	Mainly Oct–Jan	An annual, with stem-clasping oval leaves and pink papery flower-heads.
Helipterum roseum	Everlasting	Mainly Sept–Jan	Has narrow grey-green foliage and white to pink paper flower-heads. Annual.
Kennedia glabrata		Nov–Dec	Prostrate creeper with clusters of perfumed, brick red, pea-shaped flowers.
Lechenaultia biloba	Blue Lechenaultia	July–Dec	Small shrub with spectacular blue flowers.
Lechenaultia formosa	Red Lechenaultia	Mainly Mar–Nov	A variable small species. Flowers can be yellow, orange, pink, magenta, scarlet or red.
Lechenaultia tubiflora	Heath Lechenaultia	Sept–Feb	A low, fine-foliaged plant. Cream, pink or red flowers.
Thysanotus multiflorus	Fringe Lily	Nov–Mar	Has grass-like foliage, with dense heads of bright mauve flowers.
Trachymene caerulea	Rottnest Daisy	Mainly Sept–Jan	An annual, with lobed foliage and soft heads of small blue flowers.

Plant Descriptions

In this section it has been attempted to list, as concisely as possible, the major horticultural features of each plant. Common names have been stated where they are in general use, but in many cases there is no common name relating to the species.

The references to States of Australia indicate where the species originate. This information can be of assistance to the grower, as well as being of general interest. If, for example, a species is found in several or all States, it can be assumed that it is tolerant of a range of conditions; if it is restricted to one State only, it may be more specific in its requirements. But it should be noted that it is not possible to determine the needs of a plant solely on the basis of its State of origin. *Rhododendron lochae* is a native of Queensland, the 'Sunshine State', but this rhododendron is an inhabitant of Mt Bellenden Ker, the tallest peak in Queensland, where it usually grows in moist and shaded locations. Similar examples could be given in relation to plants from other areas.

To allow the maximum information to be provided without unduly enlarging the book, the cultivation requirements of each species have been given in code form. There is a logical sequence to the code, which should assist the reader to recognize immediately the conditions under which a plant may be expected to grow successfully.

H — Hot:	Tolerates sun for most of the day.
O — Open:	An open position is most suitable, but not necessarily exposed to hot sun for extended periods.
S — Shade:	Will grow well in full shade.
SS — Semi-shade:	Will grow well in situations that are shaded for some part of the day, or positions that receive dappled sunlight through overhead foliage canopy.
D — Drainage:	Will grow well in very well drained soils.
M — Moist:	Will grow well in soil that is moist for most of the year.
W — Wet:	Will withstand extended wet periods.

The next three letters used in the code refer to the soil-types that the plants can be expected to tolerate.

L — Loam:	Suitable for loam, clay-loam or clay.
SA — Sand:	Suitable for sandy soils or sandy loam.
G — Gravels:	Suitable for coarse, open gravels.

The final coding references relate to the plants' tolerance of coastal conditions and frost.

C1 — Coastal, protected:	Suitable for protected coastal situations.
C2 — Coastal, exposed:	Suitable for exposed coastal situations.
F1 — Frost:	Moderately frost resistant.
F2 — Frost:	Frost resistant at all stages of growth.

With each Plant Description there is a listing of the chart or charts in which it has been included, followed (in brackets) by any additional charts to which it is also suited. While some species, such as aquatic plants or medium to large trees, are considered to have only limited application within small gardens, others will be found in many charts, and could have even further application, such as in Plant Groupings, in which they may have not been included.

The main basis for plant selection will be found within the descriptions, and the cultivation requirements as supplied by the code used.

Acacia acinacea — Gold Dust Wattle NSW, Vic, SA
A spreading shrub, growing to around 2.5m high. Globular flower-heads are produced at the ends of the branches in August-December, and are of deep gold colour, thus resulting in the common name.
H O SS D L SA C1 F2 Chart 25 (3, 10)

Acacia aculeatissima — Thin-leaf Wattle NSW, Vic
A prostrate to low spreading wattle, growing to about 50cm high, with a width of 1-2m. It is of open habit, with short sharp phyllodes on the spreading branches. The globular flower-heads are pale to bright yellow, and flowering time is between June and November.
O SS D L SA G C1 F2 Chart 23 (2)

Acacia alata — Winged Wattle   WA
This species grows to 1-2m high, by a similar width, and has unusual, flat, winged branchlets. The globular flower-heads are borne on short stalks along the branchlets, and are cream to deep yellow. Flowering time is during September-November. Plants respond well to pruning, and it is an ideal species for growing under tall trees. Can be frost tender.
S SS D L SA G C1   Chart 27 (11)

Acacia boormanii — Snowy River Wattle NSW, Vic
Under garden conditions this wattle can grow to 3-5m high, and may sucker. The grey-green phyllodes are 5-8cm long by around 0.2cm wide. The bright yellow flowers are sweetly scented, and appear in dense racemes at the ends of the branchlets, between July and October.
H O SS D L SA G C1 F2   Charts 9, 34

Acacia browniana   WA
(previously known as *A.strigosa*)
A low-growing wattle, reaching 1-2m high by a similar width. It has hairy branches, and small dark green fern-like leaves. The yellow flower-heads are globular, and are produced on stalks longer than the leaves. Flowering is between July and October. Plants respond well to pruning.
SS D L SA G C1 F1   Chart 2

Acacia buxifolia — Box-leaf Wattle Qld, NSW, Vic
A hardy wattle, growing up to 2-4m high by a similar width. Flowering takes place between July and December, with a profuse display of yellow globular flower-heads, borne in racemes at the ends of the branches. The phyllodes are grey-green and leathery, and about 2.5cm long by 1cm wide.
H O SS D L SA G C1 F2   Chart 25 (3, 10)

Acacia cultriformis — Knife-leaf Wattle   NSW
A hardy, much-branched shrub, of up to 2-5m high, by a similar width. The dense phyllodes are about 2cm long by 1.5cm wide, triangular in shape, and grey-green in colour. Golden yellow flower-heads are borne in racemes, and form an attractive display in August - October. Plants are drought tolerant.
H O SS D L SA G C1 F2   Chart 33 (3, 12)

Acacia drummondi ssp. *affinis*   WA
(Previously known as *A.drummondii* dwarf)
A low-growing wattle, reaching 0.5-1m high by a similar width. The branches are hairy, with small fern-like green leaves. Flowering is between May and September, with profuse rod-like flower-heads of bright yellow.
O SS D L SA G C1 F1   Charts 8, 18 (25)

Acacia elongata — Slender Wattle   Qld, NSW
An open, fairly upright shrub, growing to 3-4m high. The narrow phyllodes are flat and thick, and can be up to 10cm long. Bright yellow globular flower-heads appear in clusters at the ends of branches, during August - October. This is a useful wattle for growing in heavy, wet soils.
H O SS W L SA G C1 F1   Chart 26

Acacia fimbriata — Fringed Wattle   Qld, NSW
This upright to spreading wattle grows to 5-8m high, by a width of around 4-6m. It flowers between August and October, with racemes of deep cream to yellow, globular flower-heads, produced near the ends of the branches.
O SS D W L SA G C1 F1   Chart 33

Acacia flexifolia — Bent-leaf Wattle Qld, NSW, Vic
The branches of this species are greyish, and the phyllodes of 1-2.5cm long by 0.2cm wide, are grey-green and bent near the base (resulting in the common name for the species). Plants can grow to 2m high, by a similar width. The pale yellow, globular flower-heads are fragrant, and are scattered along the branches between June and October. Plants respond well to pruning.
H O SS D L SA G C1 F2   Chart 12 (8, 25, 28)

Acacia glaucoptera — Clay Wattle   WA
For gardeners who like something a little unusual, the flat, winged, blue-green phyllodes of this species are continuous along the stems. New growth is often reddish. Plants grow to 1.5m high, with a width of up to 2-3m. They respond well to pruning. Flowering period is August-November, and the globular, bright yellow flower-heads are borne on stalks at wing notches.
SS W L SA G C1 F1   Chart 28 (2, 12)

Acacia gracilifolia   SA
This upright to spreading species, from the Flinders Ranges, has an open habit, allowing visibility through the branches, yet providing a screen from full sunlight. It grows to 5m high by 2-5m wide, with long, narrow, dark green phyllodes. The golden yellow flower-heads are produced in clusters near the ends of branchlets. Flowering is between August and October.
H O D L SA G C1 F2   Chart 10 (3, 25)

Acacia howittii — Sticky Wattle   Vic
A graceful, erect to spreading tree, of 4-6m by a similar width. The branches are pendulous. Phyllodes are up to 2.5cm long, and the new growth is slightly sticky. Fragrant pale yellow flower-heads are produced near the ends of the branchlets, between September and November.
O SS M W L SA G C1 F2   Charts 32, 33

Acacia iteaphylla — Gawler Range Wattle SA
This dense large shrub can grow to a height of 3-5m. It can grow wider than this, but responds well to pruning. The phyllodes are 5-10cm long, and blue-green in colour with pinkish new growth. In some forms the foliage is very pendulous. Pale yellow, globular flower-heads are produced between March and September. A drought tolerant species.
H O SS D L SA G C1 F2   Charts 7, 33 (10, 28)

Acacia leprosa — Cinnamon Wattle   NSW, Vic
This is a small tree of 3-12m high by 2-6m wide, often with weeping habit. The phyllodes can grow to 15cm

long, and are aromatic. Lemon-yellow flower-heads are produced during August and September.

O SS M L SA G C1 F2   Chart 29 (12, 27)

Acacia leptospermoides   **WA**

A small shrub of about 1m high, by up to 2m wide. The phyllodes are small, and blue-green in colour, on branches which are often attractively arched, making it a desirable plant, even when not in flower. Flowering occurs between May and October, when yellow globular flower-heads are produced near the ends of branchlets. A drought resistant wattle.

H O SS D L SA G C1 F1   Charts 8, 10 (25, 28)

Acacia longifolia —   Qld, NSW, Vic, Tas, SA
Sallow Wattle or Sydney Golden Wattle

A very quick growing tree, with a height of 4-8m by a similar width. The green phyllodes are 5-20cm long, by up to 2cm wide. Bright yellow, rod-like flower-heads are produced near the ends of branches, between July and October.   Chart 33

A.longifolia var *sophorae* is excellent for exposed coastal situations.

H O SS W L SA G C1 F1   Chart 40

Acacia paradoxa —   Qld, NSW, Vic, SA, WA
Hedge Wattle (Previously known as *A.armata*)

This is a very thorny plant, but is useful for restricting access to certain areas, or for giving protection to small birds. It grows 3-4m high by a similar width. The phyllodes are small, narrow, and wavy. Flowering is between August and November, when golden globular flower-heads are profuse, and well displayed.

H O SS W L SA G C1 F2   Chart 36 (34)

Acacia podalyriifolia —   Qld, NSW
Silver Wattle or Mt Morgan Wattle

This is a very attractive small tree, both in flower and foliage. It grows to about 4-6m high by 3-5m wide. The phyllodes are more or less oval, with a length of up to 5cm, and are silvery grey-green. Bright yellow, globular flower-heads are produced in loose clusters at the ends of the branches, mainly between June and October.

H O SS D L SA G C1 F1   Chart 9 (28)

Acacia pravissima — Ovens Wattle   NSW, Vic

A hardy and attractive wattle, growing 4-8m high by a similar width. The branches are often quite pendulous, bearing triangular phyllodes of up to 2cm long by about 1cm wide. The flowers are borne on recemes much longer than the foliage, with buds of reddish tonings, being followed by globular flower-heads of bright yellow. Flowering period is August-October.

H O SS M W L SA G C1 F2   Chart 33

Acacia pravissima 'Golden Carpet' is a prostrate form of the above species. It will spread to approximately 3-5m.   Chart 23

Acacia redolens   **WA**

The grey-green phyllodes of this species grow to 7cm long, by 1.5cm wide, and have a distinctive sweet fragrance, when crushed or also noticeable on a hot day. Plants grow up to 4m high, with a spread of up to 8m, but may be pruned to restrict growth if desired.

Low-growing forms are also obtainable, having been selected, and then propagated from cuttings. Small globular flower-heads are produced along the branches, between August and October.

H O SS W L SA G C1 F2   Chart 29 (3)

Acacia retinodes — Wirilda   Vic, Tas, SA

This species grows 3-5m high by 2-5m wide. The bluish-green foliage can be quite variable. The phyllodes are usually about 1cm wide, but can be wider or very narrow. New growth can often weep. Lemon yellow flower-heads are borne in clusters near the ends of the branchlets over a long period, mainly between November and May.

H O SS W L SA G C1 F2   Chart 33 (27)

Acacia spectabilis —   Qld, NSW
White Stem or Glory Wattle

A most attractive large shrub to small tree, with glaucous fern-like leaves. The trunk and branches are smooth and whitish. Plants grow to a height of 3-5m. Golden yellow flower-heads are produced in clusters near the ends of the branches, and flowering is between August and October.

H O SS D L SA G C1 F2   Chart 32 (3, 12, 28)

Acacia suaveolens —   Qld, NSW, Vic, Tas, SA
Sweet Wattle

The common name of this species is derived from the fragrant, cream to pale yellow flower-heads. They are globular, and borne in racemes, between April and October. The plant is of spreading open habit, reaching 1-3m high by 2-5m wide. Responds well to pruning. The phyllodes are bluish green, and may be up to 15cm long.

H O SS M L SA G C1 F1   Chart 29 (7, 9, 13)

Acacia terminalis —   Qld, NSW, Vic, Tas
Sunshine Wattle

(Previously known as *A.botrycephala*, and *A.discolor*) This showy wattle has dark green ferny leaves, and can reach a height of up to 6m, with a spread of 2-5m. The yellow flower-heads are produced in racemes at the ends of the branches, usually between March and July.

O SS W L SA G C1 F1   Charts 9, 27

Acacia uncinata — Round-leaf Wattle   Qld, NSW
(Previously known as *A.undulifolia*)

The main flowering time of this wattle is during the warm to hot months of September-March. Plants grow to 3-4m high by 2-4m wide, and are of open habit, with oval phyllodes to 3cm long. The globular flower-heads are bright yellow, and are borne along the ends of branchlets.

H O SS D L SA G C1 F2   Chart 5 (10, 25)

Acacia verticillata —Prickly Moses NSW, Vic, Tas, SA

This very prickly species has narrow phyllodes, grouped like wheel spokes around the stems. It grows 2-4m high by 2-3m wide. Flowering is between July and November, when pale yellow rod-shaped flower-heads are borne near the ends of the branches. A good refuge plant for small birds.

H O SS M W L SA G C1 F2   Chart 36 (27)

Acacia vestita — Hairy Wattle   NSW
This wattle grows to 3-6m high, by a similar width, with pendulous branches and dense foliage. The phyllodes are 1-2cm long, oval, hairy and grey-green. In September-October globular flower-heads of golden yellow are produced in terminal clusters.
H O SS D L SA G C1 F2   Chart 28 (12, 33)

Actinodium cunninghamii — Albany Daisy   WA
An attractive small plant for gardens or containers. It grows around 75cm high by 50cm wide, and responds well to pruning. The stem-clasping leaves are aromatic. Flower-heads are daisy-like, white and red, and of up to 3cm diameter. They are produced between August and January.
O S D M L SA C1 F1   Chart 2 (18, 25)

Actinotus helianthi — Flannel Flower   Qld, NSW
This well-known and popular annual or perennial species grows to 1.5m high by up to 1m across. The branches are woolly, and the grey-green hairy leaves are deeply lobed. Daisy-like flower-heads are borne on branched stems during August-February. They can be up to 8cm in diameter, and are white to cream tipped with grey.
O S D M L SA G C1 F1   Charts 4, 18, 38, 41 (12, 28)

Adiantum aethiopicum —   All States
Common Maidenhair Fern
This well-known fern, with delicate fronds, is ideally suited to container cultivation, or can be grown in gardens. It grows best in sheltered locations, but adapts to open, moist situations. Plants have a height of 0.3m and can spread to 1m across.
O S SS D M L SA C1 F1   Chart 21 (11)

Agonis juniperina — Juniper Myrtle   WA
An upright tree, growing 5-10m high by 3-5m wide, with fibrous bark, and branches often pendulous. The leaves are about 1cm long, narrow, and in dense clusters along the branchlets. Clusters of small white flowers with brown centres, can be seen during February to March, also August to November. An excellent species for growing in heavy wet clays.
H O SS W L SA G C1 F1   Chart 32 (26)

Alisma plantago-aquatica — Water Plantain NSW, Vic
A perennial, with a basal clump of broad, sometimes heart-shaped leaves, on long stalks. The many small, pale pink flowers are produced on branchlets from an erect stem that can be 0.5-1.5m tall. Flowering period is November-March. This plant is best grown in water, or in moist soil near the edge of a pool.
Aquatic.   Chart 39 (26)

Angophora hispida — Dwarf Apple   NSW
(Previously known as *A.cordifolia*)
A spreading tree, with a height of 3-6m by a similar width. The bark is flaky and branchlets are covered in reddish hairs. The grey-green leaves are oblong to oval, heart-shaped, and can be up to 10cm long. Following attractive buds covered with reddish hairs, cream flowers of 2cm diameter are borne in dense terminal clusters. Flowering is between November and February.
H O SS D L SA G C1 F1   Chart 32

Anigozanthos flavidus — Tall Kangaroo Paw   WA
This is the most vigorous of the Kangaroo Paws, and has long, green, strap-like leaves, forming a clump 0.5-1m high by around 1m wide. Flowering is between October and February, when tubular flowers are produced on branched stems of up to 3m high. Flowers can be yellow, green, red, orange, pink or variations and mixtures of these colours. Plants appreciate moisture, although not waterlogged conditions.
H O D M L SA G C1 F1   Charts 24, 35 (5, 14, 37)

Anigozanthos humilis — Cats Paw   WA
A small clumping perennial, with strap-like leaves up to 20cm long, by about 1cm wide. The flower stems are up to 50cm tall, bearing tubular flowers in spikes of up to 15 blooms. Flower colour varies from creamy yellow to orange, pink or red, and flowering period is June-December. The species can be deciduous, therefore if foliage appears dead, plants should not be discarded immediately.
H O D M L SA G C1 F1   Charts 16, 41 (2, 14, 37)

Anigozanthos manglesii —   WA
Red and Green Kangaroo Paw
The Floral Emblem of Western Australia. A clumping perennial, with leaves up to 20cm long. The spectacular flowers appear between June and December, on red woolly stalks to 1m tall. The flowers can be up to 7cm long, are tubular with lobes strongly turned back, and are green with a red base. It is recommended that plants be divided every 2 years. Can be frost tender.
O SS D M L SA G C1   Charts 16, 41 (2, 14, 37)

Anigozanthos pulcherrimus —   WA
Golden Kangaroo Paw
The leaves of this Kangaroo Paw are up to 75cm long, and plants form a clump to 1m wide. Flowering is mainly between November and February, with flowers borne on hairy grey-green stems 1-2m high. The golden yellow flowers are 2-3cm long, and appear as a one-sided raceme on branchlets.
H O SS D L SA G C1 F1   Chart 16 (5, 14, 37)

Anigozanthos rufus — Red Kangaroo Paw   WA
A perennial species, with leaves to 75cm tall, forming a clump up to 1m across. Flower stems are deep red and woolly, and grow up to 1.5m high. The tubular flowers are 2-3cm long, and appear during September to February, in one-sided racemes on the branchlets. They are deep red.
H O SS D L SA G C1 F1   Charts 18, 24, 35 (3, 14, 16, 37)

Anigozanthos viridis — Green Kangaroo Paw   WA
This is one of the smaller of the Kangaroo Paws, with leaves to 30cm long, forming a clump of up to 50cm wide. The leaves are dark green, and can be flat to cylindrical. Flower stems grow to 50cm tall, bearing racemes of up to 15 flowers. The flowers are woolly

yellow-green to emerald-green, and are produced between July and December.
H O D M L SA G C1 F1   Charts 24, 41 (2, 8, 14, 16, 37)

Asplenium australasius — Bird's-nest Fern Qld, NSW
This is an unusual fern, with large, erect, radiating fronds that are up to 20cm wide, and undivided. Plants grow 1-2m high by a similar width, and their shape has given rise to the common name. They prefer to have a relatively confined root system, and therefore grow well in containers.
S SS D M L SA C1 F1   Chart 21 (11, 12, 27)

Asplenium bulbiferum —   Qld, NSW, Vic, Tas, SA
Mother Spleenwort
A widely cultivated fern, suited to containers (especially hanging baskets) and gardens. It appreciates a sheltered position, and in a garden can grow 1.2m high by 1.5m wide. The soft fronds may be upright or weeping, and young plants are produced at the frond tips.
S SS D M L SA C1 F1   Chart 21 (11, 12, 27)

Asplenium simplicifrons   Qld
This fern is closely related to *A.nidus*, but has shorter and narrower fronds. It is well suited to container and garden cultivation.
S SS D M L SA C1 F1   Chart 21 (11, 12, 27)

Asterolasia asteriscophora —   NSW, Vic
Lemon Star-bush (Previously known as *A.muelleri*)
A slender shrub, growing to 1.5m high by 1m wide. The hairy leaves are 1-2.5 cm long with blunt tips, and are dull green. Lemon yellow star-shaped flowers of approx 2cm diameter are produced in September to November. Plants respond well to pruning.
S̄S̄ D M L SA G C1 F2   Chart 27 (3, 11)

Asterolasia trymalioides — Alpine Star-bush NSW, Vic
A dense low shrub of 0.5-1m high by 1m wide. The branches are hairy, with oblong, scented, dark green shiny leaves of about 1.5cm long. Profuse small yellow star-like flowers are borne in terminal clusters, during the flowering period of October to January.
O SS D M L SA G C1 F2   Charts 23, 38 (2)

Astroloma ciliatum —   WA
Candle Cranberry Heath, or Moss-leaved Heath
A small shrub, growing to 1m high by 1-2m wide. The very narrow, bright green leaves are about 1cm long, and tightly packed along the stems. The flowers are cigar-shaped, and have a red tube tipped with greenish yellow and black. Flowering period is mainly May-November. Grows well in the protection of other plants, and appreciates light pruning.
O SS D L SA G C1 F1   Chart 8 (14, 37)

Astroloma conostephioides —   NSW, Vic, SA
Flame Heath
The common name to this species provides a very apt description, and it is an eye-catching plant when in bloom, between May and February. It grows to 1.5m high by up to 2m wide, with narrow, pungent, blue-green leaves of 1-2cm long. The scarlet flowers are tubular, and up to 2cm long.
H O SS D L SA G C1 F2   Chart 8 (14, 25, 37)

Astroloma epacridis   WA
This species grows 0.3-1m high by 0.5-1m wide, and has small, dark green, pungent leaves, crowded along the branches. The small tubular flowers are pink and orange red. Flowering can be sporadic throughout the period between December and August.
O SS D L SA G C1 F1   Chart 6

Astroloma humifusum —   All states except Qld
Cranberry Heath
A ground-covering species, with a height of up to 50cm and a width of 50cm to 1.5m. The foliage is dense, with narrow, pungent, grey-green leaves. Small tubular bright red flowers are borne along the branches, between March and October, and are followed by small edible succulent green berries.
O SS D L SA G C2 F2   Chart 18 (19, 23)

Atriplex rhagodioides —   NSW, Vic, SA, WA
Silver Salt-bush
A dense shrub of up to 1.5m high by a similar width. The foliage is silvery grey, with leaves 1-3cm long. It is grown mainly for its hardiness and silver foliage, as flowers are relatively small and insignificant. Withstands hard pruning. Fire retardant.
H O SS D L SA G C1 F2   Chart 25 (33, 40)

Azolla filiculoides —   All states
Pacific Azolla or Red Azolla
A small, free-floating fern, often with brilliant reddish foliage colouration. Plants can spread rapidly to entirely cover a pool, but can be easily kept under control by raking off excess plants.
Aquatic   Chart 39

Backhousia citriodora —   Qld
Lemon Ironwood, or Sweet Verbena Myrtle
At maturity, this tree can reach 4-6m high by 3-4m wide. The leaves are about 8cm long and have a strong lemon fragrance. Flowering is mainly between August and November, with small cream flowers being borne in dense clusters. This species will withstand fairly hard pruning. Can be frost tender.
S SS M W L SA G C1   Chart 13 (3, 29)

Baeckea astarteoides   WA
This small shrub grows to around 1.5m high, often with arching branches, giving a width of up to 2m. The leaves are small and narrow, and are clustered along the branchlets. The flowers are small, pink, and resemble flowers of a tea-tree. They are profuse during the flowering period, mainly between October and January. Plants respond well to pruning.
H O SS M W L SA G C1 F1   Chart 25 (2, 4, 25)

Baeckea linifolia — Weeping Baeckea Qld, NSW, Vic
A slender shrub, of 1-3m high, with pendulous branches. The leaves are small and narrow, with new growth often reddish in colour. Between December and March, small white flowers are well displayed on the branchlets. It is an ideal species for planting near ponds, or in other situations where the weeping habit may be fully appreciated.
H O SS M W L SA G C1 F1   Chart 28 (5, 12, 26)

Baeckea ramosissima —   NSW, Vic, Tas
Rosy Heath-myrtle
A small, spreading species, with wiry branches, and small leaves. Some forms are only 30-50cm high, but can be up to 1.5m in width. The flowers are white to deep pink, and up to 1.5cm diameter. Main flowering period is between August and November. Several different forms of this species are at present in cultivation.
O SS M W L SA G C1 F2   Chart 2 (19, 23)

Baeckea virgata —   Qld, NSW, Vic, NT
Tall or Twiggy Baeckea
A hardy baeckea, with branchlets often pendulous. It can grow to a height of up to 5m, with a width usually of 2-3m. The leaves are dark green, narrow, and up to 2.5cm long. The small white flowers appear between November and March, usually in clusters near the ends of branchlets. A useful screen shrub.
H O SS W L SA G C1 F1   Charts 5, 27, 35 (11)

Banksia attenuata —   WA
Coast Banksia or Slender Banksia
There are different forms of this species, including a very useful dwarf form which can grow to 3-5m high by 3-4m wide. The stiff serrated leaves are up to 20cm long by about 1cm wide. Flowering is between October and March, when bright yellow cylindrical flower-heads of up to 25cm long are borne at the ends of branches.
H O D L SA G C1 F2   Chart 5 (10, 14)

Banksia baueri —   WA
Possum Banksia or Koala Banksia
Large flower-heads of 15-40cm long by up to 20m wide, with a fluffy grey-yellow appearance make this banksia worthy of cultivation, and have also given the species the above common names. A form with orange-brown flowers is also available. Plants grow to a height of 2-5m, and the flower-heads are nestled within the stiff serrated leaves of up to 15cm long. Flowering period is between July and November.
H O SS D L SA G C1 F2   Chart 3 (10)

Banksia baxteri — Bird's-nest Banksia   WA
During November to March this species bears large terminal dome-shaped heads of yellow-green, which are most attractive both in the garden, and as a cut flower. The leaves can be up to 15cm long, and are very stiff, with triangular lobes to the mid-rib. The new growth is rusty brown and the fruits are also decorative. Mature plants can grow to 2-3m high by similar width, but they may be pruned if desired.
H O SS D L SA G C1 F2   Chart 5 (12, 14, 25, 28, 37)

Banksia brownii — Brown's Banksia   WA
An erect shrub, with a mature height of 3-6m. The leaves are 7-12cm long by around 1cm wide, and fern-like, with the new growth often brownish. The cylindrical flower-heads are 10-20cm long, and reddish to golden brown. Flowering period is February to July. Plants respond well to pruning.
O S D L SA G C1 F1   Chart 9 (14)

Banksia caleyi — Caley's Banksia   WA
A dense shrub with many branches. It can grow to 2-4m high by a smiliar width. The dark green leaves are 5-10cm long, wedge-shaped and serrated. Flowering is between August and January, when acorn-shaped flower-heads of 7-15cm long hang down within the plant. They are deep scarlet or yellow.
H O SS D L SA C1 F2   Chart 3 (10, 14, 25)

Banksia candolleana — Propellor Banksia   WA
This banksia of 1-1.5m high by 2m wide has dense foliage, with leaves up to 20cm long, divided to the mid-rib. The flower-heads are almost globular, around 5-6cm diameter, and light green to golden orange. They are produced on the older wood of the plants, during March to July. A drought resistant species.
H O SS D L SA G C1 F2   Chart 7 (10, 14)

Banksia canei — Mountain Banksia   Vic
This small shrub of 1-3m high has stiff leaves which are serrated and prickly. It appears to be suited to container cultivation, although often not long-lived when grown in the ground. The yellow-green flower-heads are cylindrical to 10cm long. Some forms have blue-grey buds. Flowering period is from October to February.
H O SS D L SA G C1 F2   Chart 11 (5, 14, 37)

Banksia dryandroides — Dryandra-leaved Banksia WA
A small to medium shrub of 1-2m high by a similiar width. The foliage is most decorative, with shiny dark green leaves of 5-15cm long by 1-1.5cm wide, serrated to the mid-rib. The branches are hairy, and new leaf growth is a rusty brown. Between January and August, acorn-shaped flower-heads of 8cm long are produced within the shrub, on the older wood. They are light brown to greyish-brown.
H O SS D L SA G C1 F1   Chart 28 (5, 7, 9, 12, 30)

Banksia ericifolia — Heath-leaved Banksia Qld, NSW
This bushy species grows to 3-6m tall by 2-5m wide. The leaves are around 5cm long and very narrow. Flowering is between April and November, with cylindrical flower-heads of up to 25cm long, in shades of yellow, orange, deep red or cream, or combinations of these colours. Plants propagated from cuttings will retain flower colour of parent plant, however seedlings can produce variations.
H O SS D L SA G C1 F1   Charts 9, 14, 40 (34, 37)

Banksia gardneri — Prostrate Banksia   WA
(Previously known as *B.prostrata*)
A prostrate species, growing to a width of 3-4m. The deeply lobed leaves can be 15-40cm long, with new growth of rusty tones. Bronze to yellowish flower-heads of 7-12cm long by 6-8cm wide are held erect at the ends of the creeping branches. Flowering period is August to February.
H O SS D L SA G C1 F2   Chart 10 (3, 5, 23)

Banksia laricina — Rose-fruited Banksia   WA
A small, dense species, of 1-2m high by 1-3m wide. The leaves are 1-2cm long and narrow. Globular yellow flower-heads of about 4cm diameter are borne on

short branchlets inside the plant, between April and August. The seed cones are unusual, and are valued for floral art.

H O SS D L SA G C1 F1 — Chart 6 (8, 10, 25, 30)

Banksia lemanniana — WA

This is one of the relatively few banksias with flower-heads that are pendant, rather than being held upright. Flowering is between July and December, and the yellow to yellow-green heads are around 10-18cm long by 8-12cm wide. Plants reach a height of about 2-4m, by a similar width, and have wedge-shaped serrated leaves up to 10cm long. New leaf growth has a rusty appearance.

H O SS D L SA G C1 F2 — Chart 3 (10, 14, 30, 37)

Banksia marginata — Silver Banksia — Qld, NSW, Vic, Tas

A widespread banksia of eastern Australia, usually with a height of 1-6m, varying greatly under differing climatic conditions. The leaves are usually between 2cm and 10cm long, with the common name of the species resulting from their silvery under-surface. Flowering period is between March and September, with pale to bright yellow flower-heads of 4-10cm long by 4-6cm wide.

H O SS D L SA G C2 F2 — Charts 7, 9, 40 (14, 25, 37)

Banksia meisneri — Meisner's Banksia — WA

A much-branched shrub of 1-1.5m tall by up to 2m wide. The leaves are small and narrow, with yellow flower-heads of 3-4cm long being produced between March and November. The seed cones are an additional ornamental feature of this species.

H O SS D L SA G C1 F1 — Charts 7, 10 (25, 30)

Banksia ornata — Desert Banksia — Vic, SA

This bushy species grows 1-2m high by 1-3m wide. The serrated leaves are around 5-8cm long, and young growth can be very attractive when covered with rusty hairs. The flower-heads of up to 14cm long by 8cm wide are produced from March to August, and are grey and yellow to brown in colour.

H O SS D L SA G C1 F2 — Chart 7 (10, 14)

Banksia petiolaris — WA

A prostrate, spreading banksia, growing to 1-4m wide. The serrated leaves stand erect, and are up to 35cm long. Cylindrical flower-heads of 10-20cm long are borne at the ends of the branches between August and January. Flower colour is grey and yellow.

H O SS D L SA G C1 F2 — Chart 10 (3, 5, 23)

Banksia prionotes — Orange Banksia or Acorn Banksia — WA

The highly ornamental flowers of this banksia make it one of the most sought after of all the species. It is not easily grown under average garden conditions, but is suited to large containers where specific requirements can be provided. The flower buds are grey, opening to orange, acorn-shaped heads of up to 15cm long by 8cm wide. Flowering period is mainly between February and August. Plants can grow 5-12m high, but if grown in a tub would probably reach only 3-5m.

Responds well to pruning. The leaves are serrated, grey-green to dark green, and 10-35cm in length.

H O D L SA G C1 F2 — Chart 7 (10,14)

Banksia spinulosa — Hairpin Banksia — Qld, NSW, Vic

A hardy banksia from eastern Australia, growing to 3-5m high by 2-4m wide. Dwarf forms of this species are also in cultivation, and can be preferable for use under certain circumstances. The leaves are 3-8cm long and usually serrated. The flowering period is mainly between March and August, and the flower-heads can be between 5cm and 25cm long, with a width of 4-8cm. Colour can vary from amber to yellow, with black or red styles, or flower-heads of all gold.

H O SS D L SA G C1 F2 — Charts 9, 14, 37 (27)

Banksia violacea — Violet Banksia — WA

This small bushy species grows to around 1.5m high by a similar width. The leaves are blue-green, and 1-2cm long. Globular flower-heads are produced between January and July, and are around 6-8cm diameter, in shades of violet to deep purple, or almost black.

H O SS D L SA G C1 F1 — Chart 6

Bauera rubioides — Wiry Bauera — Qld, NSW, Vic, Tas, SA

A low shrub, reaching 1.5m high by up to 3m wide. It flowers throughout most of the year, with open-petalled flowers to 2cm diameter, in shades of white to pink. Several different forms of this species are available. All respond well to pruning.

H O SS SS M W L SA G C1 F2 — Charts 6, 11 (26, 27)

Bauera sessiliflora — Grampians Bauera — Vic

A lover of shaded areas, this species can grow to 2-3m high by a similar width, but responds very well to regular light pruning. The small leaflets are around 2.5cm long, and in groups of 3 on the stems. Between September and December a bright display is created by the rosy purple to magenta flowers of 1-1.5cm diameter, produced in clusters along the branches.

S SS M W L SA G F2 — Chart 11 (2, 8, 27)

Beaufortia decussata — WA

This medium shrub grows to a height of 2-3m by width of 1-2m. The oval leaves are about 1cm long, and crowded on the stems. Flowering period is mainly between January and April, when deep red flower-spikes to 10cm long are produced on the older wood.

H O SS D also W L SA G C1 F1 — Chart 25 (5, 7, 14, 37)

Beaufortia orbifolia — Ravensthorpe Bottlebrush WA

Usually a plant of upright habit, growing to 2-3m tall. The leaves are oval shaped, to 1cm long, and grey-green in colour. Flower-heads are of the bottlebrush type, around 6cm long by 4cm wide, and initially lime green with red tips, then changing to all-red. Flowering period is November to July. A hardy and adaptable species

H O SS W L SA G C1 F2 — Chart 37 (5, 7, 14, 25)

Beaufortia purpurea — WA

A very attractive small shrub, producing purple-red globular flower-heads of about 2cm diameter. Flowering is over a long period between September and April. Plants grow to about 1.5m high by 1m wide, and have small narrow leaves. Regular light pruning is beneficial.

O SS D M L SA G C1 F1 Chart 4 (6, 25)

Beaufortia schaueri WA
A spreading shrub of 0.5-1.5m high by a similar width. Different forms, varying in habit from upright to low, are obtainable. The small leaves are narrow, and crowded along the branchlets. Globular flower-heads of pink to purple are produced during the flowering period which is mainly between August and February.

H O SS D L SA G C1 F1 Chart 4 (2, 10, 25)

Beaufortia sparsa — WA
Swamp Bottlebrush or Gravel Bottlebrush
This species grows to about 2-4m high by 1-3m wide. The small green leaves of about 1cm long are dense along the branchlets. Flower-spikes of 5-7cm long are produced on the stem growth of the previous year, between December and April. They are usually bright reddish orange, although a fairly rare white form is also in cultivation. Plants respond well to light pruning.

H O SS M W L SA G C1 F1 Chart 6 (4, 14, 25, 37)

Beaufortia squarrosa — Sand Bottlebrush WA
This spreading shrub of up to 4m high by a similar width has small, opposite, oval leaves. The flower-heads of up to 3cm long appear at the ends of the branchlets between September and April. They are usually bright red, but can be orange or yellow.

H O D L SA G C1 F1 Chart 10 (4, 14, 25, 37)

Billardiera bignoniacea — Orange Bell Climber Vic, SA
(Previously known as *Marianthus bignoniaceus*)
This is a light twiner, ideal for growing amongst other plants. It has oblong dull green leaves. Flowering is mainly between September and March, and the tubular, pendant flowers can be solitary, but are often in groups of up to 3. Flower colour is a combination of orange to apricot and greenish yellow.

S SS D M L SA C1 F2 Chart 31 (2, 4, 14, 19, 27, 37)

Billardiera cymosa — NSW, Vic, SA, WA
Sweet Apple-berry
This light climber will often grow as a shrub, until able to gain support upon which to climb. The narrow oblong leaves can be quite silky. Flowering is mainly between August and December, when tubular flowers with spreading tips are borne in terminal clusters. Flower colour can be white, cream, green or pink to pale blue, and the flowers are followed by oblong reddish green berries. Plants appreciate root protection if grown in a hot location.

H O SS D L SA G C1 F2 Chart 31 (2, 4, 10, 14, 37)

Billardiera longiflora — NSW, Vic, Tas
Purple Apple-berry
This is a light climber, with dark green, shiny, narrow leaves. Flowering is between August and December, when greenish yellow tubular flowers of about 3cm long, hang from the branchlets. The flowers are followed by soft, shiny, deep bluish-purple oblong berries.

O SS S M L SA C1 F2 Charts 30, 31 (2, 11, 14, 27, 37)

Billardiera ringens — Chapman Creeper WA
This is a light climber, with deep green leaves to 10cm long. The flowers are initially orange, then deepen to red. They are produced in terminal clusters, mainly between August and March. A suitable species for growing through other plants.

H O SS D L SA G C1 F1 Chart 31 (2, 4, 19)

Billardiera scandens — Qld, NSW, Vic, Tas, SA
Common Apple-berry
A light twining plant, with soft foliage and leaves, hairy when young. The flowers are tubular and greenish yellow, and are followed by green oblong fleshy berries. Flowering can take place at any time during the year.

O S SS D M L SA G C1 F2 Chart 31 (2, 4, 11, 14, 27, 37)

Blancoa canescens — Winter Bell WA
A small clumping species, not always readily obtainable, but very worthy of cultivation. The strap-like leaves are about 30cm long, hairy and greyish green. Between June and October, hairy tubular flowers of up to 4cm long are borne on branched stems longer than the leaves. Flower colour is pink to red outside, with yellow-orange inside.

H O D M L SA G C1 F2 Chart 16 (8, 24)

Blandfordia grandiflora — Christmas Bells NSW
This small tufting species has green, grass-like leaves, and it remains inconspicuous amongst other plants, until the flowering period between November and January. Spectacular orange and yellow bells of up to 6cm long by 4cm wide, are borne in racemes, on stems above the foliage.

O SS M L SA G C1 F1 Chart 18 (4, 14, 16, 24, 37)

Blandfordia nobilis — Christmas Bells NSW
This species is similar to *B.grandiflora*, but is smaller, with bells which are more cylindrical.

O SS M L SA G C1 F1 Chart 18 (4, 14, 16, 24, 37)

Blechnum fluviatile — Ray Water-fern NSW, Vic, Tas
This is a most decorative, prostrate fern, spreading to a width of around 1m. The spreading, pale-green lobed fronds of up to 50cm long are produced in wheel-like formation. Fertile fronds stand erect, and provide additional interest.

S SS D M L SA C1 F1 Chart 21 (11, 12, 19, 27)

Blechnum minus — Qld, NSW, Vic, Tas, SA
Soft Water-fern
A hardy species, with semi-weeping, deeply divided fronds. The pinnae are slightly serrated, and new growth often attains bronze or pinkish tonings. Plants grow 0.5-1m high by similar width. The fertile fronds are narrow and held erect.

O SS D M W L SA C1 F2 Charts 21, 26 (11, 12, 19, 27)

Blechnum nudum — Qld, NSW, Vic, Tas, SA
Fishbone Water-fern
This hardy species is common in cultivation, and can

develop a trunk to 1m tall after many years. The fishbone-like fronds are about 1m long, giving plants a height of 1-2m by width of 0.5-1m.

O S SS D M W L SA C1 F2   Charts 21, 26 (11, 12, 27)

Blechnum penna-marina –   NSW, Vic, Tas
Alpine Water-fern
A hardy, creeping species, with small erect fishbone-like fronds of about 20cm tall. They are dark green, and form a mat-like cover. Ideal for containers or as a ground-cover beneath other plants in a moist situation.

O S SS M L SA C1 F2   Chart 21 (18)

Blechnum wattsii —   Qld, NSW, Vic, Tas, SA
Hard Water-fern
This hardy species was previously known as *B.procerum*. The dark green leathery fronds are deeply divided, with broad serrated pinnae. The new growth is usually shiny, and can have reddish tonings.

O S SS D M W L SA C1 F2   Chart 21 (11, 12, 26, 27, 28)

Boronia anemonifolia — Sticky Boronia NSW, Tas, Vic
This Boronia grows to 1.5m high by a similar width. The small green leaves are strongly scented. Flowering period is between August and December, when abundant, small, open-petalled flowers of pink or white are produced.

O SS D L SA G C1 F2   Chart 13 (2, 29)

Boronia crenulata   WA
A small species, growing to 1m high, with dense upright branches. The aromatic leaves are spoon-shaped, and up to 1.5cm long. The pink flowers have four open petals, and are borne near the ends of the branchlets, between July and December. A suckering form is available.

O SS D M L SA G C1 F1   Chart 27 (2, 8)

Boronia fraseri — Fraser's Boronia   NSW
A height of 1-2m by similar width is attained by this species. The pinnate leaves are smooth and usually dark green, but can have reddish tonings. Flowering is between August and November, when pink, open-petalled flowers of about 1.5cm diameter, are produced in clusters at the branchlet tips.

O S SS D M L SA C1 F1   Chart 27 (2, 11,   28)

Boronia heterophylla — Red Boronia   WA
This upright bushy boronia grows to 2-3m high by up to 2m wide. It flowers between August and November, with small reddish-pink, bell-like flowers, produced from the leaf axils near the ends of the branchlets. Flowers are profuse, and slightly fragrant. Plants respond well to pruning, and grow best if the root area receives some protection from full sun. They will withstand limited waterlogging.

O SS D M L SA G C1 F1   Charts 27, 35 (2, 13)

Boronia megastigma — Brown Boronia   WA
The well-known Brown Boronia is highly prized for its fragrance. Plants grow to 1-3m high, and for best results should be pruned regularly after flowering, which is between July and November. The small, open-bell shaped flowers are usually dark brown to reddish brown outside, with yellow to greenish inside. *B.megastigma* 'Chandleri' is a form with fragrant burgundy coloured flowers, whilst *B.megastigma* 'Lutea' also has fragrant flowers, of green-yellow. It is important that the root systems should at no time be allowed to dry out completely.

O SS D M L SA G C1 F1   Charts 11, 13, 29 (2, 8)

Boronia mollis — Soft Boronia   NSW
A bushy shrub of 1-2m high by a similar width. The foliage is pinnate, soft, and usually hairy. Open petalled flowers of bright pink are produced in terminal clusters between August and November.

S SS D M L SA G C1 F1   Chart 2 (11, 27)

Boronia molloyae — Tall Boronia   WA
(Previously known as *B.elatior*)
A highly recommended boronia, growing 1-4m high by 1-2m wide. The leaves are pinnate, 2-5cm long, hairy, dark green, and very aromatic. The bell-like flowers are pinkish red, and are seen between October and January. Plants respond very well to pruning.

O S SS D M L SA G C1 F1   Chart 2 (4, 11)

Boronia pinnata — Pinnate Boronia   Qld, NSW
An upright to spreading shrub, of 1-2m high, with smooth pinnate leaves which have a camphor-like aroma. The bright pink flowers are open-petalled, and up to 2cm diameter. They are borne in clusters along the branchlets, and flowering is between September and December.

O S SS D M L SA G C1 F2   Chart 2 (27, 29)

Boronia purdieana   WA
This small bushy shrub grows up to 1m high, with pinnate leaves to 1.5cm long. The flowers are bell-like, and borne in clusters along the branchlets, between August and November. They are greenish yellow, and highly fragrant. Plants appreciate pruning, and grow best with a protected root area.

O SS D M L SA G C1 F1   Chart 13 (2, 29)

Boronia serrulata — Native Rose   NSW
A very attractive species, growing to a height of around 1.5m. The small green leaves are oval to wedge-shaped, with a slightly serrated margin. Flowering is between August and December, with bright pink flowers of about 1.5cm diameter. They are very fragrant. Plants respond well to light pruning, and for successful cultivation must have a cool root area.

O SS D M L SA G C1 F1   Charts 11, 13 (2, 27, 29)

Bossiaea linophylla   WA
This attractive shrub grows to 2-3m high, with narrow leaves to 2.5cm long. The leaves are usually dark green, but can have bronze-red tonings, and branchlets may be reddish also. There is a profuse display of yellow and red pea-shaped flowers during the flowering period, which is between July and November.

H O SS D M L SA G C1 F1   Chart 28 (3, 12, 34)

Brachychiton populneus — Kurrajong Qld, NSW, Vic
A slow-growing small tree, which when fully grown is 8-15m high, but may be grown successfully in containers for a considerable period. The simple or lobed

The rich blue–purple flowers of the climbing *Sollya parviflora* are produced during Spring and Summer.

bottom right: Calothamnus quadrifidus is an adaptable plant that will tolerate moist or dry conditions.

below: A colourful display is provided by *Hibbertia empetrifolia*.

left: *Banksia spinulosa* is a hardy and attractive tall shrub. Plants are regularly visited by honey–eating birds, when in flower.

above: Unlike the majority of banksias, the pink flowers of *Banksia caleyi* hang in pendant form on the bush.

below: This member of the Heath family is *Epacris longiflora*. The attractive flowers are produced almost throughout the year.

leaves are 5-15cm long, and the attractive foliage has resulted in the species being grown as an indoor plant. Flowers are bell-shaped, to 2cm long, and cream with red spots inside. Flowering period is between September and December.

H O SS D L SA G C1 F2   Chart 20

Brachychiton rupestre — Bottle Tree   Qld
This species is grown primarily for its attractive narrow, lobed leaves, and bottle-like trunk. It is usually many years before plants outgrow a medium to large container. When planted in a garden situation, it has a mature height of 5-10m, with the diameter of the trunk increasing gradually with age. Plants can be deciduous. Can be frost tender.

H O SS D L SA G C1   Chart 20 (12)

Brachyscome multifida — Cut-leaf Daisy Qld, NSW, Vic
A clump-forming species, with dense, dark green, much-divided foliage. Plants grow to 50cm high by up to 1.5m wide. Flowering is through most of the year, with a main flowering season between August and March. The profuse daisy-like flowers are blue-mauve, or pink to white.

H O SS M L SA G C1 F2   Chart 24 (2, 4, 6)

Brachysema aphyllum — Ribbon Pea   WA
An unusual, leafless species, growing to 30cm high, by a spread of 1-2m. The winged branches are notched at the nodes, from where long, bright red, pea-shaped flowers are produced. Flowering is between July and October.

O SS D L SA G C1 F1   Chart 14 (2, 8, 10, 25, 37)

Brachysema lanceolatum — Dark Bush-pea   WA
This hardy and reliable species will provide good foliage contrast in a garden. It grows to 2m high by up to 3m wide. Leaves are to 10cm long and grey-green to dark-green above, silvery below. The pea-shaped flowers are bright to deep red, and are produced along the branches, mainly between June and October.

H O SS W L SA G C1 F1   Chart 25 (2, 8, 14, 37)

Brachysema praemorsum   WA
This spreading species can remain prostrate, or may grow to 1m high. The leaves are about 3cm long by 4cm wide, with a blunt apex. The pea-shaped flowers are initially cream, then age to red. They are seen mainly between May and February.

H O SS W L SA G C1 F1   Chart 15, 18 (2, 8, 11, 14, 23, 37)

Brachysema sericeum   WA
A prostrate to low species, spreading 1-3m wide. Useful as a dense groundcover plant. The green leaves are oval to oblong. Flowers are pea-shaped and cream or yellowish green. They are produced between July and January.

O SS D M L SA G C1 F1   Charts 23 (2, 8, 11, 14, 15, 37)

Calectasia cyanea — Blue Tinsel-Lily   Vic, SA, WA
An unusual, and relatively rare species, with crowded narrow leaves on the stems. It is perennial, and forms a clump about 60cm high by up to 1m across, spreading by suckering. Between September and November,

starry paper-like flowers are produced, with shiny blue to purple petals and golden anthers.

H O SS D M L SA G C1 F2   Chart 2 (16, 24)

Callistemon citrinus —   Qld, NSW, Vic
Crimson Bottlebrush
A hardy shrub of 2-8m high by 2-6m wide. Responds well to pruning. It is a variable species, and branchlets can have a weeping habit. Leaves taper to both ends and grow up to 10cm long. Bright red bottlebrush flowers are borne in profusion between September and December, and can also be produced in March-April. An excellent species for bird attraction.

H O SS W L SA G C1 F1   Chart 26 (3, 5, 10, 14, 25, 37)

Callistemon 'Harkness'   Cultivar
This bottlebrush has bright red flower-spikes, up to 15cm long by 6cm wide. They are often produced in clusters, with the main flowering between September and January. Plants grow to a height of 3-6m, by a width of 2-5m, and may be pruned if desired. New leaf growth is usually a soft pink. Flowers produce copious nectar for honey-eating birds.

H O SS W L SA G C1 F1   Chart 36 (3, 5, 10, 14, 25)

Callistemon 'Mauve Mist'   Cultivar
This callistemon, with soft hairy new leaf growth, and mauve flower-spikes, originated as a seedling from C. 'Reeves Pink'. It must be propagated from cuttings to ensure that the characteristics of the parent plant are retained. The flowering period is usually October-December.

H O SS W L SA G C1 F1   Chart 34 (3, 5, 10, 14, 25, 37)

Callistemon pallidus —   NSW, Vic, Tas
Lemon Bottlebrush
A hardy, dense shrub of 2-5m high by a similar width. The leaves are 5-10cm long, and grey-green to dark green with silvery or reddish young growth. Attractive cream to yellow flower-spikes are produced, between September and January.

H O SS W L SA G C1 F2
                    Charts 26, 40 (3, 5, 10, 14, 25,   34, 37)

Callistemon 'Reeves Pink'   Cultivar
This callistemon is similar to *C.citrinus* in foliage. It grows 2-3m high with pink flower-spikes of 10cm long by 6cm wide. Flowering period is October-December and often also March-April. Propagate from cuttings.

H O SS W L SA G C1 F1   Chart 3 (5, 10, 14, 25, 34, 37)

Callistemon salignus — Willow Bottlebrush Qld, NSW
This small tree grows 4-8m high by 2-4m wide, on a papery-barked trunk. The green leaves can be up to 15cm long, and new leaf growth is a brilliant pink to red. Flower-spikes are produced between October and December, and range from white through to deep pinks. Plants grown from cuttings will retain flower colour of parent plant, whilst seedlings can provide variations.

H O SS W L SA G C1 F1 Charts 3, 32 (10, 14, 25, 26, 34, 37)

Callistemon subulatus — NSW, Vic
Tonghi Bottlebrush
A branched shrub, growing to 2-4m high by a similar
width. The leaves are crowded, narrow and up to 5cm
long. Flowering is between October and December,
with well displayed, deep red spikes, of up to 6cm
long.
H O SS W L SA G C1 F1 Chart 14 (3, 5, 10, 25, 26, 34, 37)

Callistemon viminalis — Qld, NSW
Weeping Bottlebrush
This is a variable species, usually growing 4-10m tall
by 2-6m wide, with pendulous branches and leaves.
The bright red flower-spikes of up to 15cm long, are
borne on the branchlet tips, mainly between
November and March. Plants will adapt to a wide
range of garden conditions. Can be frost tender.
C.viminalis 'Captain Cook' is a smaller growing form,
with a height and width of about 2m.
H O SS W L SA G C1
Charts 5, 32, 40 (7, 10, 14, 25, 26, 34, 37)

Callitris columellaris — Qld, NSW, Vic, SA
White Cypress Pine
An upright conifer, suitable for garden planting or
containers. Its mature height is between 6m and 10m,
and width is 3-5m. The branchlets are pendulous, and
foliage is usually dark green.
H O SS D L SA G C1 F2 Chart 28 (12)

Callitris oblonga — Esk Cypress Pine Tas
A dense upright conifer of 2-5m high by 1-2m wide,
with bluish-green foliage, and attractive smooth grey
seed-cones.
H O SS D L SA G C1 F2 Charts 12, 35 (28)

Calocephalus brownii — Vic, Tas, SA, WA
Cushion Bush
A dense plant, with inter-twined, stiff, silvery
branches. The leaves are small, scale-like and silvery.
Plants grow 0.5-1.5m high by 1-2m wide, and provide a striking foliage contrast in a garden. Small
globular heads of cream to yellow flowers are produced between September and February.
H O D L SA G C2 F1 Charts 28, 40 (12, 18)

Calothamnus gibbosus — WA
An open, spreading shrub, of up to 1m high by 1-2m
wide. The branches are corky, and the sharp pine-like
leaves can be 8cm long. The red flowers are produced
in a one-sided spike, on the old wood, between
November and February.
H O SS D L SA G C1 F1 Chart 5 (10, 14, 25, 37)

Calothamnus quadrifidus — Common Net-bush WA
This species is quite variable, with a number of different forms being available. Plants grow from 2-4m
high by 2-5m wide, with very narrow, grey to grey-
green leaves, up to 3cm long. Flowering is mainly
between October and March. The red flowers are
arranged either in one-sided spikes or completely
around the stems, on the older wood. Excellent for
bird attraction.
H O SS W L SA G C1 F1 Chart 37 (5, 10, 14, 25)

Calothamnus rupestris — Cliff Net-bush WA
This bushy calothamnus has a mature height of 1-3m
and width of 2-3m. The dense leaves are pine-like and
up to about 5cm long. Flowering is between August
and November, with deep pink to red, one-sided
spikes being produced on the old wood.
H O SS D L SA G C1 F1 Chart 37 (3, 10, 14, 25)

Calothamnus sanguineus — Blood-red Net-bush WA
A low, spreading shrub, which usually grows no
more than 1.5m high, but can be 1-3m wide. The
dense, pine-like leaves are up to 4cm long. Flowers of
rich red are produced in one-sided spikes, during the
flowering period of October to June.
H O SS D L SA G C1 F1 Charts 10, 40 (5, 14, 25, 37)

Calothamnus villosus — Silky Net-bush WA
The hairy, pine-like leaves of up to 2.5cm long have
led to the common name given to this species. Plants
can grow to 1-3m high by a similar width, with an
upright or spreading habit. The flowering period is
between September and February, and the one-sided
spikes are bright red.
H O SS D L SA G C1 F1 Chart 25 (3, 10, 14, 37)

Calytrix alpestris — Snow Myrtle Vic, SA
A much-branched small shrub of 2-3m high by 2-4m
wide. The small leaves are hairy, and crowded on
branchlets. The flowering period is between August
and December, when pink buds open to starry
white-petalled flowers, produced along the branchlets.
O S SS M W L SA G C1 F2 Charts 2, 38 (11, 27)

Calytrix aurea — WA
This attractive species is of upright habit, growing to
between 1m and 2m high. The flowers are golden
yellow, and have a spicy fragrance. They are of about
1.5cm diameter, and are produced in clusters at the
ends of branchlets. Flowering is between September
and February.
H O SS D L SA G C1 F1 Chart 13 (4, 10, 25, 29, 38)

Calytrix fraseri — WA
A small, open, spreading plant of up to 1.5m high by a
similar width. The branches are often of arching habit,
with narrow leaves of around 0.5cm long. Starry
flowers are produced between September and May.
They are of about 2cm diameter, and pink-mauve to
purple, with conspicuous golden stamens.
H O SS D L SA G C1 F1 Charts 6, 17 (4, 10, 19, 38)

Calytrix tetragona — All States
Common Fringe-myrtle
This species grows 1-2m high by a similar width. The
branches are erect, with small narrow leaves to 0.6cm
long. White to pink starry flowers of about 1.5cm
diameter are produced between August and
November. Following flowering, the calyces are retained on the plant, providing a further display of
purplish tones.
H O SS D L SA G C1 F2 Charts 25, 35 (2, 10, 38)

Cardwellia sublima   Qld
This species grows as a large tree in tropical rain-
forests, but can also be grown as an indoor container
plant. It has large, shiny, lobed leaves. It is in the
Proteaceae family, as are many other Australian
plants, including grevilleas and hakeas.
S SS M W L SA G F1   Chart 20

Cassia artemisioides —   Qld, NSW, SA, WA, NT
Silver Cassia
A bushy shrub, growing to 3m high by about 2.5m
wide. The leaves are pinnate, with narrow silvery
leaflets. Flowering is mainly between June and December, when yellow bell-like flowers are produced
in clusters at the ends of the branches. It is a drought
resistant species.
H O D L SA G C1 F2   Chart 25 (3, 9, 10)

Cassia nemophila — Desert Cassia All mainland States
This bushy species grows to 2-3m tall by a similar
width. The leaves are pinnate and silvery. Yellow
flowers of about 1cm diameter are produced in terminal clusters, mainly between June and November.
H O D L SA G C1 F2   Chart 9 (3, 12, 25)

Castanospermum australe — Black Bean   Qld, NSW
Although this species can grow to a tree of up to 60m
high, it is also excellent for use as an indoor container
plant, and can be grown as such for quite a long
period. The large shiny, dark green leaves have many
small leaflets, and are very attractive. Plants can take
many years to flower. Flowering is between October
and March, with pea-shaped flowers, 2-4cm long, of
yellow to orange.
O S SS D M L SA C1 F1   Chart 20

Casuarina microstachya   WA
This shrub, of 1-2m high by a similar width, has many
branches and branchlets, and a leafless appearance.
The leaves have been reduced to scale-like teeth along
the branchlets. The small male and female flowers are
brown to red, and are borne on separate plants. Female
flowers are followed by interesting, spiky seed cones.
H O SS D L SA G C1 F2   Chart 28

Casuarina ramosissima   WA
This species can grow to a height of 1-2m, by a width
of up to 2.5m. The branches and branchlets are furrowed, greyish, and densely hairy. The leaves are in
the form of small scale-like teeth, giving a leafless
appearance. Flowering period is between July and
November, and is followed by the formation of cylindrical seed cones.
H O SS D L SA G C1 F2   Chart 12 (25, 28)

Celmisia asteliifolia —   NSW, Vic
Silver Daisy or Snow Daisy
A tufting perennial, with strap-like leaves to about
20cm long, forming a clump of up to about 50cm
across. The daisy-like flowers can be up to 5cm in
diameter and are white with a yellow centre. They are
borne on long stems above the foliage, between December and March.
H O SS D M L SA C1 F2   Chart 16 (1, 4, 24, 38)

Ceratopetalum gummiferum —   NSW
NSW Christmas Bush
The flowering period of this species is October-
November, when small white flowers are produced.
After the petals drop, the plant takes on another and
more spectacular display, as the calyces enlarge and
become red. This usually happens during December,
hence the common name. Plants grow 4-8m high by a
width of 3-5m, and respond well to pruning. The
green leaves have finely toothed margins.
O S SS D M L SA G C1 F1   Chart 30

Chamelaucium floriferum — Walpole Wax   WA
This species grows 1.5-3m high by a similar width.
The dense, opposite leaves are around 2.5cm long and
narrow. Open petalled flowers of about 1.5cm diameter are borne between August and November. They
are initially white, but can age to pink or purple. A
good cut flower.
H O SS D L SA G C1 F1   Charts 3, 40 (25)

Chamelaucium uncinatum — Geraldton Wax   WA
A well-known shrub, growing 2-5m high by 2-6m
wide. The fairly narrow leaves can be up to 4cm long,
and plants can be of open or dense habit. Flowering is
mainly between August and January, when waxy
open-petalled flowers of up to 2.5cm diameter are
produced. They can be reddish purple, mauve, pink or
white.
H O SS D L SA G C1 F2   Chart 10 (3, 5, 25)

Cheiranthera cyanea — Finger Flower NSW, Vic, SA
(Previously known as *C.linearis*)
An upright shrub of up to 1m high, with slender
branches, and leaves of 2-5cm long. The attractive
flowers are 3-4cm diameter, and deep blue with yellow anthers. They are held on stalks beyond the
foliage, and flowering is usually between October and
January.
H O SS D L SA G C1 F2   Chart 4 (2, 10, 25)

Chiloglottis trapeziformis —   Qld, NSW, Vic
Broad-lip Bird Orchid
This orchid is well suited to container cultivation.
Each plant has a pair of opposite basal leaves, with a
height of 0.05-0.1m. Flowering is usually between
September and November, when a purple and green
flower is produced on a stem of about 10cm tall. An
interesting feature of the flower is the mass of glands
on the labellum (lower lip).
S SS D M L SA C1 F1   Chart 22

Chorizema cordatum — Heart-leaved Flame-pea WA
A dense shrub of 1-2m high, or a semi-climber, with
heart-shaped leaves of up to 5cm long. Flowering is
mainly between July and December, when orange,
red, bright pink and yellow pea flowers are borne in
terminal racemes to about 15cm long. Can be frost
tender.
O S SS D M L SA G C1   Chart 2 (8)

Chorizema diversifolium   WA
This is a light twining shrub, with slender branches,
and leaves of around 2.5cm long by 0.5cm wide.

Pea-shaped flowers of orange, yellow, and pink to purple, are borne in loose racemes, during September and October. Frost tender.
O S SS D M L SA G C1   Charts 19, 31 (2, 15)

Cissus antarctica — Kangaroo Vine   Qld, NSW
Although this is a vigorous climber, it is suitable for growing indoors. It has shiny toothed leaves to about 15cm long, and young growth has a rusty appearance. Small greenish flowers are produced in clusters from December to March, and are followed by small, globular, black fruits. Regular pruning is often needed to restrict the plant's spread, or it can be trained on a specific course.
O S SS D M L SA C1 F1   Chart 20 (12, 15, 19, 31)

Claytonia australasica —   NSW, Vic, Tas, SA, WA
White Purslane
A creeping, layering perennial, growing 1-2m across. The leaves can be up to 10cm long. Flowering is between August and April, and the fragrant white flowers have spreading petals, giving a diameter of up to 2cm.
H O SS M W L SA G C1 F2   Charts 1, 39 (26, 38)

Clematis aristata —   Qld, NSW, Vic, Tas
Austral Clematis
A vigorous climber. Leaves are divided into 3 leaflets, and have toothed margins. The creamy-white star-like flowers are about 5cm in diameter, and are produced in clusters near the ends of the branchlets. Flowering is between August and March, followed by significant fluffy seed-heads. Will grow best if it has a cool root area.
O S SS D M L SA G C1 F2   Chart 31 (3, 5, 27, 30)

Clematis microphylla —   All States
Small-leaved Clematis
A quick-growing, dense climber. Between July and November, many greenish-cream, star-like flowers of 3-4cm diameter are produced, followed by profuse, fluffy seed-heads, which can almost cover the plant during late November to December.
H O SS D L SA G C1 F2   Chart 31 (3, 27, 30)

Clianthus formosus —   Qld, NSW, SA, WA, NT
Sturt's Desert Pea
This well-known floral emblem of South Australia can be an annual or perennial. It is prostrate, and can grow to a width of 1-4m. The branches are hairy, with grey-green pinnate leaves. Spectacular pea-shaped flowers of red and black are produced, usually between June and March. Plants are best grown in containers, or in very well-drained garden beds in warm to hot locations.
H O D L SA G C1 F2   Chart 17 (10, 41)

Conospermum amoenum — Blue Smoke-bush   WA
This small spreading shrub grows to 1m high by 1.5m wide. It has slender branches, with pine-like leaves to 2cm long. Small, light blue, tubular flowers are borne in spikes along the branches, between August and November.
H O SS D L SA G C1 F1   Chart 17 (10)

Conostylis aculeata   WA
This is a very variable species, with several subspecies. Plants form clumps of up to 50cm wide, with strap-like leaves of 40cm long, often with spiny margins. The yellow tubular flowers are borne in terminal clusters, between August and February.
H O SS D L SA G C1 F2   Chart 16 (2, 4, 24)

Conostylis bealiana   WA
This small tufting perennial grows to 20cm high by 30cm wide. The leaves are flat and grass-like, with tubular flowers of up to 3.5cm long, appearing at the base of the plant between May and September. Flower colour is usually yellow to orange, but can be greenish-purple.
O SS D M L SA G C1 F1   Chart 17 (2, 8, 14, 16, 24, 37)

Conostylis candicans — Grey Cottonheads   WA
The leaves on this tufting species are up to 50cm long by 1cm wide, and are covered in dense grey hairs. The yellow and very hairy flowers are tubular, about 1cm long, and borne in dense heads on branched stems beyond the foliage. Flowering is between July and February.
H O SS D L SA G C1 F2   Chart 16 (2, 8, 12, 24, 28)

Conostylis prolifera — Mat Cottonheads   WA
The stems of this conostylis, root at the nodes, resulting in a clump of around 30cm high by 1m wide. The narrow leaves are up to 10cm long, and can be smooth or hairy. Hairy, cream to yellow flowers of around 1cm long are borne in small clusters. Flowering is between August and February.
H O SS D M L SA G C1 F1   Chart 16 (2, 4, 19, 24)

Conostylis setigera — Bristly Cottonheads   WA
A dwarf, tufting perennial, with narrow leaves to 30cm long, forming a clump up to 50cm across. Leaf margins have prominent white hairs. Flowering is between August and December, when cream to yellow flowers of about 1cm diameter are borne on stems shorter than the leaves.
H O SS D M L SA G C1 F2   Chart 24 (1, 12, 16, 28)

Coprosma quadrifida —   NSW, Vic, Tas
Prickly Currant-bush
A light shrub of 2-5m high by up to 3m wide. It has spiny branchlets, and small green leaves. Small white flowers are produced between September and November, and these are followed by small, shiny reddish berries which are sweet, but slightly astringent.
O S SS M W L SA C1 F2   Chart 30 (27, 36)

Cordyline stricta   Qld, NSW
An erect, palm-like plant, with a height of up to 4m. The strap-like leaves are pendulous, and up to 80cm long. Many small white to purple flowers are borne on long branched stems during the flowering period of September to December. These are followed by shiny black berries, which can be retained on the plant until the next flowering period. A useful plant for narrow areas.
O S SS M W L SA G C1 F1   Charts 20, 35 (3, 12, 27, 28)

Correa alba — White Correa NSW, Vic, Tas, SA
A hardy and adaptable species, excellent for exposed situations. It is variable in growth habit, and many forms are available. The most commonly grown is a dense shrub of about 2m high by a similar width. The oval leaves are green, with a whitish underside. White starry flowers are produced mainly between November and May, with sporadic flowering at other times. Pink-flowered forms are sometimes available, and there is also a low growing form with hairy, rusty new growth.
H O S S SS D L SA G C2 F2 Chart 40 (5, 7, 25, 27, 34)

Correa backhousiana Tas, Vic
This dense shrub grows up to 2m high by a similar width. The oval leaves are green and leathery, with pendulous tubular flowers of about 2.5cm long being produced between May and November. Flower colour is cream to pale green, and the flowers are particularly attractive to honey-eating birds.
O S S SS D L SA G C2 F2 Charts 14, 40 (3, 7, 27, 37)

Correa baeuerlenii — Chef's Cap Correa NSW
This correa is easily distinguished from other species by the green tubular flowers each with a prominent, flattened calyx, giving the appearance of a chef's cap. Flowering period is between March and August. The species is adaptable to a wide range of conditions, and will grow to a dense rounded shrub of up to 2m high.
O S SS D L SA G C1 F2 Charts 27, 34 (7, 9, 11, 14, 37)

Correa decumbens SA
This low spreading shrub has a width of up to 3m. Flowering is between November and February, and the narrow tubular flowers of about 2.5m long are red with green tips. Whilst most correa flowers hang down, the flowers of this species usually are erect.
O S SS W L SA G C1 F2 Chart 23 (4, 14, 25, 37)

Correa — Dusky Bells Origin obscure
This is a hardy and adaptable species, closely allied to *C.pulchella*. It grows to 0.5m high by up to 2-3m wide, and has bright green leaves. Pink bell-shaped flowers of around 4cm long by 1cm wide are produced, mainly between March and September.
H O SS D M L SA G C1 F2 Charts 6, 23 (8, 14, 27, 37)

Correa lawrenciana — NSW, Vic, Tas
Mountain Correa
A variable species which can grow from 2m to 8m high. The leaves are leathery, and 3-8cm long. Tubular flowers are produced between March and November, and can be cream to green, or in some forms red.
O S SS D M L SA G C1 F2 Charts 11, 14 (3, 7, 9, 27, 37)

Correa 'Mannii' Cultivar
This ornamental correa grows 1-2.5m high by a similar width. It appreciates light pruning. The leaves of about 3cm long are oval, dark green and smooth. Tubular flowers of up to 4cm long are produced, mainly between March and September, and are red with a pale pink interior.
O SS D L SA G C1 F2 Charts 8, 14, 18 (6, 25, 37)

Correa pulchella SA
Different forms of this species vary, between 30cm and 1m high, with a spread of 1-3m. The leaves are 1-2cm long, and oval to elliptic. Bright orange to vermilion flowers are produced, mainly between April and September.
H O SS D L SA G C1 F2 Charts 8, 18 (6, 14, 25, 37)

Correa reflexa — Qld, NSW, Vic, Tas, SA, WA
Common Correa
This is the most variable of all correas, with a large number of forms in cultivation. Height can be between 30cm and 3m, with leaves smooth or hairy. Flowering is mainly between March and November. The pendulous flowers of 2-4cm long, are in combinations of cream, green, pink and red. A prostrate form with squat red and green bells is an ideal groundcover.
H O SS SS D L SA G C1 F2 Charts 8, 11, 18 (2, 14, 27, 37)

Correa schlechtendalii Vic, SA
A bushy, upright correa, growing 1.5-2.5m high. The leaves are dark green, elliptic, and to 4.5cm long. Between November and April, pendant flowers of about 2.5cm long are produced. The flowers are red with green lobes.
H O SS D L SA G C1 F2 Charts 35, 37 (4, 14, 25   )

Corybas diemenicus — NSW, Vic, Tas, SA
Slaty Helmet-orchid
This is a terrestrial orchid, suitable for pot culture. It has a ground-hugging, heart-shaped leaf that can develop lobes. Flowers are produced between June and October, and are on very short stems. The flowers are unusual and helmet-shaped. They are basically purplish in colour, with white markings on the labellum (lower lip).
O S SS M L SA C1 F2 Chart 22

Corybas dilatatus — NSW, Vic, Tas, SA, WA
Veined Helmet-orchid
This species is very similar to *C.diemenicus*, but the flower labellum is veined, with the veins ending in a small point to make a toothed margin. It is a resident of moist sheltered areas in its natural habitat, and can be established under similar conditions in cultivation.
S SS M L SA C1 F2 Chart 22

Crowea exalata — Small Crowea NSW, Vic
This hardy shrub grows up to 1.5m high by a similar width. The leaves of up to 5cm long, are narrow and flat, with a fragrance similar to that of aniseed. The flowers are produced over a long period between October and June. They have 5 waxy pink petals, and can be up to 2cm in diameter. Various forms of this species are available.
H O SS D L SA G C1 F2 Chart 6 (4, 25)

Cyathea cooperi Qld, NSW
This quick growing tree-fern is easily established under cultivation. It can grow 3-12m high by a width of 3-6m. The top of the trunk is most decorative, being covered with long white silky scales. Plants are

frost tender, but usually recover to produce new fronds.
O S SS D M L SA C1 Chart 21 (11, 27)

Cyathea rebeccae Qld
A most decorative tree-fern, with arching, shiny, dark green fronds. It grows to a height of 2-7m, by 3-6m wide. Plants are readily cultivated but usually need protection from frost in southern Australia.
S SS D M L SA C1 Chart 21 (11, 27)

Cyathodes juniperina — Crimson Berry Vic, Tas
A slow-growing shrub, with a mature height of between 1m and 10m. The small, heath-like leaves are narrow and prickly. Small, tubular, white flowers are produced mainly between August and January, followed by pale to deep pink fruits, which can be very spectacular.
O S SS D M L SA G C1 F2 Chart 30 (36)

Cymbidium madidum Qld, NSW
This is a hardy epiphytic orchid that grows well in containers. It can have a height of 0.3-1m by 0.2-0.5m wide. Racemes of yellow-green and brown flowers are produced, usually between August and January, and are renowned for their beautiful fragrance. There can be up to 70 flowers per raceme. The leaves grow up to about 1m in length. Can be frost tender.
S SS D M Charts 13, 22 (2)

Dampiera cauloptera WA
This species has upright, winged stems, and spreads by suckering. It grows to a height of 30cm by 1-2m wide. Leaves are up to 6cm long and glabrous. The blue flowers are borne in small terminal clusters. Flowering period is between July and December.
H O SS D L SA G C1 F1 Chart 15 (2, 23)

Dampiera cuneata WA
A species worthy of inclusion in the smallest garden. It grows to about 15cm high, but can sucker and spread to 2m across. The flowers of about 2cm diameter are deep blue with a yellow centre, and are borne in clusters. Flowering is between September and January.
H O SS D L SA G C1 F1 Charts 4, 18 (2, 19, 23)

Dampiera diversifolia WA
A prostrate species, with a width of 1-2m. Small green leaves are borne on the spreading stems. The flowers of deep blue are around 1cm in diameter, and nearly cover the plant during the flowering period between September and February.
O SS D L SA G C1 F1 Charts 1, 15, 18, 19, 23 (2, 4)

Dampiera linearis — Common Dampiera WA
This dampiera spreads by suckering. It grows to a height of around 50cm, by 1-2m wide, and has long stems with narrow leaves. The blue flowers are borne in terminal clusters, mainly between May and December.
H O SS D L SA G C1 F1 Chart 19 (2, 4, 15, 23)

Dampiera rosmarinifolia — NSW, Vic, SA, WA
Rosemary Dampiera
The small narrow leaves of this species are similar to those of Rosemary. Plants grow to around 40cm high,

with a width of 1-3m due to the suckering habit. Dense spikes of flower are produced between August and November. The most common colour form is blue, but variations of pink, purple and white are in cultivation. A drought tolerant species.
H O SS D L SA G C1 F2 Chart 23 (2)

Danthonia pallida — NSW, Vic, WA
Silver-top Wallaby Grass
This is one of the graceful native grasses, forming a dense clump of fine foliage, around 0.3-0.5m high by a similar width. The slender flower stalks can be up to 1.5m tall, bearing small flowers with red anthers. Flowering period is between October and December. Other species of *Danthonia* are also ideal for cultivation.
O S SS D W L SA C1 F2 Chart 24 (16)

Darwinia camptostylis NSW, Vic
This species is prostrate, or up to 30cm tall, with a width of around 1m. Branches can be erect or cascading, with crowded, narrow, grey-green, aromatic leaves. The small flowers are borne in clusters of 2-4, between September and December. They are initially cream, then age to pink.
O SS D M L SA G C1 F1 Chart 19 (12, 23)

Darwinia citriodora — Lemon-scented Darwinia WA
A spreading shrub, with many branches, and growing to a height of around 1.5m, by 1-2m wide. The grey-green leaves of around 2cm long are sweetly aromatic. Flowering is mainly between April and November, with flower-heads of yellow-green and red, on the ends of the branchlets. Can be damaged by frost.
O SS D M L SA G C1 Charts 9, 13 (3, 12, 14, 28, 37)

Darwinia diosmoides WA
A dense, bushy shrub, growing to 2.5m high by a similar width. The leaves are very small, narrow, and delightfully aromatic. Flowering is mainly between April and January, when small white to pale pink flower-heads are produced.
H O SS D L SA G C1 F1 Chart 29 (25, 34)

Darwinia fascicularis NSW
There are several forms of this species in cultivation, with heights varying between 30cm and 3m, and a width of 1-2m. The leaves are small and aromatic, and the small flowers are arranged in terminal heads. Flower colour is initially cream to green, ageing to red, and the main flowering period is between August and November.
O S SS D L SA G C1 F1 Charts 3, 40 (27)

Darwinia lejostyla WA
A bushy shrub of up to 1m high by similar width. The leaves are small, narrow, and dense on the branchlets. Flowering is mainly between August and February, when pinkish-red bell shaped flower-heads of about 2cm long are produced.
O SS D M L SA G C1 F1 Chart 5 (3, 14, 37)

Darwinia meeboldii — Cranbrook Bell WA
This species grows 1-3m high by up to 1.5m wide. It has small leaves, crowded on the branchlets. Flower-

ing is mainly between September and November, with bell-like flower-heads of up to 3cm long. They are usually white and red, but can be all red.

O SS D M L SA G C1 F1   Chart 17 (14)

Dendrobium x *delicatum*   Qld, NSW
This orchid is a natural hybrid between *D.kingianum* and *D.speciosum*, and grows 0.3-0.5m high by 0.5-1m wide. It is hardy, and well suited to container cultivation, growing also on rocks, tree-ferns etc. Plants produce arching terminal racemes of white or cream flowers, usually between August and October. The flowers can be tinged with pink or mauve, and can also be fragrant.

S SS M C1 F1   Chart 22

Dendrobium falcorostrum — Beech Orchid Qld, NSW
This orchid species is renowned for the beautiful fragrance of the flowers. Plants grow 0.2-0.4m high by 0.3-0.5m wide, and a long pseudo-bulb supports 4 or 5 thick oval leaves. Flowering is between August and November, and the white to cream flowers are displayed in short terminal racemes. Grows well in containers, or on slabs of tree-fern, wattle, or paperbark etc.

S SS M C1 F1   Charts 13, 22

Dendrobium x *gracilimum*   Qld, NSW
The parents of this natural hybrid are *D.gracilicaule* and *D.speciosum*. Plants grow 0.3-0.75m high by 0.5-1m wide. Flowering period is usually September-October, when small fragrant white and yellow flowers are produced in dense terminal racemes.

S SS M C1 F1   Chart 22

Dendrobium kingianum —   Qld, NSW
Pink Rock-orchid
This is a commonly cultivated species, and can grow 0.2-0.5m high by 0.5-1m wide. It forms a dense clump of pseudo-bulbs, and is suited to containers such as a pot or hanging basket, or to cultivation on slabs of rock, tree-fern or wood. The foliage often has purplish tonings. Flowering period is August-November, and the flowers are usually pink, but can be white to purple or in various combinations. Flowers can also be fragrant.

S SS M C1 F1   Chart 22

Dendrobium speciosum — Rock Orchid Qld, NSW, Vic
This is one of the hardiest Australian epiphytic orchids. It has many different forms, with large thick pseudo-bulbs, and large leathery leaves. Plants grow 0.3-1m high by 0.5-1.5m wide. Flowering is between July and November, when fragrant, white cream or yellow flowers are produced in outstanding terminal racemes containing many flowers. This orchid can be established in a container, a rock crevice, or on rocks, logs, tree-ferns etc., but usually flowers best if in a slightly sunny position.

O S SS M C1 F1   Chart 22

Dianella tasmanica — Tasman Flax-lily   Vic, Tas
A clumping plant, with dark green strap-like leaves of about 1m long by 5-6cm wide. Plants form a clump of up to 1m across. The flowers are borne on branched stems up to 1.5m high, and are star-shaped with blue petals and golden yellow anthers. Flowering is between September and February, and is followed by shiny, oblong, bluish fruits.

O S SS M W L SA G C1 F2
Charts 30, 35 (2, 4, 16, 24, 26, 27)

Dichopogon strictus — Chocolate Lily   All States
A small, grass-like perennial, with leaves to 30cm long. Purple flowers of about 2cm diameter are borne on branched stems, between October and December. The flowers have a chocolate or caramel-like fragrance.

H O SS M W L SA G F1   Chart 29 (1, 13)

Dicksonia antarctica —   Qld, NSW, Vic, Tas
Soft Tree-fern
Although this fern can grow up to 15m high, it takes many years to do so. It is the species most commonly cultivated in southern Australia. The arching fronds give it a width of 2-9m, and many soft brown hairs cover the frond butts, and the top of the trunk.

S SS D M L SA C1 F2   Chart 21 (11, 27)

Dicksonia youngiae   Qld, NSW
This tree-fern is usually quick growing when young. It has a slender trunk, and the upper part is covered with red, bristly hairs. Plants grow to 2-5m tall by a similar width. Adapts well to cultivation.

O S SS D M L SA C1 F1   Chart 21 (11, 27)

Dillwynia sericea —   NSW, Vic, Tas, SA
Showy Parrot Pea
An upright plant of 1-1.5m high, with short, narrow, hairy leaves. The pea flowers are produced in massed spikes of up to 30cm long, between September and December. Flower colour is orange, apricot, yellow or rarely pink.

H O SS D L SA G C1 F2   Charts 25, 38 (2)

Diplarrena moraea — Butterfly Flag NSW, Vic, Tas
This member of the Iris family can grow 0.5-1m high by a similar width, and has long strap-like leaves. The white flowers have 3 petals. Each flower lasts one day only, and flowers are borne in succession from a sheath on a stem of up to 1m tall. Flowering period is between November and January.

H O SS M W L SA C1 F1   Chart 24 (4, 16, 26, 38)

Diplolaena angustifolia — Yanchep Rose   WA
This shrub grows to 1m high by 1.5m wide. The leaves are about 2.5cm long and narrow. Flowering is between July and October, with pendant flowerheads of up to 3.5cm diameter. They are red to pale orange in colour, with very prominent stamens. This species will withstand lime.

O SS D SA G C1 F1   Chart 17 (2)

Diuris longifolia —   NSW, Vic, Tas, SA, WA
Wallflower Orchid or Donkey Orchid
This terrestrial orchid has for many years been grown in containers, by native orchid enthusiasts. Flowering is usually between July and November, when up to 10 flowers are borne on a stem to 0.5m tall. The flowers are distinctively shaped, and brightly coloured. They

can be pure yellow, or more commonly are a mixture of brown and yellow, with sometimes the addition of purple.

O S SS M L SA C1 F2   Chart 22

Diuris maculata —   Qld, NSW, Vic, Tas, SA
Leopard Orchid
This species is similar in many ways to *D.longifolia*. One of the main differences is that the petals have many dark brown spots.

O S SS M L SA C1 F2   Chart 22

Dodonaea adenophora   Qld, NSW, WA
A dense shrub of 2-3m high by a similar width. The leaves are pinnate, with a rough surface, and the new growth is sticky. Flowers are minute, but are followed by clusters of attractive reddish hops, produced mainly between March and October. The hops are produced only on the female plants, and therefore cutting-grown plants are recommended.

H O SS D L SA G C1 F1   Chart 30 (12, 25, 28)

Dodonaea boroniifolia —   NSW, Vic, WA
Hairy Hop-bush
This bushy shrub grows to 1-2m high. The leaves are pinnate and hairy. Flowering is spasmodic, and is followed by showy hops of green, pink or red, produced mainly between September and January.

H O SS D L SA G C1 F1   Chart 30 (12, 28)

Dodonaea procumbens — Trailing Hop-bush NSW, Vic
This spreading species grows to 50cm high, with a width of 1-2m. The leaves are wedge-shaped, and up to 2cm long. Flowering is spasmodic, but the plants are decorative both in foliage and the reddish hops.

H O SS W L SA G C1 F2   Chart 23 (12, 30)

Doodia aspera — Prickly Rasp-fern Qld, NSW, Vic
This fern has underground creeping rhizomes, and grows 0.3-0.6m tall, by 0.5-1m wide. The erect fronds of fish-bone shape are rough to touch, and often pale green. New fronds usually have bright pink to reddish new growth. Plants grow well in sunny moist locations.

O S SS D M W L SA C1 F2   Chart 21 (16, 24, 26, 27)

Doodia media — Common Rasp-fern Qld, NSW, Vic
This species is similar to *D.aspera*, but the pinnae are separated at the base of the erect fronds. New growth can be purplish red.

O S SS D M W L SA C1 F2   Chart 21 (16, 24, 26, 27)

Dryandra drummondii   WA
A decorative, clumping species, with leaves of up to 30cm long by 5cm wide, divided to the mid-rib to form triangular segments. Foliage colour is bluish green, and plants grow up to 1m across. The flower-heads are brownish yellow, and about 5cm in diameter: They are produced mainly between February and May, but are often obscured by the foliage.

O SS D L SA G C1 F1   Chart 24 (6, 12, 28)

Dryandra nivea — Couch Honeypot   WA
A clumping or spreading dryandra, growing to 1m wide. The leaves are about 30cm long by 1cm wide, and divided to the mid-rib in small triangular lobes.

Flower-heads are set amongst the leaves, and are around 5cm long by 4cm diameter. The yellow flowers are surrounded by prominent brown bracts. Flowering period is between July and October.

H O SS D L SA G C1 F2   Charts 16, 28 (2, 8, 12, 14)

Dryandra proteoides — King Dryandra   WA
This species grows 1-2m high by a similar width. The deeply lobed leaves are up to 25cm long, and have pungent tips. Flowering is between August and October, with flower-heads of about 9cm long by 7.5cm diameter. Flowers are yellow, with enveloping brown bracts.

H O SS D L SA G C1 F2   Chart 17 (3, 12, 14)

Elaeocarpus reticulatus —   Qld, NSW, Vic, Tas
Blueberry Ash
This is a small tree, growing 5-8m high. Flowering is during October and November, when delicate white flowers of around 1cm diameter are produced in racemes. These are followed by dark blue berries, also of around 1cm diameter.

S SS D M L SA G C1 F1   Chart 30 (11, 27)

Epacris impressa —   NSW, Vic, Tas, SA
Common Heath
This well-known species is usually a small plant to around 1m high, but can grow up to 2m. Leaves are small, narrow and pointed. The tubular flowers of about 2cm long are borne along the branchlets, mainly between April and November. They often form a dense spike, and can be white, or various shades of pink to red. A form from Bega NSW has orange-red bells, and is one of the most adaptable forms for gardens. Pruning after flowering is recommended.

O S SS D M L SA G C1 F2   Charts 6, 35, 37 (8, 14)

Epacris longiflora — Fuchsia Heath   NSW
An excellent small species, for gardens or containers. Plants grow to between 50cm and 2m high, by a similar width, but respond very well to pruning. The leaves are about 1cm long, dense, and slightly prickly. The attractive tubular flowers are up to 3cm long, narrow, and red with white tips. Flowering can be throughout the year, with a profuse display usually between May and January. Excellent for bird-attraction.

O S SS D M L SA G C1 F2   Charts 4, 14, 18 (8, 37)

Epacris reclinata   NSW
A small, many-branched shrub, growing up to 1.5m high. The leaves are small and sharply pointed. Flowering is between June and November, with bright pink to red tubular flowers, of about 1cm long, dense near the ends of the branchlets.

O S SS D M L SA G C1 F2   Charts 8, 35 (2)

Eremaea beaufortioides — Round-leaved Eremaea WA
This species grows 1-2m high by a similar width, and has oval leaves of around 1cm long, crowded along the branches. Showy orange flower-heads of about 2cm diameter are produced, usually between September and February.

H O SS D L SA G C1 F1   Chart 5 (10)

Eremaea violacea — Violet Eremaea　　　　　WA
A small shrub of 1-1.5m high by 1-2m wide, with small, hairy leaves. Flower-heads are composed of 2-3 purple flowers, with gold anthers, and they are produced at the branchlet tips between August and February.
H O SS D L SA G C1 F1　　　Chart 10 (5, 25)

Eremophila glabra — Tar-bush　　　　　WA
This variable species has many forms suitable for cultivation. Some have dense hairy leaves, giving a silvery appearance. Height is usually 1-1.5m, and the width 1-2m. Orange to red tubular flowers of 2-5cm long are produced, mainly between June and January. Light pruning is recommended.
H O D L SA G C1 F2　　Chart 2 (8, 10, 14, 25, 37)

Eremophila maculata 'Aurea' —
Native Fuchsia or Spotted Emu-bush
This is a yellow-flowered form of *E.maculata*. It is a much-branched shrub, with smooth leaves of about 2.5cm long. Plants grow to 1m high by 1-2m wide. The flowering is mainly between June and December, when tubular yellow flowers of 2-3cm long are produced. Light pruning is recommended.
H O SS D L SA G C1 F2　　Chart 10 (3, 9, 14, 25, 37)

Eriostemon australasius　　　　　Qld, NSW
This highly ornamental species is unfortunately not always readily obtainable, as propagation can be difficult. It is an upright shrub of 1-3m high, with thick greyish-green leaves to 7cm long. Flowering is between August and November, with profuse, mauve-pink star-like flowers of up to 4cm diameter. The petals have a waxy appearance.
O SS D L SA G C1 F2　　　Chart 17 (2)

Eriostemon myoporoides —　　　　Qld, NSW, Vic
Long-leaved Waxflower
This is the most common of the Australian waxplants in cultivation. It is hardy and adaptable, and provides a dense display of white starry flowers of 2-5cm diameter, with pink buds. Flowering period is between July and December. Plants grow 1-2m high, and the dark green leaves of up to 10cm long are sometimes warty. A sub-alpine form, known as *E.myoporoides* 'Mountain Giant' is larger in all aspects, and flowers between September and April.
H O S SS D L SA G C1 F2　　Charts 3, 11 (27)

Eriostemon spicatus — Pepper and Salt　　　WA
An open shrub of 50cm to 1.5m high, by a similar width. The leaves are small and narrow. Small deep pink to mauve flowers are produced in terminal spikes, between June and January. A white flowered form is also in cultivation. Plants respond well to pruning.
O SS D L SA G C1 F2　　　Chart 2 (19)

Eriostemon verrucosus —　　　NSW, Vic, SA, Tas
Fairy Waxflower
A variable species, with many forms which are suitable for cultivation. Plants grow 0.5-1.5m high by 1-2m wide, and the bluish-green leaves are small,

warty and leathery. The flowers are around 2cm in diameter, with pink buds opening to flowers of white or sometimes pink. Double-flowered forms including 2 from Victoria are also available. Flowering period is between June and November.
H O SS SS D L SA G C1 F2　　Charts 2, 18 (8, 10, 25)

Eucalyptus burdettiana — Burdett Gum　　　WA
A small tree growing 4-10m high. The trunk is smooth, with green-brown or light brown to cream bark, and the canopy of foliage is slightly open. The flowering period is usually between January and March. Ornamental finger-like buds are followed by clusters of yellow-green flowers, then bell-shaped fruit. Excellent for bird-attraction.
H O D L SA G C1 F1　　　Chart 32 (37)

Eucalyptus caesia — Gungurru or Gungunnu　　WA
A highly ornamental small tree, growing to between 5 and 10m high. The trunk has deciduous bark of red-brown to green-brown. The stems and leaves are grey-green, with buds and fruits silvery grey. Flowering is mainly between June and November, with pendant flowers in clusters of 3. Flower colour is pink to red with gold anthers. A large-flowered form, known as *E.caesia* 'Silver Princess' is also in cultivation. If growth is too fast, plants of this form can become top heavy. Judicious pruning while young is recommended, to reduce weight and provide a stronger trunk and framework of branches.
H O D L SA G C1 F2　　　Chart 9 (10, 37)

Eucalyptus crenulata — Silver Gum　　　　Vic
A tree of 6-15m high, with dense grey-green foliage. The young stems and flower buds are glaucous, and the leaves are heart-shaped with scalloped margins. Flowering is usually between September and December, with small white flowers borne in clusters.
H O S SS W L SA G C1 F2　　　Chart 32

Eucalyptus erythrocorys — Illyarrie　　　WA
This is usually an upright tree of 5-8m high. It has smooth white to grey bark, and leathery adult leaves. Flower buds have bright red caps, which drop off to reveal stamens of bright yellow. Flowering is mainly between February and May, but can also be sporadic. The large woody fruits are also distinctive. Plants are frost tender whilst young.
H O SS D L SA G C1　　　Chart 30 (10, 37)

Eucalyptus forrestiana —　　　　　WA
Fuchsia Gum or Forrest's Marlock
This small tree grows to 4-6m high. It has smooth, grey, deciduous bark, and dense, leathery, dark green foliage. It is most attractive in bud, flower and fruit. The pendulous flower buds are bright red to orange, and four-sided, with yellow flowers produced mainly between December and July.
H O W L SA G C1 F2　　　Chart 30 (10, 37)

Eucalyptus kruseana — Book-leaf Mallee　　　WA
This is a much-branched, spreading species, growing to 3-4m high by a similar width. The bark is smooth, and grey to grey-brown with deciduous flakes during summer. The leaves are oval, stalkless, blue-grey and

crowded near the ends of the branchlets. Pale to clear yellow flowers are produced in clusters near the branchlet tips, mainly between March and August. The decorative buds and fruits are glaucous.
H O D L SA G C1 F1   Chart 28 (10, 12, 37)

Eucalyptus lehmannii — Bushy Yate   WA
This tree of 5-10m high provides a dense canopy of deep green leaves. Flowering is mainly between July and December, with finger-like buds followed by heads of green to yellow-green flowers of up to 10cm diameter. An excellent windbreak species, and one that will tolerate saline soils.
H O SS L SA G C2 F2   Charts 33, 37, 40

Eucalyptus leucoxylon — Yellow Gum NSW, Vic, SA
This is a cream-trunked eucalypt, with typical gum leaves. Low growing forms are available from nurseries, and these grow to a height of 5-8m by similar width. Masses of flowers are produced near the ends of the branches, over a long period between March and December. They can be white, cream or in various shades from light pink to very deep pink. An excellent bird-attracting tree.
H O SS W L SA G C1 F2   Charts 37, 40

Eucalyptus macrandra — Long-flowered Marlock WA
A small tree of 5-10m high, with smooth, brown-grey trunk, and bright green leaves. Flowering is mainly between December and March, when large clusters of long narrow buds are followed by yellow-green flowers. It is excellent for bird-attraction. A drought resistant species, also suitable for saline conditions.
H O SS W L SA G C1 F2   Chart 32 (37, 40)

Eucalyptus polybractea — Blue-leaved Mallee
(Previously known as *E.fruticetorum*)   NSW, Vic
A small tree of 5-10m high. It has fibrous bark, and can be multi-trunked. The leaves are bluish-green and narrow. Small white to cream flowers are produced between March and October, and attract honey-eating birds. Plants will withstand hard pruning.
H O SS L SA G C1 F2   Chart 37 (10)

Eucalyptus preissiana — Bell-fruited Mallee   WA
A spreading, open species, with a height of 3-5m and a width of up to 3-8m. Plants may be pruned if desired. The bark is smooth and mottled grey, and leaves are grey-green and leathery. The bright yellow flowers are borne in clusters of three, and are followed by bell-shaped fruits. Flowering is between August and December.
H O D L SA G C1 F2   Chart 14 (3, 10, 30, 37)

Eucalyptus spathulata — Swamp Mallet   WA
This species usually grows as a single-trunked tree to 6-10m high by 4-8m wide. The trunk is smooth, with red-brown to grey-brown bark, and branches can form near to ground level. The leaves are narrow and dark green, and clusters of small cream flowers are produced between June and November. Plants withstand saline soils. *E.spathulata* var *grandiflora* is also an excellent ornamental form.
H O SS W L SA G C1 F2   Chart 32 (26, 37)

Eucalyptus tetraptera — Square-fruited Mallee   WA
Usually of spreading habit, this species can grow to 2-4m high by up to 6m wide. Plants benefit from pruning. The leaves are large, thick and leathery. Pink flowers are produced from the spectacular 4-angled, large, pink to red buds, and flowering is mainly between September and January.
H O D L SA G C1 F1   Chart 30 (3, 5, 10, 37)

Eucalyptus torquata — Coral Gum   WA
This small tree grows to 5-8m high, with a dense canopy of greyish green leaves. The bark on the trunk is coarse. Flowering period is mainly between September and February, when decorative ridged buds with pointed caps are followed by pink to red flowers. Grows best in a warm to hot situation.
H O D L SA G C1 F1   Chart 30 (3, 5, 10, 14, 37)

Eupomatia laurina —   Qld, NSW, Vic
Copper Laurel or Bolwarra
This shrub to small tree has a mature height of 4-8m by 3-5m wide, but can be readily pruned to a smaller size. The leaves are smooth and shiny, and green to purplish in colour, with excellent copper tonings in the cooler months of the year. Waxy cream flowers of about 2.5cm diameter are produced between September and March. Can be frost tender.
O SS D M L SA G C1   Chart 28 (5, 12, 27)

Eutaxia microphylla   All States except NT
This is a low, spreading shrub, with a width of up to 1.5m. The branchlets are often spiny, and the small narrow leaves are grey-green. Flowering is between September and November, with profuse pea-shaped flowers of yellow and orange to red.
H O SS W L SA G C1 F2   Chart 19 (2, 23, 38)

Frankenia pauciflora — Common Sea-heath All States
A dense mat species, with a width of up to 1m. The leaves are small and greyish, and open-petalled flowers of white to deep pink are produced, mainly between November and February.
H O SS D L SA G C2 F2   Chart 1 (4, 10, 18, 23, 40)

Gahnia sieberana —   Qld, NSW, Vic, Tas
Red-fruit Saw Sedge
This clumping species grows 2-3m high by 1-2m wide, with sharp-edged narrow leaves. Small cream flowers surrounded by light brown bracts, are produced in spikes on long stems above the foliage. The flowers age to black, then are followed by small shiny reddish nuts. Flowering is between September and December.
H O SS W L SA G C1 F2   Chart 24 (38)

Glischrocaryon behrii —   NSW, Vic, SA
Golden Pennants (Previously known as *Loudonia behrii*)
A clumping shrub of 0.3-0.5m high by 0.5-1m wide. The smooth, greyish-green stems are more or less leafless, bearing clusters of small, bright yellow flowers, usually between September and December.
H O SS D L SA G C1 F2   Chart 16 (10, 18, 24)

Gompholobium ecostatum — Dwarf Wedge-pea Vic, SA
An open, branched species, of 0.3-0.7m high by

0.5-1m wide. The leaves are hairy and bluish-green. Flowering is between September and January, with attractive pea-shaped flowers of apricot to orange-red on the branchlet tips.

O SS D L SA G C1 F2   Chart 25 (2)

Gompholobium huegelii —   NSW, Vic, Tas
Common Wedge-pea
This open, branched shrub has a height of 0.3-0.7m by a width of 0.5-1m. Unlike the previous species, the bluish-green foliage is not hairy. The pea-shaped flowers are pale to bright yellow, and are produced between September and February.

O SS D L SA G C1 F2   Chart 27 (2, 4)

Goodenia elongata — Lanky Goodenia NSW, Vic, Tas
A loosely matting goodenia, with basal clusters of entire or toothed, hairy leaves. Plants can spread to around 1.5m across. Yellow flowers are produced on upright stems to about 30cm tall, during the flowering season between October and March.

O S SS M W L SA G C1 F2   Chart 27 (1, 2, 4)

Goodenia geniculata —   NSW, Vic, Tas, SA
Bent Goodenia
This dense mat plant spreads by suckering, and can grow 0.5-1m wide. The leaves are dark green, oval and toothed. Flowers of bright yellow are displayed on bent stalks, mainly between October and March.

H O SS D M L SA G C1 F2   Charts 18, 23 (1, 18)

Goodenia hederacea — Ivy Goodenia   NSW, Vic
A dense mat plant, sometimes suckering, and spreading up to 2m across. The leaves are rounded and toothed, smooth and shiny. Yellow to orange flowers are produced, mainly between October and February. *G.hederacea* var *alpestris* is an excellent matting variety.

H O SS D M L SA G C1 F2   Charts 1, 23 (2, 4, 15, 18)

Goodenia humilis —   NSW, Vic, Tas, SA
Swamp Goodenia
A dense mat plant, with a width of up to 1.5m. The light green leaves are elongated and toothed. Flowering is mainly between October and March, with profuse, bright yellow flowers. An excellent species for wet or heavy soils.

H O SS M W L SA G C1 F2   Chart 26 (1, 2, 4, 18)

Goodenia lanata — Trailing Goodenia   Vic, Tas
This prostrate species spreads by rooting at the nodes, and can reach a width of around 1m. The leaves are dark green and toothed. Flowers of bright yellow are displayed on stalks above the foliage, during the flowering period of between October and March.

H O S SS M W L SA G C1 F2   Chart 19 (2, 4, 18)

Goodia lotifolia —   Qld, NSW, Vic, Tas, SA
Golden Tip
The foliage of this species is clover-like, and greyish-green. Plants are usually quick growing, and can grow 2-4m high by 2-3m wide. Slightly fragrant, yellow, pea-shaped flowers are borne in loose terminal clusters, between September and December.

O S SS D L SA G C1 F2   Chart 33 (3, 38)

Gossypium sturtianum —   Qld, NSW, SA, WA, NT
Sturt's Desert Rose
This species grows 1-2.5m high by 1-2m wide. The leaves are oval, glabrous, and blue to greyish green. Flowering is mainly between October and February, and the large pink to purple flowers have reddish blotches at the base of the petals. Frost tender.

H O D L SA G C1   Chart 17 (10)

Grevillea acanthifolia   NSW
Two forms of this grevillea are commonly grown in cultivation. One is a low, dense plant, spreading to about 4m wide, while the other is more upright and open, with a height of 2.5m. The leaves are deeply lobed, and prickly, therefore plants should not be grown close to pathways, unless to restrict access. Terminal toothbrush-shape flowers of pink to mauve are produced between September and March.

H O SS D M L SA G C1 F2   Chart 23 (3, 36)

Grevillea acerosa   WA
A small, dense shrub, of up to 1m high by 1-2m wide, with prickly fine leaves. Small, cream, woolly flowers are produced in clusters along the branches, between August and December.

H O SS D L SA G C1 F1   Chart 25 (3, 37)

Grevillea alpina —   NSW, Vic
Cat's Claw, or Mountain Grevillea
This is a most variable species, differing in growth habit, and also flower colour. Plants can grow 0.2-2.5m tall, and can be upright or to 2m across. The leaves are usually rounded to oblong, and hairy. Clusters of hairy flowers are produced between June and November, in colours of white, pink, red, yellow and orange. Excellent forms of this species, for container cultivation, are available under the following names: Grampians forms, McDonald Park form, and Goldfields form.

O SS D L SA G C1 F2   Chart 9 (3, 14, 18, 25, 37)

Grevillea aquifolium —   Vic, SA
Variable Prickly Grevillea
As the common name suggests, this is another grevillea with several different forms. It can grow between 0.2m and 3m high, by 1-4m wide, however plants respond well to pruning. The leaves are holly-like and often hairy. They are dull green to greyish, with new growth often pink to red. Toothbrush-type flowers of green and red are produced mainly between September and February. The prostrate forms are excellent as ground-covers.

H O SS D L SA G C1 F2   Charts 23, 37 (3, 5, 10, 36)

Grevillea arenaria   NSW
Two forms of this species are in cultivation, one with red flowers, and the other with yellow-green. Both are excellent for bird attraction. Plants grow about 1.5-2.5m high by a similar width, and have oblong, hairy leaves of greyish-green. The flowering period is between June and January.

H O SS D L SA G C1 F2   Chart 14 (3, 5, 34, 37)

Grevillea banksii — Banks' Grevillea   Qld
An upright, open shrub, of 2-5m tall, with greyish-

green pinnate leaves. The flowering period is mainly between July and November, when large, bright red flower-heads are produced at the ends of the branchlets. A white flowered form is also in cultivation. Can be frost tender.

H O D L SA G C1   Chart 25 (3, 9, 14)

Grevillea baueri — Bauer's Grevillea   NSW
This hardy shrub has crowded, oblong leaves, often with reddish tonings. The new growth can be particularly attractive. Plants grow 1-2m high by 1.5-2.5m wide. Flowering is between March and November, when pink, red and cream flowers are produced in terminal clusters.

H O SS D L SA G C1 F2   Chart 9 (3, 14, 25)

Grevillea bipinnatifida —   WA
Fuchsia Grevillea, or Grape Grevillea
This showy species grows as an open to dense shrub of about 1m high. The leaves are large, stiff, and deeply lobed. The flowers are arranged in pendant, terminal heads to 20cm long, with similarity to a bunch of grapes. The colour can vary from light orange-red to deep red. Flowering period is mainly between August and February.

H O SS D L SA G C1 F1   Chart 14 (3, 5, 12, 25, 28)

Grevillea brevicuspis   WA
A dense shrub of 1-2m high, with many branches. The leaves are small, divided, and prickly, and the foliage often attains reddish colouration during the colder months. Profuse white to cream flowers are borne in clusters along the branchlets, mainly between August and November.

H O SS D L SA G C1 F2   Chart 12 (3, 28, 34)

Grevillea brownii   WA
This small grevillea grows to 0.5m high, by 1-3m wide. It is of fairly dense habit, with oval green leaves. Very bright red flowers are produced in small clusters along the branches, mainly between May and November.

O SS D L SA G C1 F1   Charts 8, 18 (2, 14, 15, 23)

Grevillea buxifolia — Grey Spider-flower   NSW
The main feature of this species is the unusual grey and brown spider-like flowers. Plants grow to 2-3m high by 2m wide, with oval hairy leaves, and rusty-brown new growth. The flowering period is mainly between July and December, and the flowers are borne in heads at the ends of the branchlets.

O SS D L SA G C1 F2   Chart 27 (3, 9, 11)

Grevillea chrysophaea — Golden Grevillea   Vic
This grevillea is usually of upright, open habit, growing to a height of 1-2m. The leaves are oblong, with hairy, golden-yellow flowers borne in clusters at the ends of short branches. Flowering is between July and November.

H O SS D L SA G C1 F2   Chart 8 (2, 14, 25)

Grevillea 'Clearview David'   Cultivar
A vigorous shrub, with a height of 2-3m by width of up to 4m. Plants respond well to pruning. The leaves are narrow, dark green and prickly. Flowers of vivid

red and white are borne in dense clusters along the branchlets, mainly between July and November.

H O SS D L SA G C1 F2   Chart 34 (3, 9, 25, 36, 37)

Grevillea confertifolia — Grampians Grevillea   Vic
The commonly grown prostrate form of this species forms a dense cover up to 0.5m high by 3m wide. The leaves are narrow, and slightly prickly, with mauve to pink flowers, displayed in dense terminal heads. Flowering period is usually between August and November. There is also a taller and more upright form of this grevillea.

H Q SS D M L SA G C1 F2   Chart 3 (23, 36)

Grevillea 'Crosbie Morrison'   Cultivar
A dense, spreading shrub of 1-2m high by 2-3m wide. The leaves are small, narrow, greyish-green, and slightly prickly. Flowering is between July and November, with flowers of red to pink and cream, clustered along the branchlets.

H O SS D L SA G C1 F2   Chart 14 (3, 9, 25, 36)

Grevillea diminuta   ACT
A low, spreading shrub, of 0.5-1m high by 2-3m wide. The leaves are oval, and dark grey to green. Flowering is mainly between January and August, when small red flowers are arranged in pendant clusters, on short branchlets.

H O S SS D L SA G C1 F2   Chart 9 (14, 27, 37)

Grevillea dimorpha — Flame Grevillea   Vic
The leaves of this variable species can be thread-like, or up to 2cm wide. They are dark green above, and whitish below. Plants grow up to 2m high, by 1-3m wide, and brilliant red flowers are produced in clusters from the leaf axils. Flowering is between April and November.

O S SS D L SA G C1 F2   Chart 9 (3, 14, 37)

Grevillea endlicherana — Spindly Grevillea   WA
The narrow, grey leaves, are a feature of this usually upright grevillea, which grows to a height of 2-3m. Flowering is mainly between June and December, when white to pale pink flowers are borne in clusters at the ends of almost leafless branches. Plants respond well to pruning, and can be grown very successfully in a large container.

O SS D L SA G C1 F2   Chart 28 (10, 12, 34)

Grevillea flexuosa — Tangled Grevillea   WA
This attractive species has proved difficult to establish in gardens, but can be grown with success in containers. It is a spreading shrub of around 30cm high, with a width of up to 1.5m. Leaves are greyish-green and deeply lobed. Delicate flowers of bright pink are produced in pendant racemes, mainly between September and March.

O SS D L SA G C1 F1   Chart 17 (2, 4)

Grevillea floribunda   Qld, NSW
This species usually grows to 1-2m high by a similar width. The leaves are oblong, greyish, soft and hairy. Pendant clusters of flowers are produced, mainly between June and January. Flower colour is gold and

green, with short brown hairs giving a rusty appearance. A low spreading form is also in cultivation.
H O SS D L SA G C1 F2   Chart 9 (3, 10, 14, 25)

Grevillea x *gaudichaudii*   NSW
A comparatively recent introduction to cultivation, this natural hybrid is now amongst the most popular of all the ground-cover grevilleas. It can spread from 2-5m wide. The lobed foliage has attractive reddish new growth, and dark red to burgundy toothbrush flower-heads are produced at the ends of short branchlets over a long period, mainly between September and April.
H O SS D M L SA G C1 F2 Charts 7, 19 (3, 5, 12, 15, 23, 37)

Grevillea glabella   NSW, Vic
(Previously included under *G.rosmarinifolia*)
This is a variable species. All forms have narrow to very narrow leaves and some are prickly. The flowers of the forms known previously as *G.rosmarinifolia* 'Dwarf' are usually pink to red with varying amounts of cream. Some of these are sold labelled according to the area from which they originated, eg. *G.glabella* 'Anakie', *G.glabella* 'Lara', *G.glabella* 'Rankin Springs', *G.glabella* 'Vectis' etc. These forms usually grow 0.5-1.5m high by 1-2m wide. *G.glabella* 'Limelight' is taller, growing 1.5-2m high by 1-2m wide, and has lime-yellow to green flowers. All forms are most floriferous, and are excellent garden or container plants. Flowering period is mainly June to December.
H O SS D L SA G C1 F2   Chart 8 (2, 10, 14, 18, 25, 37)

Grevillea glabrata   WA
A fast-growing, dense shrub, which can grow 2-3m high by 2-4m wide, but may be pruned if desired. The prickly grey-green leaves are smooth and lobed, and a form with finely-lobed leaves is also available. Small white to cream flowers are produced in loose clusters along the branchlets. Flowering is between September and January.
H O SS D L SA G C1 F1   Chart 33 (12, 27, 36)

Grevillea hookerana — Toothbrush Grevillea   WA
There are several forms of this species, however the most commonly grown form is a large shrub of 1-4m high by up to 3-4m wide. It can be pruned to a small tree on a trunk if desired. The fern-like leaves are divided, with narrow leaflets. Flowering is mainly between August and December, with profuse bright red toothbrush flowers.
H O SS D L SA G C1 F1   Chart 37 (3, 10, 14, 28)

Grevillea ilicifolia — Holly Grevillea NSW, Vic, SA
This species, varying in height from prostrate to 2m tall, by a width of 1.5-3m, has many foliage forms. Most leaves are deeply lobed, but some are very fine, and others holly-like. They vary in colour from green to grey. Flowers are of toothbrush shape, and can be cream, red or combinations of these colours. Flowering is between March and November.
H O SS D L SA G C1 F2   Chart 12 (3, 7, 9, 10, 37)

Grevillea insignis   WA
An open shrub of 1.5-2.5m high by similar width. The leaves are grey-green and holly-like, with bronze to reddish new growth. Terminal clusters of pink, waxy flowers are produced, mainly between August and November.
O SS D L SA G F1   Chart 17 (12)

Grevillea intricata   WA
The unusual foliage is one of the main features of this species. The leaves are very finely lobed, and net-like, with reddish stems and new growth. Plants can grow up to 2m high by 2-3m wide. Flowering period is between August and November, with cream flowers borne in terminal spikes.
H O SS D L SA G C1 F1   Charts 12, 17 (10)

Grevillea jephcottii — Green Grevillea   Vic
This is a hardy, vigorous shrub, with a height and width of up to 2m. The oblong leaves are light green and hairy. Honey-eating birds seem particularly attracted to grevilleas with greenish flowers, and this species is no exception. The cream to green clusters of flowers are produced throughout most of the year.
H O SS D L SA G C1 F2   Chart 37 (11, 14, 27, 34)

Grevillea johnsonii   NSW
(Previously included under *G.longistyla*)
This species has handsome foliage, with fine, divided, dark green leaves on reddish stems. Plants grow up to 2-4m high by a similar width. The flowers are pink to red, and are produced in clusters at the leaf axils, or at the ends of the branchlets. Flowering period is between June and November. An excellent screening plant. Responds well to pruning.
H O SS D L SA G C1 F1   Chart 28 (3, 9, 12, 14,   34)

Grevillea juniperina — Juniper Grevillea   NSW
This is a variable species, with small, very prickly, narrow, dark green leaves. It can grow as a shrub of 2-4m high by up to 5m wide, or prostrate spreading forms are also obtainable. The shrubby form flowers mainly between July and November, when dense clusters of yellow to orange-red flowers are produced along the branches. The prostrate forms can have buff, yellow or red flowers.
H O SS D L SA G C1 F2   Charts 15, 36 (3, 9, 10, 14, 23)

Grevillea lanigera — Woolly Grevillea   NSW, Vic
This bushy species grows up to 2.5m high by 3m wide. The dense leaves are narrow, greyish-green and hairy. Flowers of red and cream are produced in clusters along the branchlets, between August and January.
H O SS D L SA G C2 F2   Chart 25 (3, 5, 14, 34, 37)

Grevillea lavandulacea —   NSW, Vic, SA
Lavender Grevillea
A species with many forms, ranging from 0.5m to 2.5m in height. Although the foliage is in some forms green, it is usually greyish, with an appearance similar to that of Lavender. Flowers are profuse, with bright pink to red clusters borne along the branches between June and November.
H O SS D L SA G C1 F2 Charts 10, 25 (2, 3, 8, 9, 14, 37)

Grevillea longifolia — Fern-leaf Grevillea   NSW
A large shrub of 2-4m high, with horizontal spreading branches, giving a width of 3-5m. Plants respond well to pruning, and can be trained onto a trunk if desired. The leaves are long, narrow, and serrated. Flowering is mainly between June and November, with profuse, bright pink-red toothbrush flowers.
H O SS D L SA G C1 F2   Chart 14 (3, 9, 28, 37)

Grevillea miqueliana — Oval-leaf Grevillea NSW, Vic
This fairly dense species grows to 3m high by 4m wide, with oval, hairy leaves. Orange-red to bright red flowers are borne in large pendulous clusters, usually between June and November. There are several forms of this species, with one known as the 'Mt Wellington' form being of compact habit, with more rigid foliage.
O S SS L SA G C1 F2   Chart 34 (3, 9, 11, 14, 27,   )

Grevillea mucronulata   NSW
A dense shrub, with a height of 1-2m by 1.5-2.5m wide. The branchlets are pendulous, with small, green, oval leaves, and new growth often bronze. The greenish flowers are relatively inconspicuous, but are extremely attractive to honey-eating birds. Plants respond well to regular pruning. Flowering is mainly between April and December. Hybrid forms are also available.
O SS D L SA G C1 F2   Chart 14 (3, 7, 9, 27, 34, 37)

Grevillea nudiflora   WA
This species can remain prostrate, or grow up to 1m high, with a width of 2-3m. It has dense, narrow foliage, and bright red flowers are produced on leafless creeping stems, which extend up to 2m beyond the foliage. Flowering is between July and December.
H O SS D L SA G C1 F2   Chart 19 (2, 8, 10, 15, 23, 37)

Grevillea phanerophlebia   WA
A spreading shrub of 1-2m high by 2-4m wide. The leaves are tri-lobed, pungent, and light green in colour. White to cream flowers are produced in clusters, between July and October. Plants withstand hard pruning if necessary.
H O SS D L SA G C1 F1   Chart 36 (25, 28)

Grevillea pilulifera   WA
This small, compact species, grows up to 1m high, and has narrow, hairy leaves. The flowers are cream, with styles that are initially yellow, changing to orange and then red. Flowering period is between July and November.
O SS D L SA G C1 F1   Chart 8 (2, 18)

Grevillea pinaster   WA
A dense shrub of up to 2.5m high by 2-4m wide. The green leaves are soft and narrow. Flowering is mainly between June and December, when loose pendant clusters of bright red flowers are produced along the branches.
H O SS D L SA G C1 F1 Chart 34 (3, 9, 10, 14, 25,   37)

Grevillea 'Pink Pearl'   Cultivar
This vigorous cultivar grows up to 2-4m high by a similar width, but will respond well to regular prun-

ing, if required. The short, narrow, pungent leaves are crowded along the stems, and bright pink flowers are produced in clusters at the ends of short branchlets. Flowering can be throughout the year, with the main display between July and October.
H O SS D L SA G C1 F2   Chart 36 (25, 33)

Grevillea 'Poorinda Beauty'   Cultivar
A hybrid grevillea, with bright red to scarlet flowers, produced in dense clusters along the branchlets. Plants are usually bushy, and grow to 2.5m high by 2-3m wide. Flowering period is between June and December.
H O SS D L SA G C1 F2   Chart 9 (3, 14, 25, 37)

Grevillea 'Poorinda Constance'   Cultivar
This much-branched shrub grows 1.5-3m high by a similar width. It has dark green, narrow, shiny leaves. Flowering is almost throughout the year, with bright red flowers produced in clusters at the ends of small side branchlets. An excellent bird-attracting shrub, or screen plant.
H O SS D L SA G C1 F1   Chart 14 (10, 25, 34, 37)

Grevillea 'Poorinda Firebird'   Cultivar
A hybrid grevillea, so named because of the bright red flowers, produced in clusters in the leaf axils, mainly between June and December. It is a spreading shrub, with a height of 1.5-3m. The leaves are narrow and dark green.
H O SS D L SA G C1 F2   Chart 34 (3, 9, 14, 25, 37)

Grevillea 'Poorinda Queen'   Cultivar
This hybrid can grow to 2-3m high by 2-4m wide, and has narrow, shiny, dark green leaves. It is very popular with honey-eating birds, due mainly to the long flowering period, which can extend almost throughout the year. Main flowering time is between July and December. The apricot to pale orange flowers are produced in dense clusters along the branches.
H O SS D L SA G C1 F2   Chart 14 (3, 9, 25, 34, 37)

Grevillea quercifolia   WA
This species grows around 0.3-0.7m high, with a width of 1-2m. The holly-like to oak-like leaves are grey-green, and have prickly lobes. Deep pink to purple flowers are arranged in terminal heads to about 2.5cm long. Flowering period is between August and November.
H O SS D L SA G C1 F1   Chart 17 (3)

Grevillea repens — Creeping Grevillea   Vic
A dense, ground-covering species, with a width of 2-4m. The leaves are holly-like, often with reddish new growth. Flowering is between October and February, when toothbrush-shaped flowers of deep red to burgundy are produced at the ends of short branchlets. There are two different forms, one from Sailors Falls, the other from Mt Slide, and they are sold under these names.
O SS D L SA G C1 F2   Chart 15 (3, 5, 14, 23, 28)

Grevillea robusta — Silky Oak   Qld
This large tree is not recommended for small gardens, but it can be grown as an ornamental foliage plant for

indoors. In Britain it is commonly used for this purpose. It has a pyramidal habit of growth, with attractive, large, deeply divided leaves. It has spectacular orange flowers, but takes several years to flower, and is not likely to flower indoors.
H O SS W L SA G C1 F2 Chart 20

Grevillea 'Robyn Gordon' Cultivar
A spectacular shrub of open habit, with deeply lobed leaves. It grows to a height of 1.5m, by 1–2m wide. Flowering can be throughout the year, with large terminal clusters of bright red flower-heads. Plants respond well to pruning.
H O SS D W L SA G C1 F1 Charts 5, 7 (10, 14, 25, 37)

Grevillea rosmarinifolia — NSW, Vic
Rosemary Grevillea
This well-known grevillea has been in cultivation for many years, and is a hardy and very useful species. It can grow to 3m high with a width of 4m or more, however plants respond well to pruning, if a smaller shrub is desired. The dark green leaves are very narrow, dense, and prickly. Dense pink to red with cream flowers are borne in clusters during the flowering period between June and December. A number of low-growing grevilleas, previously known as forms of this species, have now been included under *G.glabella*.
H O SS D L SA G C1 F2 Chart 33 (25, 37)

Grevillea sericea — Pink Spider Flower NSW
This is another species which can flower for most of the year. It grows to 2.5m high by a similar width, with a slightly open habit of growth, and narrow leaves. The flowers are borne in clusters throughout the bush, with a number of forms available, varying in colour from white through to shades of pink to mauve.
H O SS D L SA G C1 F2 Chart 9 (3, 25)

Grevillea shiressii NSW
A quick-growing species of 3–5m high by 2–4m wide, suitable for producing a dense screen. The long, olive-green leaves have undulating margins. Inconspicuous bluish-green flowers are produced, mainly between July and December, and these are highly attractive to honey-eating birds.
H O SS S W L SA C1 F2 Chart 37 (11, 14, 33, 34)

Grevillea speciosa — Red Spider Flower NSW
(Previously known as *G.punicea*)
This species grows 1.5–3m high by similar width, and is usually of slightly open growth habit. The leaves are oblong, and can be hairy. Deep red to bright red flowers are produced, mainly between June and December, in wheel-like heads.
H O SS D L SA G C1 F2 Chart 14 (3, 9, 37)

Grevillea steiglitziana — Brisbane Ranges Grevillea Vic
This spreading shrub grows 1–2m high. It has dark green, prickly, lobed, shiny leaves. The toothbrush-shaped flower-heads are red and green, and pendant. Flowering is between June and November.
H O SS D L SA G C1 F2 Chart 28 (3, 9, 12, 14,   37)

Grevillea thelemanniana — Spider-net Grevillea WA
A variable, spreading species, growing 0.3–1m high by 2–3m wide. There are several different leaf forms, one with greyish hairy leaves, and others mainly green. The flowers are borne in clusters at the ends of small branchlets, and are light to bright red. Flowering is mainly between May and December, although flowers are also produced at other times.
H O SS D L SA G C1 F1 Chart 15 (3, 9, 14, 23, 37)

Grevillea tridentifera (prostrate form) WA
This is a dense, spreading species, growing 0.5m high by 2–4m wide. It has finely divided, light green leaves. Flowering is between August and November, when scented cream flowers are borne in dense clusters near the ends of branches. Usually the main flowering branches have an upright growth habit. These should be removed after flowering if it is desired that the plant retain its low spreading habit.
H O SS D L SA G C1 F2 Chart 23 (3, 25)

Grevillea triloba WA
This dense shrub grows to 2–3m high by a similar width. The leaves are variable, and deeply lobed with coarse or narrow segments. They are light green and hairy. Dense clusters of white flowers are borne along the branchlets, between July and November.
H O SS D L SA G C1 F2 Chart 36 (25, 27, 28, 34)

Grevillea victoriae var *tenuinervis* Vic
Although the main flowering period of this species is between September and January, it can flower throughout the year, with pendant clusters of red flowers along the branches. Plants grow to 2–4m high, and have soft, narrow, light green leaves.
O S SS D M L SA G C1 F2 Chart 34 (3, 5, 14, 27, 37)

Hakea bucculenta — Red Pokers WA
This is usually an upright shrub, of 2–4m high by around 1.5–3m wide. It has long, narrow leaves, and spectacular bright red flower-spikes of up to 10cm long. Flowers are produced on the old wood, usually between July and November, and are followed by ornamental beaked fruits.
H O D L SA G C1 F1 Chart 10 (3, 9, 14, 25, 37)

Hakea costata WA
A densely branched shrub of 1–2m high by a similar width. The crowded leaves are narrow, and very prickly. Flowering is between August and November, when small white to cream flowers are produced in clusters at the leaf axils, along the branches.
H O SS D L SA G C1 F1 Chart 36 (3, 10, 25)

Hakea elliptica — Oval-leaf Hakea WA
A hardy species, of 3–5m high by 2–4m wide. The leaves are oval, and the new growth is a decorative rusty brown. Flowers of white to cream are produced in the leaf axils, usually between October and February.
H O SS D L SA G C1 F1 Chart 33 (25, 28)

Hakea laurina — Pincushion Hakea WA
This hakea can be grown as a large bush or small tree.

It has a height of 3-6m by up to 5m in width. The leaves are similar in appearance to eucalypt leaves, and new growth is bronze. Flowers are in pincushion-shaped heads, and are cream and red, deepening to all red with age. These are followed by decorative woody seed capsules. Flowering is usually between March and July, and heavy frost during these months can damage flower buds. This hakea responds well to pruning, which can be used to strengthen the trunk, particularly if plants are growing very quickly.
H O SS D L SA G C1 F1 Chart 7 (14, 25, 37)

Hakea multilineata — Grass-leaf Hakea **WA**
This shrubby species is usually of upright growth habit, with a height of 3-5m. The leaves are long and narrow, with prominent nerves. The flowering period is between March and October, when spectacular pink to red flower-heads of about 4cm long are produced in the leaf axils, forming loose spikes.
H O SS D L SA G C1 F1 Chart 37 (9, 10, 14, 25)

Hakea nodosa — Yellow Hakea **Vic, Tas, SA**
A hardy and adaptable species, growing 2-3m high by a similar width, with narrow pine-like leaves. It flowers mainly between February and May, with strongly scented, cream to yellow flowers, produced along the stems in leaf axils. Unlike most other hakeas, plants will tolerate wet conditions.
H O SS W L SA G C1 F2 Chart 26 (27)

Hakea obtusa **WA**
An upright shrub of 2-3m high by 1.5-2m wide. The leaves are oval, and flowers are produced in clusters along the older branches, usually between June and October. The flowers are initially white to cream, but deepen to pink or red.
H O SS D L SA G C1 F2 Chart 25 (3, 9, 10)

Hakea orthorrhyncha — Bird's Beak Hakea **WA**
This open shrub grows to 1.5-3m high by a similar width. It has stiff, very narrow leaves. Bright red spidery flowers are produced on the older branches, mainly between July and September. This plant is spectacular in appearance if it can be viewed with back-lighting from the sun.
H O SS D L SA G C1 F2 Chart 9 (10, 14, 25, 37)

Hakea petiolaris — Sea Urchins **WA**
The common name of this hakea refers to the cream to cream and purple, pincushion-shape flower-heads, which are produced along the branches during the flowering period of May to July. Plants grow to 3-6m high by 2-4m wide, with an upright, branched habit. The leaves are oval, and grey to green.
H O SS D M L SA G C1 F1 Chart 33 (9, 12, 25, 28, 37)

Hakea rostrata — **Vic, Tas, SA**
Beaked Hakea or Turkey Gobbler
This is an open shrub of 1-2.5m high by 1.5-3m wide, with prickly, pine-like leaves scattered along the branches. Sweetly scented white flowers are produced in the leaf axils, mainly between September and November. The common names refer to the unusual shape of the woody seed capsules.
H O SS D L SA G C1 F2 Chart 36 (27, 29, 30)

Hakea salicifolia — Willow Hakea **Qld, NSW**
(Previously known as *H.saligna*)
This fast-growing shrub has a height of 3-7m by a width of 2-5m. It has smooth, long leaves, and the new growth often has attractive reddish tonings. Small white to cream flowers are borne in clusters along the branches, at leaf axils. Flowering time is between July and Novemeber.
H O SS W L SA G C1 F2 Charts 32, 33 (25)

Hakea sericea — Silky Hakea **NSW, Vic, Tas**
This hakea grows 2-4m tall, by 1-3m wide, and has short, pungent, needle-like leaves. The stems are often reddish. Flowers are white or in various shades of pink, and are produced in the leaf axils. The main flowering is between April and September, with possible sporadic flowering at other times. An excellent refuge plant for birds.
H O SS L SA G C1 F2 Chart 36 (25, 27)

Hakea suaveolens — Sweet-scented Hakea **WA**
An open to dense shrub of 3-6m high by 3-5m wide. The leaves are smooth, and deeply lobed, with very narrow, pungent segments. Sweetly scented, white to cream flower-heads are produced in the leaf axils on the older wood. Flowering is mainly between April and June.
H O SS D L SA G C2 F1 Chart 36 (25, 27, 40)

Hakea undulata **WA**
This species usually grows as an upright shrub, 1.5-3m high by up to 2m wide. It has oval leaves, with undulating, toothed margins. Flowering is between July and September, with flowers of white to cream in the leaf axils.
H O SS D L SA G C1 F1 Chart 28 (12)

Hakea victoriae — Royal Hakea **WA**
A hakea grown mainly for its ornamental foliage. Plants grow up to 2-4m high and under favourable conditions may grow 1-3m wide. The large, pungent, stem-clasping leaves change colour as the plant ages, with tones of cream to orange. Cream and pink flowers are produced during August to October, but are usually almost hidden in the leaf axils.
H O SS D L SA G C1 F2 Chart 12 (10)

Halgania cyanea — **NSW, Vic, SA, WA, NT**
Rough Halgania
This low shrub often spreads by suckering. It grows to 0.5m high by 0.5-1m wide. Flowering is mainly between September and February, when small, open-petalled, blue flowers are produced in terminal clusters. The small toothed leaves are slightly rough to touch, and the common name refers to this feature.
H O SS D L SA G C1 F2 Chart 23 (2, 4, 10, 18, 25)

Hardenbergia comptoniana — Native Lilac **WA**
This is a quick growing, climbing species, with leaves in groups of 3. Masses of small bluish-purple to mauve flowers are produced in racemes at the ends of the branchlets, and flowering is usually between September and November. Flowers have a sweet perfume. Frost tender.
O SS D M L SA C1 Charts 29, 31 (13, 15)

Grevillea 'Robyn Gordon' is a recently introduced cultivar, worthy of a place in any garden.

The reddish new growth on *Grevillea x gaudichaudii* can be clearly seen here. This ground-covering grevillea has attractive lobed foliage, and deep red toothbrush flowers.

The daisy flowers of *Brachycome multifida* are small, but profuse. Pink, mauve and white flowered forms are available.

top left: The attractive reddish hops of *Dodonaea adenophora* are retained on the bush for a long period between March and October.

above: Eucalyptus macranda is a hardy small tree of 5–10 m high, with showy clusters of yellow–green flowers.

The attractive stems, buds and flowers of *Eucalyptus caesia* 'Silver Princess'.

Hardenbergia violacea —   Qld, NSW, Vic, Tas, SA
Purple Coral-pea, or False Sarsaparilla
This vigorous climber or trailer has oval, pointed leaves of dark green. The flowers are pea-shaped, and are borne in long racemes from the leaf axils. There are also shrub forms available, with flower colours of white, mauve, purple or pink. Flowering period is July to October.
H O SS D L SA G C1 F2   Chart 31 (15, 23, 25)

Helichrysum apiculatum —   All States
Common Everlasting
A spreading species, of 0.6m high by up to 2m wide. The leaves and stems are densely hairy, giving them a silvery appearance. Flowering is between September and February, when bright yellow flower-heads are produced in clusters, on stems above the foliage.
H O SS D L SA G C1 F2   Charts 23, 38 (2, 3, 4, 5, 10)

Helichrysum baxteri —   Vic, SA
Fringed Everlasting, or White Everlasting
This is a low, clump forming species, that can be grown to advantage in the majority of gardens. It grows to 0.5cm high by up to 1m across. Daisy-like flower-heads of about 2cm diameter, are produced on stems above the foliage, mainly between the months of October and January. The flower-heads are white with a yellow centre.
H O SS D M L SA G C1 F2

                    Charts 4, 16, 18, 38, 41 (2, 24)

Helichrysum bracteatum —   All States
Golden Everlasting
A variable species, with a height of between 0.2m and 1.5m. Some forms are annuals. The foliage is usually hairy or sticky. Flowering can be throughout the year, but is mainly between September and February. The golden papery flower-heads can be up to about 5cm diameter, and are excellent for drying and using in floral work. A spreading form, *Helichrysum bracteatum* 'Dargan Hill Monarch', and the dwarf *H. bracteatum* 'Diamond Head' are excellent as garden or container plants. Regular picking of flowers and light pruning is recommended.
H O SS D M L SA G C1 F2   Charts 4, 38, 41 (2, 23)

Helichrysum semipapposum —   All States
Clustered Everlasting
This is another variable helichrysum, the best forms for cultivation being those which retain leaf growth to ground level. Plants have greyish leaves and stems, and can grow to 1m high by 0.5-1.5m wide. Small golden yellow flower-heads are produced in dense terminal clusters, mainly between the months of October and February.
H O SS D M L SA G C1 F2   Chart 4 (2, 38)

Helipterum manglesii — Pink Everlasting   WA
This annual has greyish, stem clasping, oval leaves, and grows to a height of around 0.5m, forming a clump of similar width. Pink papery flower-heads of about 2.5cm diameter, are produced mainly between October and January. Initially they are pendant, but gradually become upright as they mature. This species

can produce an excellent massed display, and will colonize if regeneration is allowed.
H O SS D M L SA G C1 F1   Chart 41 (1, 18)

Helipterum roseum — Everlasting   WA
This annual has narrow, grey-green leaves. It grows to 1m high by 0.5m wide. The papery flower-heads are up to 4cm diameter, and can be white to pink. Flowering is mainly between September and January. An excellent cut flower.
H O SS D M L SA G C1 F2   Chart 41 (1, 18)

Hemiandra pungens — Snake Bush   WA
A low, spreading species, with narrow prickly leaves. Plants grow 1-2m wide. The flowers are mauve-pink, and are tubular with flared tips. Main flowering period is October to April. when the flowers can nearly cover the foliage.
H O D L SA G C1 F1   Chart 15 (2, 4, 6, 18, 23, 25)

Herpolirion novae-zealandiae —   NSW, Vic, Tas
Sky Lily
A small, matting plant with grass-like foliage, spreading to a width of 0.3-1m. Fragrant white and pale blue star-like flowers are nestled in the foliage. Flowering period is October to February. A relatively slow-growing species.
H O D M L SA G C1 F2   Charts 1, 13 (2, 4, 18)

Hibbertia dentata —   Qld, NSW, Vic
Trailing Guinea-flower
This is a climber or trailing plant. The leaves are up to 6cm long by 3cm wide, toothed, and shiny green. The young growth is reddish. Yellow flowers of about 4cm diameter are produced, mainly between August and December.
O SS D M L SA C1 F1   Charts 15, 31 (2, 3, 19)

Hibbertia empetrifolia —   Qld, NSW, Vic, Tas, SA
Guinea Flower (Previously known as *H.astrotricha*)
This spreading species can be ground-covering, but will climb through other plants, or cover walls and fences, if given some support. Under favourable conditions it can become quite dense, and may reach a height of 1.5m by 1-2m wide. Masses of bright yellow, open-petalled flowers are produced, usually between August and November.
O SS D M L SA G C1 F2   Chart 19 (3, 11, 23, 27)

Hibbertia fasciculata —   Qld, NSW, Vic
Bundled Guinea-flower
This is a small plant, growing to 0.5m high by a similar width. It has an upright habit of growth. The green or greyish leaves are small and hairy, and in clusters along the stems. Flowering is between June and November, when bright yellow flowers are produced along the stems.
H O SS D SA G C1 F2   Chart 2 (8, 18)

Hibbertia obtusifolia   Qld, NSW, Vic, Tas
This species has 2 forms. One is prostrate, forming a dense mat, and the other is upright to 1m high. The leaves are roughly oval, and green to greyish green. Bright yellow flowers of up to 3cm diameter are well

displayed during the flowering period of August to February.

O SS D M L SA G C1 F2 Chart 4 (18, 23)

Hibbertia procumbens — Guinea-flower Vic, Tas
A mat-forming species, which can spread to a width of 0.5-1m, layering itself as it grows. The leaves are short, narrow, and dark green. Bright yellow flowers of about 2cm diameter, are displayed in profusion during the flowering period of October to April.

H O SS D L SA G C1 F2 Charts 2, 18 (4, 23)

Hibbertia scandens — Qld, NSW
Climbing Guinea-flower
This climbing species is often slow to become established, but can then be quite vigorous. It has long trailing stems, and shiny leaves to 8cm long. Yellow flowers of up to 7cm diameter are produced almost throughout the year, the main flowering being between November and January. An excellent sand-binding species. Frost tender.

H O SS D M L SA C2 Charts 31, 40 (5, 10)

Hibbertia stellaris — Orange Stars WA
This hibbertia has a long flowering period, which can extend through the year, with main flowering between October and January. The open-petalled flowers are orange-yellow. Plants grow to 0.5m high by 0.75m wide. The fine leaves are on wiry stems, often intertwined, and new growth has reddish tonings.

H O SS D M SA G C1 F1 Charts 4, 17 (2, 18, 19)

Hibiscus heterophyllus Qld, NSW
There are a number of evergreen Australian hibiscus. This species grows 2-4m high by 2-3m wide, and has slightly prickly stems and leaves. The leaves can be entire, or with 3 lobes. Flowering is mainly between October and February, and the large flowers have slightly spreading white petals, with a dark red to purple base. There is also a yellow flowered form. Frost tender.

H O SS D M L SA G C1 Chart 25 (3, 5,   )

Homoranthus darwinioides NSW
(Previously known as *Rylstonea cernua*)
This is a compact shrub, with upright branches, and grows 0.5-1m high by a similar width. The leaves are minute, succulent, bluish-green, and sweetly aromatic. Small pink, yellow and green flowers are borne in pairs, in pendant heads. Flowering is mainly between January and July, but can be at other times also. The flowers are bird-attracting.

H O SS D L SA G C1 F1 Charts 6, 37 (5, 7, 14, 25)

Homoranthus flavescens Qld, NSW
This is an ornamental, low spreading species, with horizontal branches, and small, narrow, succulent-like greyish green leaves. Plants can grow 0.5-1m tall by 1-2m wide. Clusters of small, honey-scented, yellow flowers are produced along the branches, mainly between October and February.

H O SS D M L SA G C1 F1 Charts 12, 28 (3, 5,   23)

Hovea elliptica — Tree Hovea WA
A shrub of upright growth habit, growing to 2-5m tall by 1.5-3m wide. The leaves are olive green, and the

blue-purple pea-shaped flowers are borne in racemes from the leaf axils. Flowering is usually between August and October.

O SS D M L SA G C1 F1 Chart 27 (3, 11)

Hovea heterophylla — Qld, NSW, Vic, Tas
Common Hovea
This small species grows 0.3-0.5m high, by a similar width. It has small oval lower leaves, and narrow upper leaves. Flowering is between August and October, when pale bluish-purple pea-flowers are produced in clusters from the leaf axils.

O SS D M L SA G C1 F2 Chart 27 (2, 11, 18)

Hovea pungens WA
This is usually an upright shrub, with pungent, narrow, dark green leaves of about 2cm long. Plants grow to a height of 1-1.5m by 0.5-1m wide. Masses of bright purplish-blue pea-shaped flowers are produced along the branchlets. The main flowering period is between July and October.

H O SS D L SA G C1 F1 Chart 8 (2, 10, 18, 25)

Hoya australis Qld, NSW, WA, NT
This is a slow-growing climber, with shiny, oval, dark green leaves to about 10cm long. The waxy, white flowers are fragrant, and are borne in clusters of 20-30 flowers. Flowering period is between September and November. Frost tender.

O SS D L SA G C1 Chart 15 (19, 31)

Hymenosporum flavum — Qld, NSW
Native Frangipani
An upright tree, growing 5-10m high by 2.5-5m wide, with shiny, dark green leaves. Flowering is between October and December, when cream and yellow flowers of about 3cm long by 2cm wide are produced. The flowers have a delightful fragrance.

H O SS D M L SA G C1 F1 Charts 13, 29, 32 (3, 10, 25)

Hypocalymma angustifolium — White Myrtle WA
A many-branched shrub of 1-1.5m high by 1-2m wide. The leaves are small and narrow, and combine with small flowers clustered in the leaf axils, to produce a most attractive display. The flowers may be initially white, deepening to pink, or there is also an all-white form. Main flowering is between June and December.

H O SS M W L SA G C1 F1 Chart 25 (2, 8,   )

Hypocalymma cordifolium WA
This small shrub grows to 1.5m high by 1-2m wide. It has stem-clasping, round leaves of light green, which combine attractively with the new stem growth, which is usually red. Plants respond well to regular light pruning, which promotes the attractive new growth. There is also a variegated form, known as *H. cordifolium* 'Golden Veil'. Flowering is between September and November, when white flowers are produced on short stems in the leaf axils.

O SS M W L SA G C1 F1 Chart 12 (2, 11, 25, 27, 28)

Hypocalymma puniceum — Large Myrtle WA
A much-branched, spreading shrub, with a height of 0.5-1m, by 1-1.5m wide. The leaves are short and narrow, and the pink to reddish flowers are the largest

of all hypocalymma species, being up to 2cm in diameter. Flowering is between November and April.

H O SS D M L SA G C1 F1   Chart 17 (4)

Hypocalymma robustum — Swan River Myrtle   WA
An upright shrub, growing to 1.5m high. The leaves are narrow, to about 1.5cm long. Showy pink flowers of about 1cm diameter are tightly clustered in the leaf axils during the flowering period between July and November. The flowers are pleasantly fragrant.

H O SS D L SA G C1 F1   Chart 3 (25)

Hypocalymma strictum   WA
This species has an upright growth habit, with a height of 0.5m-1m, by similar width. The leaves are short and narrow. Pink flowers are produced in the leaf axils, near the branchlet tips, during the flowering period of December to April.

H O SS D M L SA G C1 F1   Charts 6, 38 (4)

Indigofera australis — Austral Indigo   All States
This upright, open shrub, has slender branches, and attractive fern-like grey-green leaves. It grows up to 2.5m high by 1-2m wide. Flowering is between September and December, when pale to bright lilac pea-flowers are produced in racemes. The flowers have a delicate fragrance. A white-flowered form is also in cultivation, although not common.

O SS M W L SA G C1 F2   Charts 11, 13 (3, 27, 29, 38)

Isopogon anethifolius — Conebush   NSW
A hardy shrub of 1.5-3m high by 1-2m wide, with upright branches, and finely divided leaves. Yellow flower-heads of about 4cm diameter are produced at the branchlet tips, mainly between August and November. The flowers are followed by almost globular seed cones.

H O SS D L SA G C1 F2   Charts 12, 35 (3, 28)

Isopogon latifolius   WA
Although this showy species is not readily grown under garden conditions, it can be successfully cultivated in a medium to large container. Plants grow to 2.5m high by a similar width, but appreciate regular pruning. The leaves are long, flat, and light green. Deep purple-pink flower-heads of up to 8cm diameter are produced at the ends of the branches. Flowering period is October-November.

H O SS D L SA G C1 F1   Chart 17 (3)

Jacksonia scoparia   Qld, NSW
This is an upright shrub, of 3-5m high by 1.5-3m wide, with narrow, greyish-green foliage. A profuse display of yellow to orange pea-shaped flowers is produced between September and November. The flowers have a delicate perfume.

H O SS D L SA G C1 F2   Charts 13, 29, 35, 38 (3, 28)

Jasminum suavissimum — Sweet Jasmine   Qld, NSW
This species will grow as a shrub, but if given some framework, or grown near other plants, it will act as a climber. The leaves are simple, narrow, and light green. Highly fragrant white flowers are produced, usually in clusters of 3-5, or there may be odd single

flowers. Flowering is mainly October-February. This species has been sold as *J.lineare*.

H O SS D L SA C1 F2   Charts 29, 31 (3, 5, 19, 38)

Kennedia beckxiana   WA
This is a strong climber, with blue-green leaves. The pea-shaped flowers of up to 5cm long are bright red with green, and the main flowering period is August-December. A good bird attracting species.

H O SS D L SA G C1 F1   Chart 31 (37)

Kennedia eximia   WA
This species is usually prostrate, growing 1-3m wide. It has slender stems, with oval, crinkled leaves of dark green. The pea-shaped flowers are up to 2cm long, and dark red. They are produced in short racemes along the stems, during the flowering period of August to December.

O SS D L SA G C1 F1   Chart 15 (3, 23)

Kennedia glabrata   WA
This prostrate kennedia grows to a width of 1-2m. It is usually very quick growing, but can sometimes be short-lived. The leaves are shiny dark green, and are held above the trailing stems. Flowering is usually around November to December, when profuse brick-red pea-shaped flowers are borne in racemes, and held upright. The flowers are perfumed. Frost tender.

O SS D L SA G C1   Charts 13, 41 (3, 15, 23)

Kennedia microphylla   WA
This species forms a dense mat, covering an area of up to 1-2m. The spreading stems are covered with small, dark green leaves, and deep brick-red pea-shaped flowers are borne in profusion between August and November. Frost tender.

O SS D M L SA G C1   Charts 15, 19 (2, 23)

Kennedia prostrata — Running Postman   All States
A quick-growing ground-cover, with greyish green clover-like leaves. Plants can spread to 1-3m wide. The pea-shaped flowers are bright red with yellow, and although they can be seen sporadically through the year, the main flowering is between August and November.

H O SS D L SA G C1 F2   Chart 15 (3, 23)

Kunzea baxteri   WA
This shrub to small tree can grow to 2-4m high by a similar width. The foliage is dense, with short, oblong leaves. Bright red flower-spikes with gold tips are produced at the ends of the branchlets, mainly between May and October. These have a similar shape to that of the callistemons, and can be up to 7cm long by 5cm wide. It can take a number of years for some plants to flower. Recommended for coastal areas.

H O SS D L SA G C2 F1   Chart 37 (3, 7, 9, 10, 25, 40)

Kunzea ericifolia   WA
An upright, branched shrub, of 2-3m high by 1.5-2m wide, with soft, small, narrow leaves. Globular yellow flower-heads are produced at the ends of the branchlets, between September and November.

O SS D M L SA G C1 F1   Chart 34 (3)

Kunzea parvifolia — Violet Kunzea   NSW, Vic
There are two forms of this species, one being an open branched shrub of up to 2.5m high by 1-2m wide, and the other, commonly known as the 'dwarf form' being of compact habit, and excellent for containers, or small areas. The leaves are very small, narrow, and stem clasping. Flowering is between September and January, when mauve to magenta flower-heads of up to 1.5cm diameter are produced on the branchlet tips.
H O SS D M L SA G C1 F2   Charts 2, 26 (3)

Kunzea pomifera — Muntries   Vic, SA
This dense, spreading species, grows 1-3m wide, but can be slow growing. It has small, light green, crowded oval leaves. The flowers are white to cream, and are borne in clusters along the branches. Flowering is between September and November, and is followed by edible bluish berries. Plants can be slow to flower in cultivation.
H O SS D L SA G C2 F2   Charts 23, 40 (10)

Kunzea recurva var *montana*   WA
This species grows 3-4m high by 2-3m wide, and is of upright growth with slender branches and small soft leaves. It is quick-growing. Globular yellow flower-heads are produced on the branchlet tips, usually between September and November.
H O SS D M L SA G C1 F1   Chart 33 (3)

Lambertia ericifolia   WA
This is a much branched shrub of 2.5-3.5m high by a slightly smaller width, but it is not dense, having scattered, narrow, pine-like leaves. Showy tubular flowers of orange-red, are produced in terminal clusters at various times throughout the year.
H O SS D L SA G C1 F1   Chart 10 (14, 25, 37)

Lambertia formosa —   NSW
Mountain Devil, or Honey Flower
This lambertia, as with previous species, can flower throughout the year, with the main flowering time usually being February-April. Plants grow 2-3m high by a similar width, and have rigid branches with narrow, pungent, dark green leaves. The flowers are orange-red to bright red, and are in terminal clusters. The common name of Mountain Devil is derived from the unusual shape of the woody seed capsules.
H O SS D L SA G C1 F2   Charts 7, 14 (30, 37)

Lasiopetalum behrii —   NSW, Vic, SA
Pink Velvet Bush
This much-branched shrub grows 1-1.5m high by a similar width. The leaves are up to 6cm long, oblong and greyish green. Small cream to pink flowers are produced in loose clusters during the flowering period of August-December.
H O SS D L SA G C1 F2   Chart 12 (10, 25)

Lastreopsis shepherdii —   Qld, NSW, Vic, Tas, SA
Shiny Shield-fern
This hardy fern has a tufted rhizome, and grows 0.5-1m high by a similar width. The arching fronds are shiny, and have toothed pinnae.
O SS SS D M L SA C1 F2   Chart 21 (11, 12, 27, 28)

Lechenaultia biloba — Blue Lechenaultia   WA
This twiggy small shrub of 0.5-1m high by a similar width, is renowned for its spectacular blue flowers. The leaves are small and narrow, and the flowers are arranged in terminal clusters. Flowering is mainly between July and December. There are various colour forms available, from pale blue or blue with white, to a rich deep blue. Branches tend to be brittle, and protection from strong winds is advisable. Pruning after flowering is recommended. Any clippings can be used for propagation by cuttings, as plants usually strike readily.
O SS D M L SA G C1 F1   Charts 2, 41 (8, 18, 19)

Lechenaultia floribunda   WA
A small, much branched shrub, of up to 0.5m high by 1m wide. The leaves are very small and dense. Small white, cream or lilac to blue flowers are produced in terminal clusters, usually between September and January. Flowering is profuse, and the flowers can have a delicate fragrance. Plants sometimes spread by suckering.
H O SS D M L SA G C1 F2   Chart 13 (2, 4, 19)

Lechenaultia formosa — Red Lechenaultia   WA
This is the most variable lechenaultia, in growth habit and flower. Plants can be prostrate, or up to 0.6m high by 0.5-1m wide. Flower colour varies, and includes yellow, orange, pink, magenta, scarlet and red, or combinations of these colours. Flowering period is mainly between March and November, and the flowers, although solitary, are profuse. The foliage is small and often grey-green. Plants can spread by suckering.
H O SS D M L SA G C1 F1   Charts 8, 19, 41 (2, 25)

Lechenaultia laricina   WA
A many-branched shrub of up to 0.5m high by 0.5-1m wide. The leaves are short and small, and bright orange-red flowers are well displayed during the flowering period of October to February.
H O SS D M L SA G C1 F1   Chart 4 (2, 10, 19, 25)

Lechenaultia tubiflora — Heath Lechenaultia   WA
This species is variable in growth habit, from being mat-like, to up to 0.5m tall. It spreads 0.5-1m wide. The foliage is dense, with small grey-green leaves. Flowering is usually between September and February, when small tubular flowers of cream, pink or red, stand erect from the leaf axils.
H O SS D M L SA G C1 F1   Charts 1, 41 (2, 4, 18, 19)

Lemna minor — Common Duckweed   All States
A small, free-floating species, with oval to round, bright green leaves. It spreads rapidly in still water, and can literally cover the surface. It can however be controlled by raking off excess plants.
Aquatic   Chart 39

Lepidozamia peroffskyana   Qld, NSW
This is a member of the Cycad family, and is slow growing. It is an excellent species for containers, and has deeply lobed, shiny palm-like foliage. Frost tender.
S SS D M L SA C1   Chart 20 (11, 27)

Leptospermum epacridoideum NSW
A many-branched shrub, of 1.5-2.5m tall, by 1.5-2m
wide, with dense foliage and very short, oval leaves.
The white, or rarely pinkish flowers, are of about 1cm
diameter, and are produced at the ends of short
branchlets. Main flowering period is between December and February.
H O SS M W L SA G C1 F1 Chart 5 (26, 38)

Leptospermum flavescens — Tantoon Qld, NSW
A large, many-branched shrub, of 3-4m high by a
similar width. The branchlets are usually pendulous,
with reddish new stems, and the leaves are flat,
narrow, and blunt tipped. Flowering is between September and December, when white to cream, strongly
sweet-scented flowers are produced.
H O SS M W L SA G C1 F1 Chart 33 (26, 27, 38)

Leptospermum 'Horizontalis' Cultivar
This is a dense, ground-covering shrub, with a height
of 0.5-1m and width of 2-4m. The leaves are broad,
and somewhat prickly. Profuse white flowers almost
cover the horizontal branches during the flowering
period between October and December.
H O SS W L SA G C2 F1 Charts 23, 38, 40 (3, 26)

Leptospermum humifusum Tas
This is a variable, spreading, dwarf shrub, with a
height of 0.2-1m by 1-2m wide. The leaves are small
and dark green, and scattered along slender branches.
Small white flowers are produced, mainly between
September and November.
H O SS W L SA G C1 F2 Chart 23 (26)

Leptospermum lanigerum — Qld, NSW, Vic, Tas, SA
Woolly Tea-tree
This dense shrub grows to 2-4m high by 1-2m wide.
The leaves are small and green to grey, whilst new
growth can be silky and reddish. White flowers of up
to 2cm diameter are produced along the branchlets,
mainly between November and January. There is also
a form available with weeping foliage.
H O SS W L SA G C1 F2 Charts 26, 33 (27, 38)

Leptospermum nitidum 'Copper Sheen' Cultivar
This dense shrub has smooth leaves, with dark reddish
tonings, particularly in the young growth. Plants
grow to 2.5m high by 2-3m wide. Flowering is between September and November, when pale lime-
yellow flowers of about 2.5cm diameter are produced
along the branchlets.
H O SS M W L SA G C1 F1 Chart 12 (3, 28, 38)

Leptospermum petersonii — Qld
Lemon-scented Tea-tree
A soft-foliaged shrub, of 2-5m high by 2-3m wide.
The smooth, narrow, green leaves are lemon scented,
and new foliage growth can be reddish. White to
cream flowers are produced, mainly between De-
cember and February. Can be frost tender.
O SS M W L SA G C1 Charts 13, 29 (26, 27)

Leptospermum phylicoides — Burgan Qld, NSW, Vic
This is a large shrub to small tree, of 3-6m high by
2-4m wide. It has crowded, narrow leaves, which in
some forms have reddish tonings. The flowers are

white to pale pink, and are borne in clusters near the
ends of the branchlets. Flowering period is November
to February.
H O SS M W L SA G C1 F2 Charts 26, 32, 33 (27)

Leptospermum scoparium var *rotundifolium* NSW
Usually a spreading shrub of 1.5-2.5m high by 2-3m
wide. The leaves are more or less oval, and the profuse
white to pale pink flowers are 2-3cm in diameter.
Flowering is mainly between October and December.
A form from Jervis Bay is more upright than the
above, and the flowers are a deep mauve-pink with a
tinge of blue.
H O SS M W L SA G C1 F2 Chart 3 (26, 34)

Leptospermum squarrosum — Peach Tea-tree NSW
A many-branched shrub of 1-3m high by a similar
width, with prickly, narrow, dark green leaves. The
flowers are white to deep pink, and are produced in
large numbers on the older wood of branches. Flowering is between February and April.
H O SS M W L SA G C1 F2 Charts 7, 40 (26)

Liparis reflexa — Yellow Rock-orchid Qld, NSW
This is a most reliable species for container culture. It
grows 0.2-0.5m wide, and has pear-shaped pseudo-
bulbs, with broad leaves up to 30cm long. The small,
pale greenish-white to yellow-green flowers are produced on erect racemes, that are about the same length
as the leaves. Flowering period is March to May, and
the flowers occasionally emit an unpleasant aroma.
O S SS M C1 F1 Chart 22

Lomandra filiformis — Qld, NSW, Vic
Wattle Mat-rush
This tuft-forming perennial species grows to 0.5m
high by a similar width. The green leaves are narrow,
and grass-like. Small cream to yellow flowers are
borne in clusters along a branched stem, between September and December.
O SS M L SA G C1 F2 Chart 16 (18, 27)

Lomatia polymorpha — Mountain Lomatia Tas
This shrub of up to 2.5m high by a similar width, has
narrow leaves to about 5cm long, sometimes being
lobed. Clusters of cream flowers are produced near the
ends of the branchlets, during the flowering period of
December to February.
O SS D L SA G C1 F2 Chart 27 (5, 11)

Ludwigia peploides — Qld, NSW, Vic, SA
Clove Strip, or Water Primrose
A perennial, with trailing stems, rooting at the nodes.
The leaves are oblong. Attractive, small, buttercup-
like flowers of bright yellow are produced between
October and April. Plants can be grown in shallow
water, or in soil near the edges of pools.
Aquatic Chart 39

Marsilea drummondii — Qld, NSW, Vic, SA, WA
Common Nardoo
A perennial aquatic fern, with branching, creeping
rhizomes. The 4-leaved, clover-like leaves float on the
surface of the water. Suitable for growing in water, or

in bog gardens. The Aborigines gathered the spore cases, and ground them to make a flour.
Aquatic   Chart 39

Mazus pumilio —   Qld, NSW, Vic, Tas, SA
Swamp Mazus
This vigorous, suckering mat plant can spread to a width of 1-2m. The leaves are oblong and shiny, with lobed largins. Small tubular flowers of mauve or white are produced mainly between November and April.
H O SS M W L SA C1 F1   Chart 1 (23, 26)

Melaleuca armillaris —   Qld, NSW, Vic
Bracelet Honey-myrtle
This very worthwhile large shrub to small tree will grow to 4-8m high by 3-6m wide. The leaves are narrow, up to 2.5cm long and dark green. Flowering is between August and January, with cream spikes of up to 7.5cm long. Honey-eating birds are regular visitors when plants are in flower. Reddish bracts are often prominent before the flowers open. Execellent for exposed coastal conditions.
H O SS W L SA G C1 F1   Charts 32, 33 (26, 36, 40)

Melaleuca coccinea — Goldfields Bottlebrush   WA
This melaleuca can grow 1.5-2.5m high by up to 2m wide. The leaves are almost oval, and arranged opposite each other along the branches. Brilliant red brushes of about 8cm long by 5cm wide, are produced on the older wood. Flowering is usually between November and February.
H O SS D L SA G C1 F1   Chart 5 (10, 14, 25, 37)

Melaleuca cordata   WA
An open, branched shrub of 1-2m high by a similar width. The name *cordata* refers to the heart-shaped leaves which are grey-green, and about 1-1.5cm long. Pink to red, globular flower-heads of up to 2cm diameter, are produced at the ends of the branchlets, between September and December.
H O SS D L SA G C1 F2   Chart 2 (10, 12, 25, 28)

Melaleuca decussata — Totem Poles   Vic, SA
A dense shrub of 2-4m high by a similar width, with branches sometimes pendulous. The leaves are small and narrow, opposite, and grey-green. Flowering is between September and January, when pale to deep mauve brushes of 2-3cm long are produced. A white-flowered form is also available. The common name refers to the woody seed capsules, which are embedded in the stems.
H O SS W L SA G C1 F2   Charts 3, 26 (5, 34)

Melaleuca diosmifolia   WA
This dense bushy shrub can grow to 2-4m high by a similar width. The branches are stiff, with crowded, green, oblong to oval leaves. The foliage will last for a long time after picking, and is useful for floral art purposes. Flowering is between October and December, when lime-green brushes of up to 8cm long by 5cm wide are produced. Plants grown from seed can take some years to flower, while those propagated

from cuttings of selected plants, or grown under harsh conditions, appear to flower best. Frost tender.
H O SS M W L SA G C1   Chart 12 (26, 34, 37)

Melaleuca elliptica — Granite Honey-myrtle   WA
A dense shrub of 2-3m high by a similar width. The branches are stiff, and the oval, grey-green leaves are opposite. Deep red flower brushes up to 7.5cm long are produced between November and February.
H O SS W L SA G C1 F1   Chart 5 (10, 14, 25, 37)

Melaleuca ericifolia —   NSW, Vic, Tas
Swamp Paper-bark
This is an upright shrub to small tree, growing 4-8m high by 2-4m wide. The botanical and common names of this species indicate some of the features it possesses. The bark on mature plants is papery. The leaves are very small, narrow, and crowded on the branchlets, similar to those of the plant family, *Erica*. Plants are tolerant of wet soils. Flowering is usually around October-November, with cream brushes of about 4cm long by 2cm wide.
H O SS W L SA G C1 F2   Chart 26 (27, 40)

Melaleuca fulgens — Scarlet Honey-myrtle   WA
A much-branched, slightly open shrub, of 1.5-3m high by a similar width. The narrow, smooth, greyish-green leaves are up to 2cm long. Flowering is between September and December, with brushes of scarlet to deep pink, with gold anthers. A salmon coloured form is also available, and the various forms should be propagated from cuttings to retain the true colours. The flowers are produced on short lateral branchlets from the older wood.
H O SS D W L SA G C1 F1   Chart 3 (10, 14, 25, 37)

Melaleuca gibbosa —   Vic, Tas, SA
Slender Honey-myrtle
This melaleuca grows 1-2m high by a similar width. The small leaves or about 0.5cm long are oval, curved, and crowded on the stems. The lilac to mauve flowers are produced in globular heads, or short spikes. Flowering is usually between October and January.
H O SS M W L SA G C1 F1   Chart 26 (4, 5, 10)

Melaleuca huegelii — Chenille Honey-myrtle   WA
A dense shrub of 2-4m high by a similar width, with very small, crowded triangular leaves. The flower buds are pink, opening to cream-white spikes of up to 12cm long. Flowers are profuse, and often in clusters at the branchlet tips. Flowering period is between November and January.
H O SS M L SA G C1 F1   Chart 5 (10, 25, 34)

Melaleuca hypericifolia — Hillock Bush   NSW
This dense shrub can grow to 3-6m high by 2-5m wide. The branchlets are pendulous, and the leaves are up to 2.5cm long, often gaining reddish tonings in cold weather. Orange-red flower-spikes of up to 8cm long are produced on the older wood, usually between September and February. Excellent for bird-attracting, and an ideal plant for use as an informal hedge.
H O SS W L SA G C1 F1   Chart 37 (25, 26, 34)

Melaleuca incana — Grey Honey-myrtle WA
This shrub of around 2-3m high has weeping pendulous branches, and grey-green foliage. The leaves are around 1.5cm long, narrow, and crowded along the branchlets. A green-leaved form can also be obtained, but it is not common. Flowering is between September and December, when many pale yellow flower-spikes of up to 5cm long are produced.
H O SS M W L SA G C1 F1   Chart 12 (3, 10, 25, 28)

Melaleuca lanceolata —   Qld, NSW, Vic, SA, WA
Moonah (Previously known as *M.pubescens*)
This slow-growing small tree, of 3-8m high by 2-6m wide, is excellent for exposed coastal regions. It has a dark, hard-barked trunk, and the small linear leaves of about 1cm long form a dense canopy. Small white to cream brushes are displayed between October and February, and in a good season the foliage can be literally covered with flower-brushes.
H O SS L SA G C2 F1   Chart 40 (25, 32)

Melaleuca lateritia — Red Robin Bush WA
An open shrub of 2-4m high by 1.5-3m wide. The leaves are narrow, 1-2cm long, and light green. Bright orange-red flower-spikes to 10cm long, are borne on the old wood, and can be partially hidden by the foliage. Flowering can be sporadic through the year, with the main flowering between November and April.
H O SS W L SA G C1 F2   Chart 7 (5, 10, 25, 26, 37)

Melaleuca linariifolia — Snow in Summer Qld, NSW
A well-known small tree, with soft papery bark. Plants grow 5-10m high by 3-6m wide. The light green leaves are narrow, pointed, and up to 4cm long. White to light cream flowers are produced in dense terminal clusters, which can literally cover the foliage. Flowering is usually between November and February.
H O SS W L SA G C1 F2   Charts 5, 32 (26)

Melaleuca megacephala WA
A much-branched shrub of 1.5-3m high by a similiar width. The green to grey-green leaves are broad and thick, and up to 2.5cm long. Deep cream to yellow, globular flower-heads of about 2-3cm diameter, are produced on branchlet tips, between the months of September and December.
H O SS D L SA G C1 F2   Chart 3 (10, 25)

Melaleuca micromera WA
This is initially an upright, dense shrub, of up to 2.5m high, but it can spread with age to a width of 1-2m. The leaves are very small, giving a conifer-like appearance. Globular yellow flower-heads, which look similar to those of a wattle, are produced during the flowering season of August-September.
H O SS M W L SA G C1 F2   Charts 28, 35 (3, 10, 12, 25)

Melaleuca nematophylla — Wiry Honey-myrtle WA
(Previously known as *M.filifolia*)
This species grows to 2.5m high by 2m wide. The needle-like leaves are up to 10cm long, but are smooth and not prickly. The flower-heads are globular, up to 3cm in diameter, and are mauve-pink with gold anthers. They are produced on the ends of the branchlets. Flowering is mainly between August and November, but can also be at other times throughout the year.
H·O SS D L SA G C1 F2   Chart 25 (3, 10)

Melaleuca nesophila — Showy Honey-myrtle WA
A hardy, and relatively dense shrub, growing to 3-6m high by 2-5m wide. The dark green leaves are leathery, and oblong to 2.5cm long. New growth is often bronze. Globular flower-heads of about 2.5cm diameter are produced usually between December and March. They are an attractive mauve-pink with gold anthers.
H O SS W L SA G C1 F1   Charts 5, 40 (26, 34)

Melaleuca pulchella — Claw Flower WA
A small shrub of 1-1.5m high by up to 2m wide. The leaves are oval, to 0.5cm long, crowded, and grey-green. Flowering is between November and February, when mauve-pink flowers with claw-like stamens are produced along the branches.
H O SS M W L SA G C1 F1   Chart 4 (2, 10, 25)

Melaleuca seriata WA
This upright species grows to a height of 1.5-2m. The leaves are silvery-green, narrow, and up to about 2cm long. Pink flower-heads are produced at the ends of the branchlets, with the main flowering period being from November to January.
H O SS D L SA G C1 F1   Charts 28, 35 (5, 12, 25)

Melaleuca spathulata WA
This species is initially an upright plant to 2m high, later spreading to a width of 1-1.5m. The leaves are spoon-shaped to 1cm long. Deep pink globular flower-heads are produced in dense clusters at the ends of the branchlets. Flowering period is October to December.
H O SS M W L SA G C1 F1   Charts 26, 35 (3)

Melaleuca thymifolia —   Qld, NSW
Thyme Honey-myrtle
A compact shrub of 0.5-1.5m tall by 1-1.5m wide. The leaves are narrow, to 1cm long, greyish-green and crowded. Flowers are mauve to purple, with claw-like stamens. They are produced on short spikes, scattered along the older wood. The main flowering period is between October and April. A useful small shrub for a moist situation.
H O SS M W L SA C1 F1   Charts 4, 18, 26 (2, 6)

Melaleuca violacea WA
This species often grows as a flat-topped shrub, with a height of 1-2m by a similar width. The leaves are opposite, heart-shaped, stalkless, about 1cm long, and greyish-green. Flowers are purple to violet, and may be in clusters along the old wood, or terminal. Flowering period is mainly September-October. A prostrate form of this species is also available.
H O SS W L SA G C1 F1   Chart 26 (3)

Melaleuca wilsonii — Violet Honey-myrtle Vic, SA
An open to fairly dense shrub, of 1-2.5m high by 1-3m wide. The leaves are narrow, to 1.5cm long, and dull

green. The flowers are lilac to reddish pink, and are borne in clusters of up to 10cm in length, along the older branches. Flowering is mainly during September-October. Excellent for bird-attraction.
H O SS W L SA G C1 F2   Chart 37 (3, 10, 25)

Mentha diemenica —   NSW, Vic, Tas, SA
Slender Mint (Previously known as *M.gracilis*)
This species spreads by suckering, and grows to 0.2m high by 0.5-1m wide. The leaves of about 2-3cm long are oval to oblong, and aromatic. Small mauve flowers are produced in terminal spikes, mainly between September and February.
H O SS M W L SA C1 F2   Charts 1, 29 (13, 26, 27)

Micromyrtus ciliata — Fringed Heath-myrtle Vic, SA
A spreading shrub of 0.1m-1m high by 1-2m wide. The minute leaves are aromatic, and crowded along the stems, often overlapping. Flowering is between May and November, with a profuse display of small flowers along the branchlets. The buds are white to pink, opening to white flowers, which then deepen with age to red.
O SS M W L SA G C1 F2   Chart 2 (8, 23, 25)

Mirbelia dilatata   WA
This much-branched shrub grows to 2-3m high by 1-2m wide. The leaves are 2-4cm long, and are wedge-shaped with a pungent, wavy, toothed margin at the tip. Profuse blue to rosy purple pea-shaped flowers are borne, either individually or in clusters, during the flowering period of September to November.
H O SS L SA G C1 F1   Chart 12 (3, 10, 25, 36)

Mirbelia oxyloboides — Mountain Mirbelia NSW, Vic
A bushy shrub of 2-3m high by a similar width. The dark green leaves are oblong, and about 0.5cm long. During the flowering period of October to December, there is a profuse display of bright yellow and red pea-shaped flowers of about 1cm diameter. The seed pods are hairy and decorative.
O SS L SA G F2   Chart 34 (3, 38)

Myoporum debile — Sprawling Myoporum Qld, NSW
This matting plant spreads to around 1m wide, and will cascade if in a suitable situation. The stems are reddish, and the dark green leaves are lance-shaped, often with toothed margins. Small white to pink flowers are produced along the stems at various times throughout the year, and these are followed by pink to reddish berries.
H O SS D M L SA G C1 F1   Chart 30 (15, 18, 19, 23)

Myoporum floribundum —   NSW, Vic
Slender Myoporum
A graceful shrub, usually with horizontal branches. It grows to a height of 2.5-4m, by 2-3m wide. The drooping leaves are very narrow, up to 10cm long, dark green and smooth. Small white, scented flowers, are borne in clusters on the upper side of the branchlets. Main flowering period is November to January.
O SS D L SA G C1 F2   Chart 12 (5, 27, 37)

Myoporum parvifolium —   Vic, Tas, SA, WA
Creeping Myoporum
This prostrate species grows 1-3m wide, and spreads by layering. The bright green, narrow leaves are about 2-4cm long, and a form with purplish foliage can also be obtained. Flowering is between November and March, when small flowers of white or rarely pink are displayed along the branchlets, near the tips.
H O SS W L SA G C2 F2   Charts 19, 23, 40 (4, 10, 15)

Myriophyllum propinquum — Water-milfoil All States
This species will form a dense mat in wet soils, or in shallow water. It has bright green, conifer-like branchlets. Small white or pink flowers are produced in clusters, on erect stems, mainly from September to April.
Aquatic   Chart 39 (26)

Nephrolepis cordifolia —   Qld, NSW, WA, NT
Fish-bone Fern
This fern is very well-known in cultivation. It grows 0.5-1m high, and spreads by runners, creating a dense clump 0.5-2m wide. It is tolerant of a wide range of conditions, including full sun. Suitable also for cultivation indoors.
·**O SS SS D M L SA C1 F1**   Chart 21 (11, 12, 27, 28)

Nothofagus cunninghamii — Myrtle Beech   Vic, Tas
This is a relatively slow-growing tree, with a mature height of 5-15m, by 3-6m wide. The foliage is dense, with smooth, shiny, oval, toothed leaves of 1-2cm long. New growth is reddish to bronze. Small brownish flowers are produced in clusters at the ends of branchlets, between November and January.
O SS S M W L SA C1 F2   Chart 20 (11, 12)

Olearia ciliata —   NSW, Vic, Tas, SA, WA
Fringed Daisy-bush
A dwarf shrub of 0.3-0.5m high by 0.5m wide. The leaves are stiff, narrow, pointed, and up to 2.5cm long. They are clustered along the branchlets. Flowering period is mainly between October and January, when pale to bright purple, daisy-shaped flowerheads, of up to 3cm diameter, are produced on long stalks.
H O SS D L SA G C1 F2   Charts 2, 38 (4, 10, 25)

Olearia frostii — Bogong Daisy-bush   Vic
This shrub grows to 1.5m high by a similar width. The leaves are woolly grey-green, and oblong, to a length of about 2.5cm. Daisy-shaped flowers of 2-3cm diameter are borne on long stems above the foliage. They are commonly mauve, but can be pink or white. Flowering is usually between November and February. Regular tip pruning is recommended for this species.
O SS D M L SA G F2   Chart 4 (38)

Olearia iodochroa — Violet Daisy-bush   NSW, Vic
A rounded shrub of 1-1.5m high by a similar width, with many branches. The leaves are oval, to 0.5cm long, with a shiny, dark green upper surface. Flowering is between September and November, when large numbers of daisy flowers, of up to 2cm in diameter are

produced. The flowers have a violet centre, with white to violet rays.

O SS D M L SA G C1 F2   Chart 27 (2, 38)

Olearia phlogopappa —   NSW, Vic, Tas
Dusty Daisy-bush
This is a fast-growing, upright shrub, with a height of 1.5-2.5m by width of 1-2m. The oblong leaves of around 5cm long, often have wavy margins, and are greyish green and hairy. Daisy flowers of up to 2cm diameter are borne in profusion between July and November. Flower colour can be white, pink, blue or purple. Regular tip pruning is recommended.

O SS D M L SA G C1 F2   Chart 33 (3, 11, 38)

Olearia teretifolia —   NSW, Vic, SA
Cypress Daisy-bush
The foliage of this species has a similar appearance to that of a conifer, with leaves of under 0.5cm long, dark green, sticky, and crowded on the branchlets. Plants can grow 1-2m high by 0.5-1.5m wide, but a dwarf form, sold as *O.teretifolia* 'Compact Form', is the most commonly available. A profuse display of small white daisy-flowers of up to 1cm diameter can be seen during September-November. The flowers are borne in dense terminal clusters.

O SS D M L SA G C1 F2   Chart 12 (2, 28, 38)

Olearia tomentosus — Toothed Daisy-bush   NSW, Vic
(Previously known as *O.dentata*)
This species grows to 3m high by 1-3m wide, and plants are of a variable dense, to open habit. The soft, oval leaves have toothed margins. Daisy flowers of 2-4cm diameter are produced on long stalks above the foliage, usually between August and November. Flower colour is commonly white, or rarely pale mauve. Regular tip pruning is recommended.

O SS D M L SA C1 F2   Chart 11 (2, 3, 38)

Orthrosanthus laxus — Morning Iris   WA
This is a tufting perennial, with erect, narrow, strap-like leaves, forming a clump 0.3-0.6m high by around 0.5m wide. Flowering is between August and November, and although the flowers open for 1 day only, they are produced over a long period. Clusters of up to 3, pale to deep blue flowers, are borne on loosely branched stems, and each flower is 2-3cm in diameter, with 6 open petals.

O SS D M L SA G C1 F1   Chart 16 (2, 18, 24)

Orthrosanthus multiflorus — Morning Flag Vic, SA, WA
This species is very similar to *O.laxus*, but usually has a more robust growth habit, growing to 0.75m high by up to 1m wide. The flowers are normally in clusters of 4 or more.

O SS D M L SA G C1 F1   Chart 24 (2, 16, 18)

Oxylobium tricuspidatum   WA
This prostrate ground-covering species spreads to a width of around 1m. The wedge-shaped, grey-green leaves are opposite, and each has 3 small prickles at the tip. Pea-shaped flowers of orange and yellow with brown are produced along the branchlet tips, usually between September and November.

O SS D M L SA C1 F1   Charts 15, 19 (2, 18, 23)

Pandorea jasminoides — Bower Climber   Qld, NSW
A vigorous climber, with shiny, dark green, pinnate leaves. The flowers are trumpet-like, and white to pink with a deep red hairy throat. Flowering period is mainly December to March. Frost tender.

O SS D M L SA C1   Chart 31 (5)

Pandorea pandorana —   Qld, NSW, Vic, Tas
Wonga Vine
This strong climber is variable in foliage and flower. The leaves are pinnate, and fine to coarse. The flowers are tubular, and cream to brown, with cream to red-dish throats. They are produced in loose terminal clusters, with the main flowering between July and November.

O S SS D M L SA C1 F1   Chart 31 (3, 27)

Passiflora cinnabarina — Red Passion-flower NSW, Vic
This climber is usually vigorous in cultivation. The leaves are tri-lobed, to 10cm across, and dark green. Bright coppery-red flowers of up to 5cm diameter, hang on individual stalks from the leaf axils, and are produced mainly between September and December. Flowers are followed by oval green fruits of about 3cm diameter, which do not have a pleasant taste.

O SS D M W L SA G C1 F1   Chart 31 (38)

Patersonia fragilis —   Qld, NSW, Vic, Tas, SA
Short Purple Flag
A tufted perennial, with narrow, rush-like leaves to 0.5m high, forming a clump of similar width. The purple flowers have 3 petals, and are borne on stems shorter than the leaves. Flowering is over a long period between October and February, with each flower lasting one day only.

H O SS M L SA G C1 F2   Chart 16 (2, 4, 18, 24, 38)

Patersonia occidentalis — Purple Flags Vic, Tas, SA, WA
This species now includes the form previously known as *P. longiscapa*. Plants are of similar habit to *P. fragilis*, however the flowers are borne on stems which are either the same length as the leaves or longer. An excellent small clump-forming plant for moist to wet areas. Plants in this species are the most commonly cultivated of the Patersonias.

H O SS M W L SA G C1 F1   Charts 24, 35 (2, 4, 16, 18, 26, 38)

Patersonia sericea — Silky Purple Flag Qld, NSW, Vic
The leaves of this species are narrow and grass-like. It is of similar habit to the other patersonias previously described, but flowering is mainly between September and December, with deep purple-blue flowers borne on woolly stems of about 30cm long. The bracts are also woolly.

H O SS M L SA G C1 F2   Chart 1 (2, 10, 16, 18, 25, 38)

Pellaea falcata — Sickle Fern   Qld, NSW, Vic, Tas
This hardy fern spreads by creeping rhizomes. It grows 0.3-0.6m high by 0.5-1m wide. The fronds are of fish-bone shape, and are more or less erect. They have narrow pinnae, with undulating margins.

O S SS D M L SA C1 F2   Chart 21 (11, 12, 27, 28)

Persoonia pinifolia —   Qld, NSW
Pine-leaved Geebung
This is a most attractive shrub, but it can be difficult to propagate, and therefore plants are not always readily obtainable. It grows 2-5m high by 2-3m wide, with fine green foliage, and often reddish new growth. Small yellow flowers are produced in terminal spikes of up to 20cm long. Flowering period is mainly from December through to May, and the flowers are followed by attractive clusters of fleshy, greenish fruits.
O SS D L SA G C1 F2   Chart 5 (7, 28, 30, 34)

Petrophile biloba — Granite Petrophile   WA
This is usually an upright shrub of 1-2m high. The two-lobed leaves are stiff, prickly, and hairy when young. Clusters of small, pink and grey flowers, are produced in the upper axils. Flowering period is between July and September.
H O SS D L SA G C1 F1   Chart 10 (3, 9, 25)

Petrophile serruriae —   WA
This species grows to 2-3m high by a similiar width. The branches are arching and the leaves finely divided and prickly. Flowering is profuse, with clusters of pink to yellow flowers, borne in the upper leaf axils, during the period October-December.
H O SS D L SA G C1 F2   Chart 3 (10, 12. 25, 36)

Phebalium bullatum — Desert Phebalium   Vic, SA
An open shrub, of 0.5-1.5m high by 1m wide. The leaves are small and scaly, with a silver undersurface. Small, bright yellow, star-like flowers are produced in terminal clusters during the flowering period of September to December.
H O SS D L SA G F2   Chart 10 (3, 25)

Phebalium lamprophyllum —   NSW, Vic
Shiny Phebalium
A bushy shrub, growing to 1-2m high by 1-1.5m wide. The leaves are oval to oblong, and are shiny dark green. Flowering is between September and December, when white to cream flowers are borne in dense terminal clusters.
O SS D M L SA G F2   Chart 11 (2, 27, 38)

Phebalium squamulosum ssp *ozothamnoides* NSW, Vic
(Previously known as *P.ozothamnoides*)
This is a busy shrub of 1-3m high by 1-2m wide. It has smooth, oblong, blunt leaves of about 1cm long, with a white undersurface. Small, bright yellow flowers are produced in dense terminal clusters, usually between October and January.
H O SS D L SA G C1 F2   Chart 25 (3, 5, 38)

Pimelea ferruginea —   WA
A dense shrub of 0.5-1.5m high by a similar width. The leaves are about 1.25cm long, oblong, shiny, and crowded along the branchlets. Pink flower-heads of about 3cm diameter are borne on the branchlet tips, and provide a massed display mainly between July and October. Plants respond well to pruning.
O SS D M L SA C2 F1   Charts 2, 38, 40 (8)

Pimelea spectabilis —   WA
This species can prove difficult under garden conditions, however it can be grown successfully in con-

tainers, and even if it is not long-lived, the spectacular display it provides makes it worthy of growing. Plants grow to 0.5-1.5m high by a similar width, and have narrow, smooth, grey-green leaves to 4cm long. Flower-heads of up to 5cm diameter are produced on branchlet tips, mainly between September and November. Flowering is profuse, with flower colour mainly white, sometimes tinged with pink. Plants respond well to pruning.
SS D M L SA C1 F1   Charts 17, 38 (2, 3)

Pittosporum phillyraeoides —   Qld, NSW, Vic, SA,
Butterbush   WA, NT
An upright shrub to small tree, with a height of 3-6m, by width of 1.5-3m. The bark is often whitish, and branches are usually pendulous. The leaves are 5-10cm long, narrow, flat and leathery. Yellow, scented flowers of 1-2cm wide are produced, either individually or in clusters, during the period September-November. The flowers are followed by decorative yellow fruits of about 1.5cm long.
H O SS D L SA G C1 F2   Chart 30 (27, 32)

Platycerium bifurcatum — Elkhorn   Qld, NSW
This is the most common, and widespread, Elkhorn fern in Australia. Whilst listed as suitable for container growing, plants grow best if they are not actually in containers, but are grown as epiphytes, and tied to slabs of tree-fern or timber. They can form quite large clumps, and require little attention apart from watering, and light applications of fertilizer. Plants may also be grown successfully on large tree trunks.
S SS D C1 F1   Chart 21

Platytheca verticillata — Platytheca   WA
This is a dwarf shrub of open habit. It grows to a height of around 0.5m, by a width of 0.5-1m. The leaves are up to 2cm long, very narrow, and in whorls around the branchlets. Flowering continues over a long period, mainly between March and December, with pendant, purple flowers to 2cm diameter, scattered throughout the bush.
O SS D M L SA F1   Chart 6 (2, 8, 18)

Plectranthus argentatus —   Qld
This is dense, rounded shrub, of 0.5-1m high by 1-2m wide. The toothed leaves are about 8cm long by 4cm wide, and are hairy, greyish and aromatic. Small pale blue flowers, with a spicy fragrance, are produced in long terminal spikes, mainly between September and April. This species has been available as *P.spectabilis*.
O SS SS D L SA G C1 F1   Chart 29 (12, 13, 27, 28)

Poa caespitosa — Snow Grass   All States
This is a soft grass, which often attains greyish tonings. It usually grows as a clump of 0.1-0.3m high by 0.5-1m wide. The flower-heads can be quite decorative, with purplish tonings. Flowering is between October and February. Plants are often sold as *Poa australis*.
H O SS D M L SA C1 F2   Chart 24 (16)

Podocarpus lawrencei —   NSW, Vic, Tas
Mountain Plum Pine
A dwarf conifer, of 1-2m high by a similar width. The

ornamental, narrow-oblong leaves are about 1.5cm long, and are dark green to grey-green, rigid, leathery, and aromatic. On mature plants the bark is papery, brown, and quite ornamental. Sometimes sold as *P.alpina*.

O SS D M L SA C1 F2   Chart 12 (11, 27, 28)

Polyscias sambucifolius —   Qld, NSW, Vic
Elderberry Panax (Previously known as *Tieghemopanax sambucifolius*)
An upright species, growing 4–6m high by 1–3m wide. The stems are often purplish, with olive-green, pinnate leaves, of up to 30cm long. Small greenish flowers are produced in September to December, and these are followed by bluish berries.

O S SS D M W L SA C1 F2   Chart 30 (11, 12, 27)

Polystichum proliferum —   NSW, Vic, Tas
Mother Shield-fern
This fern is commonly cultivated, because of its adaptability. It grows 0.5–1.5m high by 1–2m wide. The arching fronds are dark dull green, and divided. The frond stems have many brown scales, and young plants are often produced at the frond tips.

O S SS D M L SA C1 F2   Chart 21 (11, 12, 27, 28)

Pomaderris lanigera —   Qld, NSW, Vic
Woolly Pomaderris
This species grows as an upright shrub, to 2–4m high by 1.5–3m wide, and has an open habit. The branches are hairy, and the leaves of around 6cm by 3cm are soft and woolly. Small yellow flowers arranged in dense terminal clusters are produced, mainly between September and November.

O S SS D M L SA F1   Chart 27 (3)

Pratia erecta   Qld
This is a dense spreading ground cover, covering an area of up to 1m. It has narrow, light green leaves, and small white flowers are held erect on short stems above the foliage. Flowering is mainly between September and February.

H O SS M W L SA C1 F1   Chart 18 (2, 4, 19, 23, 38)

Pratia pedunculata   NSW, Vic, Tas
This prostrate species forms a dense carpeting plant of 0.5–2m wide. The leaves are small, oval, and toothed. Small star-like flowers of blue or white are borne in profusion, mainly between October and April.

H O SS M W L SA C1 F2   Charts 1, 18, 38 (2, 4, 6, 23)

Prostanthera aspalathoides   NSW, Vic, SA
This dense, dwarf shrub, grows to 0.5m high by 0.3–1m wide. The leaves are fine and narrow, and are strongly aromatic. The flowers are narrow-tubular, being broadest at the tip. They are produced in the leaf axils, and various colour forms including red, orange, yellow, and rarely white, are obtainable. Flowering is mainly between September and February, but sporadic flowering can occur at other times also.

O SS D L SA G C1 F2   Chart 10 (2, 4, 25, 29)

Prostanthera chlorantha — Green Mint-bush   SA
A low, spreading, open shrub of up to 0.5m high by 1m wide. The branches are hairy, with minute, hairy, aromatic leaves. Flowering is mainly between August and March, when pale green tubular flowers of around 2cm long are produced. Honey-eating birds are attracted to these flowers.

O SS D L SA G C1 F2   Chart 37 (2, 4, 6, 14, 29)

Prostanthera cuneata —   NSW, Vic, Tas
Alpine Mint-bush
There are several forms of this species, ranging from 0.3–1.5m high by 0.5–1.5m wide. A low spreading form is the most commonly cultivated. It is a dense shrub, with oval, lobed, smooth, dark green, highly aromatic leaves, to 1cm long. Flowering period is October to March, when tubular white flowers with purple or yellow blotches inside the throat, are produced from the leaf axils. Mauve to pink flowered forms are also sometimes available.

O S SS D M L SA C1 F2   Chart 11 (2, 4, 27, 29)

Prostanthera hirtula (prostrate form) —   NSW
Hairy Mint-bush
(Often incorrectly known as *P.denticulata*)
This is a variable species, and the form chosen for inclusion here is commonly sold as 'Prostrate Form'. It usually grows 0.1–0.5m high by 1–1.5m wide. The foliage is dense, with small aromatic leaves scattered along the branches. Flowering is between September and December, when mauve to purple flowers are produced in terminal clusters.

O SS D M L SA C1 F1   Chart 3 (23, 29)

Prostanthera incana   Qld, NSW
A bushy shrub of 1–2m high by a similar width. The leaves are about 1.5cm long, and are soft, hairy, wrinkled and often grey-green. Flowering period is August–November, when tubular flowers are borne in profuse clusters near the ends of the branchlets. Flower colour can be lavender to blue, or white.

O S SS D M L SA C1 F1   Chart 28 (3, 11)

Prostanthera incisa   Qld, NSW, Vic
A spreading shrub of 1–2m high by a similar width. The leaves are 1–2cm long, oval, toothed, and very aromatic. The flowers are usually purple, but pink flowered forms are also available. Profuse clusters of flowers are borne at the ends of branchlets, usually between September and November.

O S SS D M L SA C1 F2   Chart 29 (3, 11, 13, 27)

Prostanthera lasianthos —   Qld, NSW, Vic, Tas
Victorian Christmas Bush
This is a shrub to small tree, growing to 2–6m high by 2–3m wide. The dark green leaves are about 10cm long, and have toothed margins. Tubular flowers are produced in dense heads near the ends of the branchlets. They are usually white with purple dots in the throat, but pale mauve, and pink forms are also available. Flowering time is November–January.

O S SS D M W L SA C1 F2   Chart 11 (5, 27, 29)

Prostanthera melissifolia — Balm Mint-bush   Vic
A bushy, compact shrub, of 1.5–3m high by 1–2m wide. The dark green leaves are strongly aromatic, 2.5–5cm long, oval, and sometimes toothed. Tubular

flowers of violet to deep lilac are borne in dense terminal clusters near the ends of the branches. Flowering period is October to January.
O S SS D M W L SA C1 F2   Charts 11, 13 (3, 27, 29)

Prostanthera microphylla — Qld, NSW, Vic, SA, WA
Small-leaf Mint-bush
This low shrub of 0.3-0.5m tall by 1m wide, is of relatively open, dwarf habit. The leaves are small, hairy, scattered along the branches, and aromatic. Flowering period is between September and February, when red or bluish green, tubular flowers, are scattered over the plant. An excellent bird-attracting species.
H O SS D L SA G C1 F2   Chart 14 (2, 4, 37)

Prostanthera ovalifolia   Qld, NSW
This is the best known of the Australian Mint-bushes. It is an upright to spreading shrub of 2-4m high by 2-3m wide. Leaves are oval, to 1.5cm long, sometimes toothed, and strongly aromatic. The flowers are usually purple, but there are also pink and white forms. They are produced in dense clusters near the ends of the branchlets. Flowering is mainly between September and December. There are several forms of this species, including low-growing, compact forms. Plants respond well to pruning.
O SS D M L SA C1 F2   Chart 27 (3, 13, 29)

Prostanthera rotundifolia —   NSW, Vic, Tas, SA
Round-leaf Mint-bush
This is a variable species, with many forms ranging in height from 1.5-2.5m by a width of 1-3m. Plants are usually fairly compact, with aromatic round to oval leaves, up to 1.5cm long, sometimes toothed. Mauve to purple flowers are borne in profusion near the ends of branchlets. There is also a pink flowered form, known as *P.rotundifolia* 'Rosea'. The flowering period is August to November.
O S SS D M L SA C1 F2   Charts 13, 27 (3, 11, 29)

Prostanthera spinosa — Spiny Mint-bush NSW, Vic, SA
A variable species of 1-1.5m high by 1-2m wide. A dense, spreading form from the Grampians (Vic) is common in cultivation. It has spreading branches, with narrow spines, and very small oval leaves. Lilac to lavender flowers are produced at the ends of short branchlets. A white-flowered form is also obtainable. Flowering period is September-March.
O S SS D L SA G C1 F2   Chart 36 (3, 5)

Prostanthera stricta   NSW
This species grows to 1-2m high by a similar width. It is of dense habit, with spreading branches, and hairy leaves of about 0.5cm long. Flowering period is around September-October, when deep purple flowers are produced in the leaf axils, near the ends of the branchlets.
O S SS D M L SA G C1 F2   Chart 34 (3, 11, 29)

Prostanthera violacea   NSW
This dense, much-branched shrub, grows to 1-2m tall by a similar width. The leaves are very small, oval, wrinkled and aromatic. Violet coloured flowers are produced in small heads, near the ends of the branchlets. The flowering period is August-December.
O SS D M L SA G C1 F2   Chart 29 (2, 11, 13, 27)

Prostanthera walteri —   NSW, Vic
Monkey Mint-bush
A spreading species of up to 1m high by 2m wide. The leaves are up to 4cm long, oval to oblong, and dark green. The unusual flowers are greenish with purple streaks. They are 2-3cm long, and produced in heads from the leaf axils. Flowering period is mainly from November-February.
O S SS D L SA G C1 F2   Chart 11 (5, 23, 27)

Pterostylis concinna —   Qld, NSW, Vic, Tas
Trim Greenhood
This terrestrial orchid grows well in containers, often forming dense colonies. It has a basal rosette, supporting a slender flower-stem of up to 0.3m high. Each stem bears a solitary green and white striped flower, with brown markings. Flowering period is May to October.
Pterostylis species do not appreciate watering during their dormancy period, and protection from slugs and snails is vital for successful cultivation.
O S SS L SA C1 F2   Chart 22

Pterostylis curta —   Qld, NSW, Vic, Tas
Blunt Greenhood
This species forms a basal rosette of wavy leaves, and produces single flowers on stems up to 0.3m high. Flowering is between July and October. The flowers are mainly green, but have red and brown markings. The lobes are very fine, erect and very short. Cultivation requirements are similar to that *P.concinna*.
O S SS L SA C1 F2   Chart 22

Pterostylis nutans —   Qld, NSW, Vic, Tas, SA
Nodding Greenhood
This is a very distinctive greenhood, which forms a basal rosette of about 5 wavy-edged leaves. It flowers between July and November, and has nodding, translucent green flowers, on stems up to 0.3m high. It is one of the easiest *Pterostylis* species to grow, and will form dense colonies. Cultivation requirements are as mentioned for *P.concinna*.
O S SS L SA C1 F2   Chart 22

Pterostylis pedunculata —   Qld, NSW, Vic, Tas, SA
Maroonhood
The flowers on this species are borne on slender stems up to 0.3m high. They usually have green and white stripes, with the hood tip mainly maroon or reddish-brown. There is a basal rosette of 3-6 heavily veined leaves. Flowering is between July and November. See *P.concinna* for cultivation requirements.
O S SS L SA C1 F2   Chart 22

Pultenaea daphnoides —   NSW, Vic, Tas, SA
Large-leaved Bush-pea
This species, which grows 1.5-2m high by 1-2m wide, is of open to fairly dense growth. The olive-green leaves are 2-4cm long, and wedge-shaped. Small pea-shaped flowers of yellow with red or brown, are borne

in terminal heads during the flowering period of September-November.

O S SS D L SA G C1 F1   Chart 11 (3, 27, 38)

Pultenaea graveolens — Scented Bush-pea   Vic, SA
A compact shrub of 1-1.5m high by a similar width. The branchlets are pendulous, and the small, narrow leaves are often hairy, and have a spicy aroma. Pea-shaped flowers of yellow with red are produced in the leaf axils. Flowering period is mainly October-November.

O SS D L SA G C1 F2   Chart 29 (2, 11, 13)

Pultenaea pedunculata —   NSW, Vic, Tas, SA
Matted Bush-pea
This spreading plant grows to 0.5m high by 1-2m wide, and will often layer. The small leaves give the foliage a moss-like appearance. Flowering period is September-December, when there is a profuse display of pea-shaped flowers. Usual flower colour is orange or yellow with red, but a pink flowered form is also available.

H O SS M L SA G C1 F2   Charts 1, 19, 38 (2, 18, 23)

Pultenaea subalpina — Rosy Bush-pea   Vic
This compact shrub grows 0.5-1.5m high by 1-1.5m wide. The leaves are small, narrow, blunt and greyish-green. The flower colour of pink to purple is unusual for this genus, and the pea-shaped flowers are produced in terminal clusters, mainly between September and December.

O SS D L SA G F2   Chart 17 (2, 3)

Pultenaea subternata   NSW
A small shrub of 1-1.5m high by a similar width, with branchlets sometimes pendulous. The greyish green leaves are up to 1cm long, oval, pungent pointed, and often in threes. Flowering is between September and December, when yellow with red pea-flowers are produced in the upper leaf axils.

O SS D L SA G F2   Chart 28 (3, 12)

Pyrrosia rupestris — Rock Felt-fern   Qld, NSW, Vic
This fern has creeping rhizomes, and grows 0.1-0.2m high by 0.5-1m wide. The fronds are strap-like, and covered with soft hairs, which can give them a rusty appearance. Plants will grow well on a slab of timber, tree-fern, or rock, or on a large tree. Suitable also for hanging baskets.

O S SS D C1 F2   Chart 21

Ranunculus collinus —   NSW, Vic, Tas
Strawberry Buttercup
This perennial species is usually a small prostrate plant, of 0.5-1.5m wide, with shiny, lobed leaves. Bright yellow flowers of 1-2cm diameter are produced, mainly between November and January. Plants are sometimes sold as *R.rivularis*.

H O SS M W L SA C1 F2   Charts 26, 39 (1, 4, 23)

Regelia ciliata   WA
This species grows 1.5-2.5m high by 2-3m wide. The leaves are small, stem-hugging, and hairy. Globular mauve to purple flower-heads of about 2cm diameter,

are produced at the ends of the branchlets, during the flowering period of November-March.

H O SS W L SA G C1 F1   Charts 10, 34 (5, 25)

Regelia cymbifolia   WA
An upright shrub, growing to 2.5m high by 1-2m wide. The leaves are oval, small, opposite, and crowded flat against the branches. The purplish-red flower-heads are in loose spikes of up to 2cm long. They are produced on the branchlet tips, mainly between September and December.

H O SS D L SA G C1 F2   Chart 10 (3, 25)

Regelia velutina   WA
This is an upright shrub of 2.5-4m high by 1-2m wide. The leaves are opposite, and hairy giving a greyish appearance. The flower-spikes are up to 4cm long, and bright red with gold tips. They are produced on the ends of the branchlets, between August and January. This species can take a number of years before the first flowering.

H O SS D L SA G C2 F2   Charts 12, 40 (3, 5, 10, 14, 25, 37)

Restio tetraphyllus —   All States except WA
Tassel-cord Rush
This is a decorative rush, with upright green stems bearing soft foliage at the tips. Plants grow 1.5-2m high by 1-2m wide. Tassels of brown or reddish flowers are produced along the tips, mainly between September and December. A very attractive plant for use beside a pond.

H O SS M W L SA C1 F2   Charts 24, 39 (12, 26, 28)

Rhagodia spinescens —   Inland regions of all States
Hedge Saltbush
A dense, spreading perennial, with greyish hairy triangular leaves. Plants often remain prostrate, but will sometimes grow to about 1m high. An excellent ground-cover. Plants of this species are sometimes sold as *Rhagodia* species, or *R.nutans*. Flowers are insignificant.

H O SS L SA G C2 F2   Chart 28 (10, 12, 23)

Rhododendron lochae   Qld
This Australian rhododendron will grow 1-1.5m high by 1-2m wide under garden conditions. It has red stems, with oval, smooth, shiny leaves to 10cm long by 5cm wide. Flowering is mainly between January and April, when waxy, red, bell-shaped flowers to 5cm long are produced in terminal heads.

S SS D M L SA F1   Charts 6, 11, 18 (27)

Scaevola aemula —   NSW, Vic, Tas, SA, WA
Fairy Fan-flower
This is a variable species. It can form a clump to 0.7m high, or spread as a ground-cover to 1.5m wide. The light green leaves are oblong, with toothed margins, and are slightly hairy. Fan-shaped flowers, about 2-3cm wide, and blue with yellow, are borne along the ends of the branchlets. Flowering is mainly between September and February, but sporadic flowering also occurs at other times.

O S SS D M L SA C1 F2   Chart 15 (2, 5, 18, 19, 23)

Scaevola hookeri —   NSW, Vic, Tas
Creeping Fan-flower
A mat plant from sub-alpine regions. Plants spread
0.5-1m wide, and have small shiny leaves with
toothed margins. The flowering period is November
to March, when there is a profuse display of small
white to mauve flowers, produced in the upper leaf
axils.
H O SS M W L SA C1 F2   Charts 26, 38 (2, 4, 23)

Scaevola microphylla   WA
This is a medium to dense carpeting species, growing
0.2m high by 1-2m wide. The small leaves are oblong,
toothed and hairy. Small pale blue fan-shaped flowers
are produced at the ends of the branchlets. Flowering
is profuse between October and January, with
sporadic flowers at other times.
O SS D M L SA C1 F1   Chart 19 (2, 4, 15, 23)

Scaevola phlebopetala — Royal Robe   WA
A loosely spreading perennial, growing 0.2-0.3m
high by 0.5-2m wide. The leaves are an elongated
wedge-shape, to 6cm long, and hairy. The flowers are
deep purple with gold (hence the common name of
Royal Robe) and are produced mainly between
November and May.
O SS D M L SA C1 F1   Chart 15 (4, 6, 19, 23)

Scaevola striata — Royal Robe   WA
This species has spreading stems, and grows 0.2-0.5m
high by 1-2m wide. It can spread by suckering. The
leaves are about 5cm long by 2.5cm wide, wedge-
shaped, with toothed margins, hairy and leathery.
Mauve to bluish-purple flowers of about 2.5cm
diameter are produced at the ends of short branchlets.
Main flowering period is October to February. Can be
frost tender.
O SS D M L SA C1   Charts 5, 38 (2, 3, 4, 23)

Schefflera actinophylla — Umbrella Tree   Qld, NT
This small tree grows 5-8m high by 3-4m wide. It has
an upright trunk and a canopy of large shiny leaves
radiating from the branch tips. Small red flowers are
produced in long racemes during the flowering period
of March to September. Plants are frost tender, and are
best grown indoors in southern Australia.
H O SS D M L SA C1   Chart 20 (10)

Scholtzia involucrata   WA
This species grows 0.5-1m high by about 1m wide. It
has spreading branches, and small, smooth, oval
leaves, crowded along the branchlets. Pale pink tea-
tree-like flowers are produced in long, dense clusters
near the ends of the branchlets. Flowering is usually
sporadic throughout the year.
O SS D M L SA G C1 F1   Chart 4 (2, 6, 25)

Scleranthus biflorus — Knawel   Qld, NSW, Vic, Tas
This moss-like plant has bright green foliage, and
provides an attractive contrast among other plants. It
is ideal for containers, or for use in conjunction with
rocks or logs. Plants have a cushion-like habit of
growth, and can spread 0.5-1m wide.
H O SS D M L SA C1 F2   Charts 1, 18 (23, 28)

Sollya heterophylla — Bluebell Creeper   WA
A dense climber, with bright green oblong leaves to
6cm long. The flowers can be blue, pink or white, and
are produced in pendant clusters from branchlet tips.
The main flowering is between September and February.
H O SS M W L SA C1 F1   Chart 31 (3, 5)

Sollya parviflora   WA
This species is a lighter climber than *S.heterophylla*,
and has narrower leaves. The flowers are of light to
deep blue, and are produced in clusters of 1-3.
H O SS M W L SA C1 F1   Chart 31 (3, 5, 15, 19)

Sowerbaea juncea —   Qld, NSW, Vic
Rush Lily, or Vanilla Lily
A clump-forming species, with grass-like foliage.
Plants grow 0.3-0.5m high by 0.5m wide. Flowering
is between October and December, when mauve
flowers are borne in globular clusters, at the ends of
fine stems longer than the foliage. The flowers have a
fragrance similar to chocolate or caramel.
H O SS M W L SA C1 F1

         Charts 16, 38 (1, 2, 13, 18, 24, 26, 29)

Spyridium cinereum — Tiny Spyridium   Vic
A prostrate species, spreading to 1m wide, with small,
greyish, wedge-shaped leaves. The flowers are relatively inconspicuous, and form small flat terminal
clusters. They are produced usually between September and April.
O SS D M L SA G C2 F1   Charts 18, 23 (12, 19, 28)

Spyridium obcordatum   Tas
This species grows 0.5-1m wide. It is usually of compact, prostrate habit, but if given support by other
plants it can reach 0.5-1m high. It has wiry branches
and small, oval green leaves. Cream flowers are produced in small dense heads, usually between September and January.
O SS D M L SA G C1 F2   Chart 4 (2, 11, 23, 27)

Spyridium parvifolium —   NSW, Vic, Tas, SA
Australian Dusty Miller
An upright shrub of 1-3m tall by 1-2m wide. The
leaves are up to 2cm long, oval, wrinkled, and sometimes hairy. Small white to cream flowers are produced in dense terminal heads, and surrounded by
grey floral leaves. Flowering period is usually
September-February. A prostrate form, *S.parvifolium*
'Austraflora Nimbus', is an excellent ground-cover or
container plant.
O SS D L SA G C1 F2   Chart 11 (12, 27, 28)

Stenocarpus sinuatus — Firewheel Tree   Qld, NSW
Under suitable garden conditions, this tree can grow
to a height of 6-15m by 3-5m wide. The leaves are
large, simple or lobed, and shiny dark green. Orange
to red flowers, arranged in wheel-like formation, are
produced mainly between January and May. A bird-
attracting species. Plants can be frost tender, especially
when young.
H O SS D M W L SA G C1   Chart 20

Stylidium bulbiferum — Circus Trigger-plant   WA
This is a low tufting plant, of 0.03-0.1m high by 0.3-0.5m wide. It has crowded narrow leaves, and plants spread by putting down aerial roots. Red, pink, or white flowers are produced on short stems, usually between September and December, and the flowers can literally cover the plant.
O SS D M L SA G C1 F1   Chart 1 (2, 4, 18, 23, 24)

Stylidium graminifolium —   Qld, NSW, Vic, Tas
Grass Trigger-plant
This clumping perennial has grass-like foliage, and grows to a height of 0.1-0.2m by width of 0.2-0.3m. Erect flower-stems of up to 1m high are produced, mainly between November and January, and bear small pale to dark pink flowers. The flowers of all trigger-plants have an unusual trigger-like pollinating mechanism.
O SS D M L SA G C1 F2   Chart 16 (1, 2, 4, 24)

Stypandra caespitosa — Tufted Lily Qld, NSW, Vic, Tas
This is a perennial, with greyish-green, grass-like leaves of 0.3-0.5m long, forming a tuft of up to 0.5m wide. The flowers have blue petals and yellow stamens, and are borne on branching upright stems of about 60cm long. There is also a cream-flowered form. Flowering is mainly between October and February.
O SS D M L SA G C1 F2   Chart 16 (2, 4, 18, 24)

Stypandra glauca —   Qld, NSW, Vic, SA
Nodding Blue-lily
This species forms a clump 1-1.5m high by a similiar width. It has blue-green grass-like leaves, which sheath the stems. The flowers usually have blue petals with yellow stamens, but a white-flowered form is also available. The flowers are produced in pendant terminal racemes, mainly between September and November.
H O SS D L SA G C1 F2   Chart 24 (2, 3, 16)

Swainsonia galegifolia — Darling Pea Qld, NSW, SA
An open, branched shrub, of 1-2m high by a similar width. The leaves are fern-like, soft, and greyish-green. Pea-shaped flowers of about 1.5cm long are displayed in terminal racemes, and can be blue to pink, through to red or brownish red. Flowering is between October and February, and is followed by decorative inflated seed pods.
H O SS W L SA G C1 F2   Chart 25 (3, 5, 10)

Symphionema montanum   NSW
This species has a compact growth habit, with a height of 0.3-1m by a similar width. It has soft stems, with light green divided leaves of 2-4cm long. The flowers are small and white, and are produced in terminal racemes. Flowering period is between October and January.
O SS D M L SA G C1 F2   Chart 28 (2, 4, 11, 18, 27)

Syzygium coolminianum   NSW
(Previously known as *Eugenia cyanocarpa*)
A small tree of 4-10m high by 3-6m wide, with dense foliage. The shiny green leaves are about 12cm long.

Delicate white flowers are produced in terminal clusters during November to January, and are followed by purple to bluish berries of about 2cm diameter.
O S SS D M L SA C1 F1   Chart 30 (32)

Telopea speciosissima — NSW Waratah   NSW
This well-known species can grow to an upright shrub of 3-5m tall by 2-3m wide. It responds well to pruning, and can be pruned to ground level every few years if desired. The leaves are up to 20cm long, oblong, tapering to the base, toothed, and dark green. Spectacular red flower-heads with decorative red bracts are produced on the ends of the branches, usually between September and November. A bird-attracting species.
O SS D M L SA G C1 F2   Chart 3 (14, 25, 37)

Templetonia retusa — Cockies Tongues   SA, WA
This species is usually of upright growth, but spreads more under coastal conditions. It has a height of 1.5-2.5m, by a width of 1-2m. The leaves are grey-green, wedge-shaped, and leathery. The pea flowers are usually pink to red, but a cream flowered form is also in cultivation. They are produced in terminal clusters to 6cm long. Flowering period is usually May-October. An excellent species for limestone soils. Plants can be frost tender, especially when young.
H O SS D W L SA G C2   Charts 9, 35, 40 (3, 10, 14, 25, 37)

Tetratheca ciliata — Pink Bells   Vic, Tas, SA
This species grows as a small clump of up to 0.5m high by 0.5-1m wide. It has upright stems, and oval leaves in threes or fours, encircling the stems. Pendant pink flowers are produced near the ends of the branchlets, between July and December. A white flowered form is also in cultivation.
O SS D M L SA G C1 F2   Chart 19 (1, 2, 8, 11, 24, 27)

Tetratheca thymifolia   Qld, NSW, Vic
A clumping perennial, of 0.5-1m tall by a similiar width. It has upright hairy stems, with leaves in groups of 3-5 surrounding the stems. The flowers are pink, pendant, and profuse during the period of August to December.
O SS D M L SA G C1 F2   Charts 24, 35 (2, 27)

Themeda australis — Kangaroo Grass   All States
This is a native grass, which forms dense tussocks of 0.5-1m high by 0.3-0.5m wide. The flowers, although very small, are decorative, and have orange-red to violet anthers that are enclosed in leaf-like bracts. They are produced on stems above the foliage, usually between October and January.
H O SS D L SA C1 F2   Chart 24 (16)

Thomasia grandiflora   WA
This is a spreading, much-branched species, which can grow to a height of 1m, by up to 1.5m wide. The dark green leaves of 4cm by 1cm are crinkled, and wavy edged. Flowering period is August to November, when pendant pink to mauve, star-like flowers of papery appearance are produced at the ends of the branchlets. *T.grandiflora* var *angustifolia* is very similar, but has narrow foliage, and smaller flowers.
O SS D L SA G C1 F1   Chart 19 (2, 11, 27)

Thomasia macrocarpa   WA
A dense-foliaged species, of 1-2m high by a similar
width. The leaves are oval to heart-shaped, up to
4-6cm long, with lobed or toothed margins, and are
covered in fine hairs, giving a light greyish appearance. Flowering period is September to November,
when mauve-pink flowers are produced in short
terminal heads.
O SS D L SA G C1 F1   Chart 34 (3, 12, 28)

Thomasia petalocalyx — Paper Flower Vic, SA, WA
This is a spreading shrub of up to 1m high by 1-2m
wide. The foliage is dense, with hairy, blunt oblong
leaves of 2-5cm long. Pendant mauve-pink flowers are
produced in terminal racemes during the flowering
period of October-December. Excellent for coastal
situations.
O SS D L SA G C2 F1   Chart 23 (2, 3, 40)

Thryptomene baeckeacea   WA
A low shrub, with arching branches. Plants can grow
0.5-1.5m high by 1-1.5m wide. The minute leaves are
aromatic, and crowded along the branches. Small
mauve-pink, tea-tree-like flowers are produced in
dense clusters in the upper leaf axils. Flowering is
mainly between March and July.
O SS D M L SA G C1 F1   Chart 6 (8, 18)

Thryptomene saxicola — Rock Thryptomene WA
This is a spreading shrub of 0.5-1.5m high by 1-2m
wide. Small aromatic leaves are crowded along the
arching branches. Flowering is mainly between April
and October, but can extend through most of the year,
with clusters of pale to deep pink flowers, produced
near the ends of the branchlets. A good cut-flower
species, and plants respond well to flower-picking, or
pruning. This species now includes *Thryptomene*
'Paynei'.
H O SS D L SA G C1 F1   Chart 8 (2, 3, 6, 7, 9, 25)

Thysanotus multiflorus — Fringe-lily   WA
A clump-forming perennial, of up to 0.5m high, with
grass-like foliage. Flowering is between November
and March, when dense heads of bright mauve flowers are produced on stems taller than the foliage. The
flower petals have a delicate fringe.
O SS D M L SA G C1 F1   Charts 16, 38, 41 (1, 4, 24)

Thysanotus tuberosus —   Qld, NSW, Vic
Common Fringe-lily
This is a perennial species, with a few, small, grass-
like leaves. Flowering is between October and
January, when mauve to rosy-purple flowers are
borne on light branched stems of about 20-30cm tall.
O S SS D M L SA G C1 F2   Chart 27 (1, 2, 4, 38)

Todea barbara — King Fern Qld, NSW, Vic, Tas, SA
The distinguishing feature of this fern is its short,
broad trunk, which can develop multiple heads of
fronds. It is a slow-growing species, but can reach a
height of 3m by a width of 2-4m. The fronds are
leathery, divided, and bright shiny green.
O S SS D M W L SA C1 F2   Chart 21 (11, 12, 26, 27)

Trachymene caerulea — Rottnest Daisy   WA
An annual species, growing up to 1m high, and flowering mainly between September and January. The
foliage is lobed, and the blue flowers are in soft heads
of up to 6cm diameter. Plants re-seed readily, and are
ideal for mass planting. Frost tender.
H O SS D M L SA C1   Chart 41

Triglochin procera — Water Ribbons   All States
A perennial with long, strap-like leaves. It has a
flower-spike about 25cm long, and produces many
small green to reddish flowers. Flowering period is
mainly September-April.
Aquatic   Chart 39

Triglochin striata — Streaked Arrow-grass All States
A creeping perennial, with rush-like or slightly flattened leaves to 50cm long. The small flowers are
borne in a spike on an erect stem to 30cm long, mainly
between September and April. Grows best in shallow
water.
Aquatic   Chart 39

Utricularia gibba   Qld, NSW, NT
A bladderwort with submerged leaves, and small yellow flowers well-displayed above the water. It is very
suitable for cultivation in shallow pools with a clay
base. Alternatively it can be planted near the edges, in
moist soil. It often spreads rapidly, and while in flower
provides an attractive display of bright yellow. Flowering is mainly September-March.
H O SS M W L SA C1 F1   Chart 39 (26)

Vallisneria spiralis —   All States
Ribbon Weed, or Eel Grass
A submerged, spreading perennial, with long, flat,
ribbon-like leaves. The female flowers are tubular and
attached to a long stem, which becomes spiralled as
the seeds develop. Flowering period is November to
June.
Aquatic   Chart 39

Verticorda densiflora   WA
This small shrub of 0.5-1m high by a similar width, is
of compact habit, with many branches. The leaves are
narrow, grey-green and aromatic. Small feathery
flowers of white to pink are produced in dense terminal heads. Flowering is profuse, mainly between
November and February.
H O SS D L SA G C1 F1   Chart 17 (2, 4, 10, 25, 38)

Verticordia monodelpha —   WA
Woolly Feather-flower
An upright to rounded shrub of 1m high by a similar
width. The grey-green leaves are aromatic, narrow
and to 1.5cm long. Small, pink woolly flowers are
produced in terminal clusters during the flowering
period of November-December. Flowering is profuse.
H O D L SA G C1 F1   Chart 10 (4, 25, 38)

Verticordia plumosa   WA
A dense shrub of up to 1m high by a similar width.
The small narrow leaves are aromatic, grey-green,

and crowded on the stems. Flowering is between September and December, when small, mauve-pink, feathery flowers are arranged in dense globular heads.
H O SS D L SA G C1 F1   Chart 25 (2, 3, 10, 38)

Villarsia reniformis —   NSW, Vic, Tas, SA
Running Marsh-flower
A perennial species that will grow in shallow water, or soils which are permanently moist to wet. It has spreading runners, and oval to kidney-shaped leaves, on long stalks. Bright yellow, 5-petalled, bearded flowers, are produced on branched stems to 1m tall. Flowering period is September to March.
Villarsia exaltata, from Qld, NSW, Vic and Tas, is very similar, but has leaves which are more pointed, and it grows as a tufted plant.
H O SS M W L SA C1 F1   Chart 39 (26)

Viola betonicifolia —   Qld, NSW, Vic, Tas, SA
Showy Violet
A tuft-forming perennial, of 0.1m high by 0.2-0.3m wide. The leaves are oblong, and on a long stalk. The flowering period is mainly September to December, when violet to purple flowers of about 2cm diameter are produced on stems up to 10cm long. The flowers are not fragrant.
O SS D M L SA F2   Chart 1 (2, 16, 18, 24)

Viola hederacea —   Qld, NSW, Vic, Tas, SA
Ivy-leaved Violet
A spreading, perennial herb, of 0.1m high by up to 1-2m wide. The leaves are kidney-shaped. Plants can flower throughout the year, but the main flowering is usually between September and March. The flowers are purple-blue and white, and some of the small flowered forms are perfumed.
O S SS M W L SA C1 F2 Charts 6, 18, 27 (2, 4, 11, 19, 23, 26)

Viola sieberana — Tiny Violet   NSW, Vic, Tas, SA
This prostrate species grows to 0.5-1.5m wide, and is very similar to *V.hederacea*, but smaller in all respects. A good matting plant.
O S SS M W L SA C1 F2   Chart 1 (2, 4, 6, 11, 23, 26)

Wahlenbergia gloriosa —   NSW, Vic, Tas
Royal Bluebell
A prostrate species, which spreads by suckering. The leaves are oblong, to 2-3cm long, with wavy margins, and plants can spread to around 0.5-1m in diameter. Deep bluish purple flowers of 2-3cm diameter, are

produced on individual stems beyond the foliage. Flowering is between November and March.
H O SS D M L SA C1 F2   Chart 1 (4, 6, 18, 23)

Westringia fruticosa — Coast Rosemary   Qld, NSW
This is a hardy, dense shrub, growing up to 2.5m high by 2-3m wide. The leaves are dark green above, and white below, and are up to 3cm long. White flowers, with purple markings on the throat, are produced sporadically throughout the year, with a main flowering time around September-October. A good low windbreak.
H O SS W L SA G C2 F2   Chart 33 (3, 40)

Westringia glabra — Violet Westringia Qld, NSW, Vic
A bushy shrub of 1-2m high by a similar width. The leaves are up to 2.5cm long, broad, and in whorls of four. Lilac coloured, flattened tubular flowers are produced in the upper leaf axils. Flowering is mainly between August and December, but can be sporadic throughout the year.
O SS D M L SA G C1 F1   Chart 34 (3)

Westringia linifolia   NSW
A quick-growing bushy species, of 1.5-2.5m high by 1-2m wide. The leaves are narrow, and in whorls of three. White to lilac flowers are scattered over the foliage, mainly between September and January, but with sporadic flowering at other times. Plants respond well to pruning.
O SS D M L SA G C1 F1   Chart 11 (3, 5, 34)

Xanthorrhoea australis —   NSW, Vic, Tas, SA
Austral Grass-tree
Xanthorrhoea species are grown in cultivation mainly for the attractive clump of long slender grass-like leaves they produce. Plants grow to over 1m tall, but this takes many many years. Similarly, flowering on cultivated plants is not common, and plant selection should not rely on this feature.
H O SS D L SA C1 F2   Chart 18 (12, 24)

Xanthosia rotundifolia — Southern Cross   WA
This is a perennial, with a height of up to 0.3m by a width of 0.5-2m. The leaves are broad and toothed, and sheath the stems at intervals. Flowering can be throughout the year, but is mainly between August and November. Small cream flowers are borne in clusters with decorative bracts, and they are produced in the form of a cross.
O S SS D M L SA C1 F1   Chart 27 (2, 3, 23)

Glossary of terms used

acute Bearing a short, sharp point.

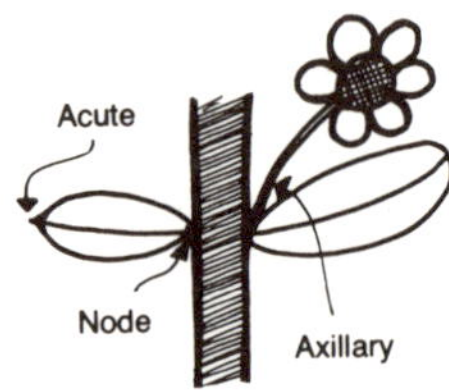

alternate Of leaves, occurring first on one side of a branch and then on the other.

annual A plant that completes its life cycle within one year.

axil The angle formed by a leaf and the stem which bears it.

axillary Produced within the angle of a leaf and a stem.

bipinnate Of leaves or fronds, twice divided.

bracts Modified leaves at the base of flower-stalk, or surrounding clusters of small individual flowers.

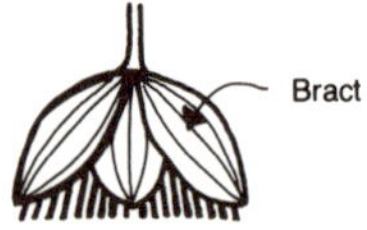

calyces Plural of calyx.

calyx Outer covering of flower-base; protector of buds.

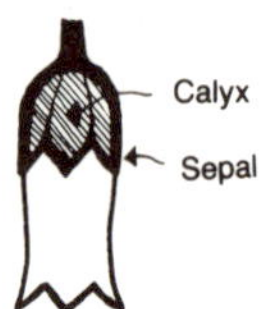

compound leaf A leaf divided into separate leaflets.

cultivar Horticultural variety of a plant.

decussate Leaves in opposite pairs, alternately at right angles along the stem.

elliptic Oval, and tapering at both ends.

epiphyte A plant which grows on another plant but is not parasitic.

erect Upright.

frond The leaf of a fern.

glabrous Smooth, without hairs.

gland A fluid-secreting organ, usually on leaves.

head A dense cluster of flowers.

labellum Modified front petal of an orchid; appears as a 'lip' or 'tongue'.

linear Long, narrow, with parallel edges.

lobe A division of a leaf, petal or sepal.

nerve The main vein or mid-rib of a leaf.

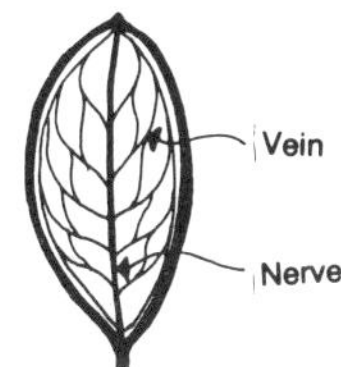

node The point on a stem where leaves or bracts arise.
opposite Of leaves, arranged opposite each other on stem.

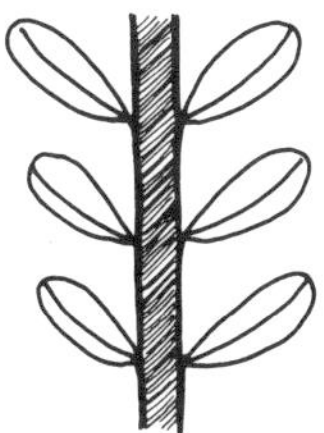

pendant Hanging down.

pendulous Hanging down.
phyllode Modified leaf stalk acting as a leaf, as in most *Acacia* species.
pinna First division of a compound leaf.

pinnae Plural of pinna.
pinnate Of leaves or fronds, compound — divided once.

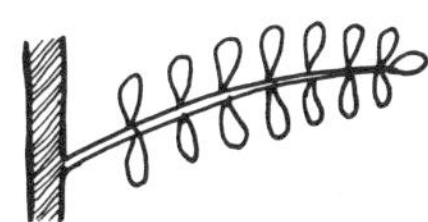

pinnules The smallest divisions of a compound leaf.
pod A dry, non-fleshy fruit that splits when ripe to release its seed.
procumbent Non-rooting stems that lie flat on the ground for most of their length.

prostrate Lying flat on the ground.
pungent Ending in a stiff sharp point or tip.
raceme Equally-stalked flowers along a single stem.

rhizome An underground stem.
sepal A lobe that is portion of the calyx.
serrated With sharp teeth along the margins.

simple Undivided.
sp Species: classification of closely related plants within a genus.
ssp Sub species: a sub group within a species.
spike Stalkless flowers arranged along a single stem.

terminal At the apex or end.

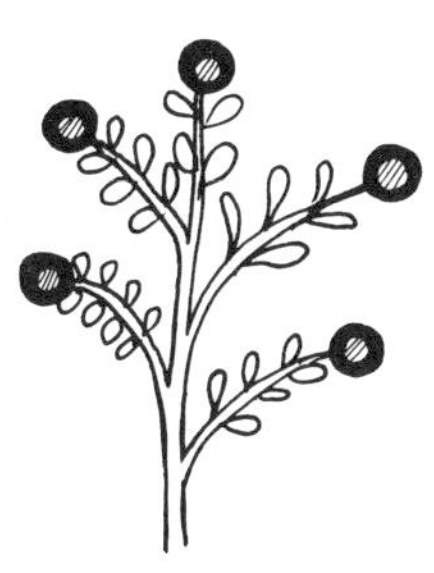

trifoliate   A compound leaf with three leaflets.

var   A sub division of a species.
vein   The sap-carrying tissue of a leaf.
whorl   A ring of flowers or leaves around a stem.

x   Used in nomenclature to indicate a hybrid that has occurred in the natural habitat of the parent plants.